Guatemala

Blood in the Cornfields

Bonnie Dilger

PublishAmerica
Baltimore

First printing

ISBN: 1-4137-6492-4
PUBLISHED BY PUBLISHAMERICA, LLLP
www.publishamerica.com
Baltimore

Printed in the United States of America

For my children and their children,
especially for Jeannette and Pete who have brought to the world a
message of hope and peace through the dark days of Guatemala
with their hauntingly beautiful music.
And for Michael, who with insightful eyes,
saw this work in print long before I did.
My deepest gratitude to Father George Dyer,
who has loved and cared for the Guatemalan people,
and has considered their suffering as his own.
And for those who have not...
"...There's still a chance that they may see..."
Also for Jeanne,
who hugged away my fears when there was nothing else to do.
And to the courageous people of Guatemala:
I've tried to make this story as much yours as mine.
I salute you!

In appreciation to the staff of PublishAmerica
(Jen, Jeni, Jeannette, Shawn, Laurie)
who, with their integrity, objectivity and literary courage,
made it possible for this story to be told.

SOME COMMENTS BY AUTHORS AND OTHERS FAMILIAR WITH THE SITUATION IN CENTRAL AMERICA

"There is no way of reading this material without being moved.... Though all of it is arresting, the most important part of it is that it is eye-witness history colored by righteous rage...a fine and worthwhile book." —John Daniel and Company Publishers.

"My God, this is great! If this doesn't reach Middle America, nothing will." —Charles Clement, M.D. Former Vietnam War Pilot, Peace Activist, Health Worker in El Salvador: author, *Witness to War.*

"I'm not only moved by your writing, but I'm overwhelmed by the challenge of your thought and your defense to injustice. You have moved me deeply." —Mario Velasquez, director, Medical Aid to El Salvador.

"I'm moved by this account for all its passionate intensity, concern, love and deep humanity. You are indeed in the company of angels!" —Michael Krasny, Ph.D., professor of literature, radio journalist.

INTRODUCTION
Institute of
Terror

It is the year 1980, Guatemala City. The year at its beginning, ushered in upon waves of terror, culminates in a raging sea of fear and destruction. Stories of violent crime fill every page of the local newspapers. Grisly, stomach-churning photographs accompany these articles. A young mother lies dead in a cornfield. Her small children find her. They see that her body is horribly mutilated. Her hands have been chopped off at the wrists. She managed a *"cooperativo"* in the rural area of *Comalapa.*

A youth lies bleeding to death in a huge ravine. This cavernous hell lies underneath the highway just outside the capital. The boy's genitals have been hacked off and jammed into his mouth. Barely in his twenties, he is a member of an active labor union.

Published daily is a long list of the names of the dead. A separate list categorizes the *desaparecidos,* those who have simply disappeared. The intelligent eyes of a bearded young man gaze from a photo reprinted in *El Grafico.* The large print is labeled, *ROGAMOS*—WE PRAY.

We the parents beg the captors of our son to return him home safely and in good health. He is not political. He is a person dedicated exclusively to his studies and sports. Each of these articles end in a benediction: *God bless you and reward you for your kindness.* The young man is of course already dead by the time the article reaches the press. He was a student of the San Carlos University. The capital normally teeming with activity has come to an almost standstill, commerce nearly ceased. Murder is the only business carried out with precise regularity. Citizens who must leave their homes look furtively in all directions before entering the streets. They avoid walking whenever possible. No one lingers, for to do so is to court death.

People rush to their parked cars, slam the doors behind them and quickly drive away.

Those who depend upon the municipal transportation services race to the nearest corner only when the buses are in view.

Even the perennial beggars are scarcer in number these days and many of their sidewalk turfs are now vacant.

The streets are filled with litter. The gutters overflow with garbage. The whole city reeks with an acrid odor. It is not lack of maintenance that demobilizes the city, but the prevailing stench of fear itself.

Military trucks roll by, filled to capacity with their uniformed, armed passengers. Death squads are on the prowl. When seen cruising the capital at their leisure, they are merely preserving law and order. Four to six men occupy the black and white police cars marked *La Policia.* The policemen wear the standard blue uniforms. Machine guns jut from the open windows. It is imperative that no signs of fear be detected in anyone within range of these "guardians of justice." Fear of the police casts suspicion upon the person showing it. They could be *subversivos* and may be targeted for death.

When members of the police are on a mission, their work is singularly motivated . They become the mysterious *desconocidos—* unknown persons. They speed through the capital, their vehicles bearing no license plates; they have no identity, their uniforms changed for civilian dress. If their victim is driving, they blow up his car. The use of explosives presents grave danger to both victim and assassin. It is to his extreme advantage when the victim can be overtaken on foot. He is gunned down in the street, Mafia style. The unidentified vehicle roars away into the night, mission accomplished.

The bleeding and dying man is a *comunista*. His assassin is a respected agent of the Guatemalan Government. As in the capital, the whole country is at war with itself. The rural Indians, too, are being drawn into the conflict. For centuries they have preferred to live as a separate society—have remained apolitical. For the first time, they begin to align themselves with the "Ladino groups" in their struggle against the government. Always non-violent in the past, they begin to take up arms.

The lush volcanoes and the rugged terrain of the mountains, inhabited by the Mayan tribes, have become a haven for the guerrilla groups. They are rising from obscurity and making their presence felt in all sectors of the country. * Formed in the 1960s, the four principle bands of guerrillas, once scattered and alienated—never having been able to agree on their modus operandi—lay aside their differences and unite.

In the early morning hours, the pueblos in the highlands and the barrios of the cities resemble heavy snowfall. The earth is thick with the profusion of leaflets dropped by the *campesinos*. Dissemination of the literature has to be due to massive effort. Very little technology is available to them. Their groups are too poor to own a helicopter. The message is bold and startling: "We are being slaughtered like animals. The soldiers enter our homes and rape our daughters. They murder our old men and women and our sons who resist the draft. For years the military has raided our fiestas, kidnapping our young men and forcing them into the army. After their brain-washing techniques, the army's madmen own them. They can never again be reintegrated into the village of their birth. They have become cold-blooded killers. The person who directs this ever-present terror against us is the bloodiest, most repressive dictator ever to live, General Romeo Lucas Garcia. Will you help us to establish peace? Will you help us rid the country of his government?" The President General Lucas Garcia also senses the mood of the country's political unrest as never before under his dominance. He feels the hot breath of opposition all about him.

His fear and rage are echoed from the headline news: *"NO ME SACARAN COMO SACARON SOMOZA!"*—They will not kick me out like they kicked out Somoza!

Somoza, seething with injured pride, discloses his intentions publicly concerning the Nicaragua now lost to him. These boastful words are among his last: "I feel the vigor of youth. It does not matter what that bastard Carter (Jimmy) thinks of me. I will return to Nicaragua. I will conquer Nicaragua!"

In just a few days following this boastful statement, Anastasio Debayle Somoza is dead—his car bombed while coming from a nightclub in Asunción, Paraguay where he lived in exile following the overthrow of his government by Nicaragua's Sandinistas.

Here in Guatemala, Somoza's death sparks a fresh fury of paranoia in the Lucas regime. Hundreds are murdered at random while just following their normal daily activities. Men and women in the city jails serving sentences for only minor offences, and those incarcerated before the benefit of a trial, are taken from their cells and murdered. The screams of the prisoners can be heard for blocks away.

An entire family, including the children, is shot to death on the street, machine-gunned down while entering a funeral parlor. The other family members lie in coffins, also murdered. The local police arrive on the scene, sirens screaming, pistols waving overhead…much running and dodging behind parked cars…Children scramble for safety as the police stage a street drama of "cops and bad guys." The walls of the funeral parlor serve as a fortress while the police are in hot pursuit of the murderer(s).

Amid the chaos the Red Cross arrives. The workers jump out and carry the fresh corpses into the funeral parlor as someone from within quickly opens and slams the door behind them. Pooling of blood replaces the victims' bodies where they have fallen, staining the sidewalks a bright red…an entire family wiped out. Fresh coffins will be provided. Perhaps the dignity of a funeral is still possible—can be worked out by someone in charge.

Screaming, shrill and hysterical, splits the air, the sound of many terrified voices. No one person hears the other. The deafening roar of explosives blasts the city. The whine of bullets tells the gruesome story—institutionalized terror.

Over the Palacio Nacional a huge banner of blue and white silk waves in the warm autumn breeze. Emblazoned upon it are the words: JIMMY CASTRO-FIDEL CARTER.

A crowd gathers below the windows of the presidential palace, presumably awaiting word from their president regarding the country's turmoil. *El Presidente* Romeo Lucas, flanked by his bodyguards and attaché, walks down the gilded halls of the palace, out onto the balcony and into the bright sunlight. Resplendent in military uniform, the president looks down a moment at his chest to assure that his buttons and numerous medals are all in place, before addressing the crowd.

After a brief greeting to his countrymen and a smart salute to his cabinet, General Romeo Lucas begins the issuance of a stern warning... "No communistic or other subversive activity will be tolerated in Guatemala. The priests and other religious persons are to confine their work to the saving of souls, not meddling in the affairs of the government."

He says that there are bad *Guatemaltecos* among the loyal citizens of Guatemala desiring to take over the country. Before the president concludes his message he says that hope for Guatemala is just around the corner—when Ronald Reagan becomes president of the United States, no further problems are anticipated from their neighbors of the North.

The full implications of the President general's message undoubtedly have not yet registered in the minds of most of the listeners. For the average North American his oratory would make no sense whatsoever. Most are confident, however, that our leaders, whether Democrats or Republicans, have nothing to share with murderers.

The guerrilla bands are named and dated as follows: CNT (la Central Nacional de Trabajadores) 1960; FAR (Fuerzas Armadas Rebeldes) 1962; ORPA (Oranización del Pueblo en Armas) 1967; PGT (Partido Guatamalteco del Trabajo) 1948; EGP (Ejército Guerillero de los Pobres) 1972; CUC (el Comité de Unidad Campesina)1980; FERG (Frente Estudiantil Robin Garcia) 1980.

LEAVING HOME
Central America (1973)

Acquaintance with Central America for me begins in 1973. An announcement at the family dinner table facilitates my decision to travel…four sets of eyes that burn with excitement in four young faces, begging me not to make a scene, not to cry. Two sons and two daughters inform me that they want to see the world, and of all things without me!

In the evening as I prepare for bed, and I contemplate the future without my children, I grudgingly admit that the news they have just imparted may not be all bad! This time of family transition may be the catalyst for growth in all of us, including me. I still have ahead of me, after all, a long-awaited dream to pursue a writing career.

Coincident to the recent turn of events in my life, the state of being without any family ties, though an unmarried parent for many years, a young lady from El Salvador invites me to spend the summer with her in San Salvador, her home and the country's capital. She and I work at the same hospital, and though my job can scarcely be termed exciting, my friend, Angela, has the duller position. However, it is obvious that the files over which she, without any attempt at disguise, yawns, are but stepping-stones in her life. Her real vocation she works toward is fulfilled at UCLA where she majors in Sociology.

June arrives—a lovely month of the year, and Angela leaves for El Salvador, where she plans to spend the entire school vacation with her father. Prior to leaving, she again extends invitation for me to visit.

This seems quite normal to me, having grown up in Tucson, Arizona, where there was a large ethnic influence of Latin Americans and who, when neighbors, were high on my list as favorites.

Since I plan to travel, I feel fortunate to know someone in another country, particularly when that someone is as gracious as Angela. In spite of the differences in age and nationality, we had gravitated toward each other in easy camaraderie.

After a few months of being friends with Angela, I was, however, freshly conscious of the fact that even friends have their conflicts. Angela had a maddening habit of always being late for appointments, that is when she bothered to keep them at all. The most frustrating part of it all is that no apology was ever offered. I sometimes showed extreme annoyance with her for this very quality but she had only looked at me in wide-eyed surprise, as if she couldn't believe that I, her friend, could ever be displeased with her.

I think the only reason Angela gets by with conducting her life as she does is that she is endowed with exceptional beauty. She has a trophy, which is tangible proof that she is beautiful. She was Miss El Salvador two years ago, but the standard of prettiness sometimes associated with beauty contests does not describe her. Angela's complexion is the color of rich cream. Her eyes are the darkest shade of velvet, the tone of her voice musical and sweet. A Spanish accent pervades her English, which seems half contrived, half a foreign innocence, but either way it is a complimenting factor.

As I begin my last-minute preparations for my trip to El Salvador I need to know that her invitation has not been just a part of an impulsive hospitality syndrome; I, therefore, call Angela at her home in San Salvador to ensure a welcome and opportune visit. Over the telephone and across the miles, the charm she radiates is as vivid as ever. "*Si,*" she answers, "*como no, venga.*"—Yes, why not, come.

EL SALVADOR
(1973)

As I walk toward the terminal and proceed through customs with the other passengers, I look around, hoping to catch a glimpse of Angela. She at the moment is not to be seen. While my bags are being searched I visually search the airport. While the plane was landing, I had felt that Angela's usual habit of tardiness might prevent her from meeting me here, but then I had ruled it out. (Guests invited from another country are usually greeted upon arrival.) But a further look around tells me that my apprehension is proving to be warranted after all. There is no sign of Angela anywhere.

Not only is my friend not present to meet me but also I question fearfully if I've come to the right place. The terminal is filled with sights and sounds of human misery. Added to my fear is dismay.

Dirty, ragged children roam the airport in search of a handout. They push and shove to get to us, the airline passengers, first, apparently apprised of the foreigners' arrival time.

Afflictions long believed to have vanished by us of the "privileged segment" of the Western world are present here at El Salvador's terminal.

It is difficult to assimilate the information conveyed initially only to my five senses. A middle-aged man makes his way slowly, painstakingly, through the crowd of disembarking tourists…groping, as a misplaced actor from a play featuring an epochal tragedy. His face at a distance looks as if a nylon stocking has been stretched over his face and head, his expression blank. But as he comes closer and I can see him well, it is obvious that he is blind, and has only hideous-looking scars where eyes have been. Their empty sockets give the impression that his eyes have been gouged out. The telltale sores of leprosy are present on more than one person.

The body of a young woman supports a huge and scaly limb of elephantiasis. It juts grotesquely beneath her skirt beside a normal, well-proportioned leg. A young man with a handsome face and luminous dark eyes hops on all fours toward me. His inability to walk uprightly presumably is the result of poliomyelitis, never treated.

While I stare in astonishment, my mind makes an attempt to reject the information transmitted through my vision: Surely this can't be the sophisticated little country described in the pretty travel brochures I had come to visit! To expect the lush Garden of Eden the literature describes is unreal to be sure; no such utopia exists in a real world, but my first glimpse of San Salvador, El Salvador's capital, is unbelievable.

I want to go home but where is home? I had burned the proverbial bridges behind me and I am here—like it or not—in El Salvador!

I'm mad at Angela for her failure to explain to me what her country is really like. I'm mad at the whole damn world for what I see here. This isn't the twentieth century. It is the abyss of the dark ages for God's sake. Here in this miserable aggregate of people are the greatly maligned citizens of the Third World we read about. I want to weep, but the entire picture presented here defies the luxury of tears.

It becomes obvious that Angela is either going to be very late or is not coming at all—it's the same story just another country—and with those cynical thoughts in mind, I go to change some dollars into colones, El Salvador's currency, wondering at the same time who among the airport's "welcoming committee" has the greater need.

While in the process of attempting to interact with San Salvador's poor people, a handsome, energetic-looking man hurries toward me. As he approaches I see that he is somewhat breathless with hurry, but as he greets me—enthusiastically—I still don't know who he is…then sudden recognition…Angela's father. I had met him on only one occasion…in Los Angeles when he was visiting Angela. Although not exactly engulfed in well-being, my sense of abandonment is greatly ameliorated by his presence. He picks up my bags with an accustomed efficiency—as a person used to playing host to visitors—and beckons me to follow him, where presumably outside the terminal there is a waiting automobile.

Four to five men crowd me out of the way and begin a marathon-like hike behind "my Salvadoran host." I can only assume they all work for him, as they all defer to him as *Jefe*, which I remember from my high school Spanish, means boss. I'm still in the rear of this small procession when I reach the car and the door opens. Gabriel, seated behind the wheel, pats the seat beside him in a companionable manner, motioning for me to get in the car beside him.

The men who had followed Gabriel to the car scatter and go running after another man with luggage, calling him *Jefe* also. Perhaps their efforts will be rewarded and a tip will be in order.

We quickly leave the airport and pass through the nucleus of the city. Gabriel drives very fast, and judging from the cars whizzing by on the highways so do most Salvadoran motorists—I see things only in a segmented fashion. Gabriel, like Angela, is polite and gracious; he asks, "Is your family well? Was your trip pleasant? Have you been waiting long?" His first two questions can be answered truthfully; the third cannot. I had waited two hours in that airport and had I stopped to consider for a moment that the events of my imagination would become a reality, I'd not have come here. However, in fairness to Gabriel, the irritation I feel for Angela has nothing to do with her father—or so I concede at the time.

Obviously in a horrendous hurry, Gabriel still takes the time to point out sites he thinks will interest me—the commercial buildings, the centers of industry—and as we leave the city, he shows me a new shopping center that closely resembles those of the United States. Unlike the city's architecture, in a general state of disrepair, these structures are conspicuous in their newness.

Gabriel presently takes a wide boulevard. We enter a residential area, pleasant and with lovely landscaping. Tropical plants flourish and the streets are lined with flowers. There is a profusion of magnificent trees and their fiery brilliance seems to be produced by their leaves alone.

Gabriel tells me that these are the *arboles de fuego*—fire trees, for which El Salvador is famous. The ambience here is a true representation of the beauty described in travelogues of El Salvador.

Nothing here suggests poverty—that is, nothing other than the jagged glass that juts from the very top of the walls surrounding the homes in the neighborhood. The multi-colored pieces shine incongruously in the sun, the sharp edges discouraging to the most skillful of thieves.

They could be ripped to pieces on any attempt to scale the garden walls. Policemen who wear the identical uniform as the city cops stand guard outside these homes.

Gabriel sees the question on my face regarding these members of the law enforcement agency and answers me before my curiosity has been voiced. "The guards," he explains, "are the same faction as the local police, though the home-owners pay them." He elaborates further to say that all law enforcement agencies, including the members of the military, receive their orders from only one source. From what I gather at this point, their orders are dispersed and filtered down through the echelon's apex, the presidential palace. This information gives me some insight into the judicial system practiced in El Salvador.

As necessary as these guards seem to be, and though I have no intention of being other than a law-abiding guest in El Salvador, I hope that I can avoid dealing with them at any time. They are scary just to look at. Each of them carry the hardware necessary for their jobs and, though their machine guns appear to be carelessly slung over their shoulders, their faces, dark and smoldering, belie the impression that their masters' wealth is other than assiduously guarded.

The home on the block belonging to Gabriel would probably be classified as a mansion in El Salvador, but anywhere else it would be considered very beautiful, its brick structure styled after the classic Spanish era following the conquest. Bougainvillea shades the house. Their hues range from shades of deep pink to purple. Noting my admiration, Gabriel says it is not unusual to see them growing higher than a two-story house in both El Salvador and Guatemala.

Inside Gabriel's home, my predominately negative thoughts of El Salvador recede somewhat. In spite of the oppressive heat and the lack of air conditioning, the house is invitingly cool. The shutters are drawn to protect the rooms from the fierceness of the midday sun. The tile floors, pleasant in floral pattern, shine with cleanliness. The smell of wax and other household cleaning agents blend with the aromas escaping from the kitchen—the simmering of black beans, coffee perking and tortillas in the making. In the hand-painted vases, there are fresh-cut flowers wherever you look. The entire picture presented here is one of a well-kept home, orderly and serene.

Someone in the house has magically appeared and, without being seen, has whisked away my bags, presumably to the room I'm to occupy while a guest in the home.

Gabriel tells me that he must hurry back to work, but that he will try to get off early so that we can become acquainted later. He calls to me as he quickly vanishes through the door, *"Mi casa es su casa,"* that thoroughly delightful, hospitable expression of which most of us are already familiar.

I would be completely happy now, were it not for one thing that has nagged me since my arrival at the airport: Where is Angela?—the person I've come to see.

One of the servants comes into the living room and asks if I would like to rest. She shows me the bedroom where, at a glance, I see my luggage. With my limited knowledge of Spanish, I'm able to ask her if she resides here, does she have a family, is she an established employee—all the usual questions people ask upon acquaintance. I explain that I'm from the United States and have come to visit Angela—"And where may I ask is she?"

The maid doesn't answer me, but averts her eyes and looks at the floor, gives a little shrug of the shoulders. There is, however, a certain expression, which implies that she is not at liberty to divulge this information. Now I begin to really worry. Suppose Angela is not here at all? I feel that I should approach the subject to Gabriel as soon as possible. I had seen a telephone in the hall and wonder if it's possible to call him at his office.

I feel ridiculous that I had not mentioned Angela's absence on the way here from the airport. While sorting out these thoughts, trying to separate justifiable fear from the hysteria of so rapid a change, I hear footsteps outside the door. They are, however, halting and not at all like the sound of Angela's walking. I know her walk to be brisk and self-assured. When I open the door to her knocking I know immediately that something is wrong. Though Angela's figure has retained its youthful firmness, she has gained about twenty pounds. She is slumping, something I've never seen her do before. Her lovely skin is marred by angry, red eruptions. But the most noticeable sign of all, other than the fact that she is not her happiest self, is the absence of her beautiful smile. In its place is a look of frustration, bordering on anguish. I open my arms to her and she warms to my embrace. Almost immediately, though, she bursts into tears. I listen incredulously as she tells me that she and her father no longer speak. She is not allowed to use the car—the reason she gives for not having met me at the airport—and that she is barely allowed the "privilege" of dining at the same table with him now. The reason for all this misery and estrangement seems to be involved with Gabriel's latest mistress. She now dictates, it seems, the rules of the household. Angela tells me that her place has been totally usurped by this wench who has taken over the home.

Though I'm disturbed by Angela's distress, I find myself responding to this tearful story with a sense of recognition—it is certainly nothing new for children to feel resentful about another person entering their parents' homes.

I am further reminded of the Angela I knew in Los Angeles, the spoiled and mercurial girl. Whatever her mood her father was somehow responsible. When she was happy she was his good, sweet darlin', the favorite among his children. The other three siblings are boys, so as a consequence apparently never having been a threat to her. In her dark moods, Angela mentioned her father only for his errors. He alone was to blame that she never had enough money, that she couldn't go to Europe, that she was not now married to the young man of her choice; whatever her unhappy plight at the time, her father was always blamed.

But these storms passed as quickly as they came. The amiable, lovable Angela I was beginning to know so well emerged. Long forgotten were her "miserable poverty," her state of unfulfilled love and her father's failure to understand her.

Because of what I know about Angela, I attempt to console her by pointing out that one day she will decide to marry and, when she does, her father will have little to say about the matter. His rights will be limited to a blessing for her and the intended in her life. To this she reacts so violently that I don't know what to do next. She flings herself down on the bed, shouting, "But you don't understand. Even you don't understand!"

I stare distractedly at a space between the bed and a chair where there lies a fluffy throw rug. Angela rises and sinks down in it, as if comfort will be obtained by its softness, and cries brokenly. Because of her misery, I am greatly torn by pity, but I say nothing more. I am at the moment powerless to help her.

I begin to wish that whatever is wrong, the problem would go away by itself—or that nothing more is involved than an emotional and immature outburst on Angela's part when something has not gone her way. And with these thoughts, I hear the key turn and, with the opened door, there drifts the fragrance of a man's cologne.

It is by now late in the afternoon; the sky outside the window is a deep and mysterious purple. Gabriel calls to Angela and me, and as we three meet in the narrow hallway, father and daughter greet each other amiably, though I sense tension between them. Despite Angela's earlier account, that of being denied her father's company at mealtimes, the three of us sit down together for dinner.

From the dining room through the window, the sky can be seen darkening. A soft rain begins to fall, soothing to my spirits, following the feeling of jet lag and the disturbing events of the day.

Angel and Gabriel seem to be carefully avoiding any mention of words that could lead to an open quarrel. The exchange between them is polite and cheerful, if a bit strained.

Soon the rainfall gets heavier, becomes even heavier and begins to beat the roof with a vengeance. A loud clap of a cloudburst is accompanied by great peals of thunder. Sporadic streaks of lightening illuminate the room, left dark from lack of power. The lights had gone out with the first deluge.

The conversation, which the three of us began in a well-lit ambience, continues by candlelight and the weather—a safe subject anywhere it appears—becomes the topic of discussion. Though the rain brings nothing but further humidity to El Salvador's shores, the present season is still considered winter, there being in El Salvador but two—wet and dry.

We retire to the living room to drink our demitasse, and after the first sip of the mellow, delicious coffee, an imposing knock resounds loudly. Angela gets up from her chair to answer, but not before a second intrusive knock is heard. A slight frown creases her pretty forehead, her thoughts mirrored only too clearly: *Who could be calling at this hour and in all this rain?* Seeing who's at the door, Angela's expression changes from mere annoyance to incredulous rage. Shrieking, she tries to evict the visitor. Gabriel rises uncertainly, his handsome mouth twitching slightly, but once on his feet, he quickly leaves the room.

I move into a position where I am better able to see and my view reveals a young woman planted firmly in the doorway, also angry, very determined, not easily turned away from her mission.

I move again, even with the open door, so that I now have a clear view of both Angela and her caller—and the girl, though she talks with Angela in a loud voice and with troubled expression, exhibits nothing formidable. Her features are clouded by fright, childish. She bends to pick up something and it turns out to be one of those little plastic carriers in which mothers carry their infants. It is by now obvious that somewhere in the blue and yellow blankets lining the carrier, a baby is enclosed, and this seems to be the reason for Angela's distress.

I'm not able to follow the conversation entirely (if it can be called that) between Angela and the young woman. I have a bare knowledge of their language but even if I spoke Spanish fluently, I doubt that I could thoroughly understand the problem as it exists at the moment.

The girl, with the baby still in her arms, pushes her way aggressively into the living room. Angela, having been unable to block her entry, begins to shout at the girl, pushing her backward, demanding that she leave immediately. The young girl pushes her back in retaliation, shouting also. The baby in the mother's arms is between the two of them.

The girls are making so much noise, there is no way either of them can hear the other.

Words just now seem to have no particular significance. The battle here represents rights of territory not the logic of order.

Though Angela's anger is strong the girl will not be dissuaded. She is fiercely motivated and will not leave without some kind of recognition. Not knowing quite what to do, it seems that my part in this Salvadoran drama is to take the baby. I manage to extract the bundle from the arms of its mother…the infant feels very warm and good against my chest.

While the girls are still engaged in battle, Gabriel returns. If he feels any awkward sense of embarrassment, he doesn't show it. He strides across the room, takes the baby peaceful in sleep from me and looks down on the silkish black head of hair, surfacing from where he has removed the bonnet. He begins to remove the rest of the baby's clothing and, when examining the infant's anatomy, notes happily that the baby is a boy. He holds the tiny human up to me for comment. "Do you think this little guy looks like me?" In low and timid tones, I give my answer: "Oh, yes, he looks just like you." By his pleased expression it is obvious that these words are what Gabriel, like any other new father, longs to hear.

The young mother, having accomplished her purpose, leaves the house as quickly as she came in, the child once more bundled up against the rain and the infant in her arms.

It becomes clear that not only has Angela to contend with her father's present mistress, but the seeds of past sexual unions on her father's part still blow upon her doorstep, haunting her, making her miserable. I am beginning to understand the reason for Angela's distress, a state that Gabriel seems intent upon ignoring. It seems she will not let him—he cannot but feel the scorn cast in his direction, transmitted through dark, burning eyes. Turning toward his daughter he matches her disdain. "Must I remind you, señorita, that I'm still the master of this house. What takes place here is really none of your business."

More bitter words ensue and a full-blown argument is now in progress. The exchange of angry accusations continues well into the night. I hear Angela threaten to walk out the door and never return. Gabriel agrees that this is exactly what she should do, if she continues to treat her father this way—that she should never have come back to El Salvador, but should have stayed in the United States with her mother. She now acts more like a "*gringa* than a *Salvadoreña*. A Salvadoran girl respects her father." A slight cough is then heard and a change of tenor on Gabriel's part to a dramatic humility. "I had thought that when you first returned, you no longer loved me; now I am certain of it!"

These words are said in a variety of ways until finally it seems there remains nothing left unsaid.

When the shouting comes to an end a modicum of tranquility seems restored. But the absence of vitriolic expression, I would soon be reminded, by no means represents peace. During the course of the argument I had gone to the room designated for my occupancy as a guest in the home. I had hoped to get some sleep—it has been a long day. But rest is not to be had at this time.

Angela enters the room, her father following closely behind her. She sits on the bed and so does he. She pouts and he sticks out his lip, affecting a similar expression, mocking her. He then tries teasing her—charmingly—attempting at the same time to cradle his head in her lap. He calls her his "*Angelita*," his "*Negrita*," in tones so low and soft, that they could almost be interpreted as seductive. To all of this Angela reacts by pushing her father away from her; undoubtedly she sees all of this as a false attempt at reconciliation. Gabriel in turn, is infuriated with Angela, and the two of them storm out of the room to resume their quarrel elsewhere in the house for another hour or so.

At some point a weeping Angela comes back to my room. Her huge eyes are brimming with tears and she needs to confide further in me—that is obvious. In view of all that has happened, I can't imagine what there is left to be said. However, according to Angela, tonight's drama was no unusual event. Like a lifetime plague, her father's sexual indiscretions have afflicted the entire family. Not only for Angela and her brothers have they been a source of searing pain and anger, but they are what drove her mother away from home.

Angela begins relating a tale to me so fantastic that it seems fabricated. But after the events of the day here in this Salvadoran household, it can readily be understood as unquestionably true.

She describes the way she was introduced to the wonderful and mysterious world of "adult behavior"—the knowledge came into her life through a violent and rude awakening.

Angela's mother had suspected for some time that her husband, Gabriel, was having an affair with one of the maids in the home. Pretending to be asleep, she saw and heard her husband leave the nuptial bed. Believing her sleep genuine, Gabriel went directly to the maid's quarters.

His wife followed him there. Upon having her suspicions of his infidelity confirmed, the irate wife went to the garage, got into the car and drove it straight into the living room through a huge picture window. Fortunately, no one suffered any physical Injury.

Angela asks now in a voice thick with rage and torment, "Do you know how old she was?"—meaning the maid seduced by her father—and of course there is no way I can answer; presumably she was very young. Angela shouts out the answer, "She was thirteen! Do you know how old I was?—fourteen!" As if part of the same subject, the next exclamation of information Angela imparts is, "Do you know that my mother also hates me?" (I have seen the two together, mother and daughter, and I readily agree this is so.) I know at the moment, however, that I've no advice to give this tormented girl.

Sometime in the early morning hours I fall asleep, but awaken in a few minutes, my thoughts filled with the devastating scene at the airport; vying for attention inside my skull are the echoes of the loud and bitter arguments I've heard.

The violence of nature ceases; in the calm the rain falls softly, unobtrusively on the roof and window panes, bathing the wounds of this home in its softness. In that somnolent state between sleeping and being awake, I wonder, *What has any of this to do with me?*

The next morning, the quarrels of the household, like the hungry and the distressing scene at the airport, seem but something I dreamed. I awaken to the tantalizing aroma of brewing coffee. Indeed I am offered a cup, along with hot tortillas, fried beans and eggs. Both Angela and the maid keep heaping more portions on my plate.

It is my second or third day in El Salvador—I am unsure which— when I am again surprised. I meet the person who seems to be the continuing cause for contention in the household. I had imagined Angela's "enemy numero uno" strong and in control, a full-bodied woman. But Gabriel's mistress is little different from the girl who had appeared at the door with the baby on the night I arrived. Dressed in a uniform of grade school, she is as defenseless-appearing as a baby doe. Her body still has the slender grace of a child. Her features are delicate and sweet.

I begin to plan a departure that will be as graceful as possible. I know that I must come up with some reason. In spite of the distressing state of the household, neither Angela nor Gabriel have in any way ill-treated me. To the contrary, they have been warm and hospitable. I think that I am ready to go. In the time I spend with Angela, I see that there is really very little to enjoy about the city of San Salvador. As in the airport, beggars walk alongside the well-dressed and the elegant. When the begging children ask for money and are rewarded, they make the sign of the cross and add, "God bless you," a more condemning action than were they to curse me to my face.

The city is so crowded. There seems to be not enough space to accommodate all these people.

Angela and I weave in and out of traffic in the congested city; more than once I feel a speeding motorist's bumper against my calves as we run across the street. I feel unseen hands touching me, presumably searching for money. The months Angela and I had spent together in the U.S. seem far away...as if the conversations we had in the

Westwood coffee houses took place in another world, another lifetime. Had it only been a few months ago? Over late lunches of fruit and good wines our conversations invariably led to politics. Angela would begin to condemn the U.S. Government for its role in the third-world countries, for its perpetuating the crimes of dictators all over the world—for the advantage it takes of the small, weak nations. My counter-offensive to these attacks always varied somewhat, but I never failed to point out that without the cooperation of the dictators in the small, weak nations she spoke of, control would never have been possible.

Sometimes these arguments became so noisy that they attracted the attention of people at nearby tables. Frequently the young intellectuals from among the students of UCLA joined us and, though they admitted they did not really know much about the Third World, like most people when politics surface in conversation, they gave their opinions anyway. Sometimes they agreed with Angela, sometimes with me, but a lively debate that continued well into the night would often ensue.

Here in the steamy, over-crowded city of San Salvador, the politics Angela and I had discussed in "civilized surroundings" now seem absurdly irrelevant.

Angela and I thread our way through the congestion of pedestrians, street vendors, dodging buses and motorcycles, I in a state of panic each time we must cross the street. The sidewalks are occupied with endless rows of restless-looking young men. They lean against the window ledges of the shops ogling all the women going by. As Angela and I pass them, they make hissing noises and stare with mean, lustful eyes. Only the most forlorn of women could possibly be flattered by their attentions.

"Don't any of these men ever work?" I ask Angela.

"No," she replies with an irritated sigh. "There are not enough jobs to go around."

The hungry people, the idle men who would be working and cannot because there are not enough jobs for them, the overpopulated city, these are all visible signs of unrest in El Salvador.

But there is also an aura about the country, if the capital here is an indication, like its smoldering volcanoes, seems ready to explode. Indefinable as the feeling may be, you sense that it is there. The impoverished masses seem to call out to "How long, how long can we endure?"

San Salvador is a thoroughly depressing city; its inhabitants seem equally depressing.

Back at the home, Gabriel now brings a loaded gun to the table where he dines. The weapon lies alongside his plate with his napkin—with it he threatens Angela and the whole human race. He says that he would have everyone killed who does not produce.

I hope that Gabriel is not referring to me! I am normally quite industrious and I am about to tell him so when he, to some degree, clarifies his rambling. He says that he is talking about the lazy people, the infirm and the mentally retarded of his country.

I have heard quite enough and gracefully or otherwise, I know I must leave immediately. I hope that Angela will see her way clear to leave with me. The thought of leaving her is intolerable to me.

The phone rings and it is my son, David, calling me from Guatemala. He tells me that there is a beautiful lake in the mountains—El Lago Atitlán—and since I don't sound overly enthusiastic about El Salvador, perhaps I would like to come there—to Guatemala. He will wait for me. This is good timing, perfect. The reason I need for leaving is wonderfully provided.

Within twenty-four hours, I am on the plane bound for Guatemala. Angela is with me and we begin to make plans for the near future, now that plans are again possible.

Angela informs me—that is, if I'm in agreement—we will run around the mountains together, and then she will return to the States where she will resume her studies in Sociology. I hope that life will be kinder to her there.

Angela is a good conversationalist, intelligent and respectful, and now that she is leaving her problems behind, the sense of humor I had found so charming in Los Angeles returns. Even now as she teases there is no real derision in her voice. "So, Bōney,"—this is Spanish for Bonnie—"Were you ready for El Salvador and was it ready for you?"

Angela and I easily chat away the short time it takes to reach Guatemala by air, our camaraderie restored.

GUATEMALA

My initial impression of Guatemala after coming directly here—from San Salvador to Guatemala's capital city—is one of extreme surprise. Here at the airport, I note with relief that there are no signs of the stark poverty of an oppressed nation—an absence of the over crowdedness of El Salvador's airport, no beggars about.

High windows in the balconies allow a cool breeze to circulate, giving it the name for which Guatemala is famous—*La Tierra de la Primavera Eterna*—the Land of Eternal Springtime. Garments of every size and fashion are on display in the small stores at the terminal, but what separates them from conventional fashion is that they are all made from brilliant, hand-woven cloth, giving the terminal a look of festivity, undoubtedly as pleasing to the eyes of every tourist as it is to me. These smart boutiques also offer belts, table cloths and matching napkins with the Quetzal, Guatemala's national bird, woven into their designs. Bright green stones gleam from bracelets, rings and necklaces; the shop clerks tell us that the jade is plentiful in Guatemala. The only indication that Guatemala, too, has its economic problems, is that five or more porters rush to the baggage room to be of service when Angela and I claim our luggage, making choice very difficult. Once outside the airport, there are a number of *choferes* clamoring for our taxi fare and we cannot patronize them all. Somehow the need for choosing a *chofer* has been removed and the winning porter settles us down in one of the taxis in our luggage struggle.

As we leave the airport for the downtown section, the driver takes a route that reveals one of the most beautiful areas I've ever seen. Gigantic trees line the sides of the wide asphalt roadway; many shades of shimmering green sway in the soft breeze. "American Embassy." The driver points out a building whose identity is comfortingly obvious. The red, white and blue of the U.S. flag billows in the warm air. The homes in this area cannot be seen, only the tops of the trees and climbing foliage from the gardens, but little imagination is required to envision immense wealth hidden behind the towering walls.

Angela asks the driver to take us to a nice, but relatively inexpensive hotel. He understands and complies with this request. We are shown a small hotel whose architecture is colonial, red brick and built around a beautiful garden. Roses in reds and yellows flourish and birds gather to drink at a fountain in the center of the garden.

Angela is pleased with the taxi driver's recommendation; I am ecstatic. The room is tastefully furnished and even the bed linens are spotlessly clean. The concierge had asked us for only ten dollars for the room. We didn't even have to go to the trouble of money exchange. Guatemala's currency, the Quetzal, is exactly the equivalent to an American dollar.

Life's meaning begins to assume a more pleasant prospect. I am to meet my youngest son in the mountains here in Guatemala. I realize how much I've missed him. I begin to feel particularly well and rested after a nap and a typical Guatemalan meal of tortillas and black beans with an assortment of vegetables. Angela's demeanor tells me that she, too, is feeling better.

At Angela's suggestion, we take a stroll through the city. I'm looking forward to sightseeing now that we are no longer in El Salvador. However, just a few blocks away from the hotel, more toward the central part of the city, conditions reveal that they are little different from El Salvador. Many beggars line the sidewalks. Some are blind and play accordions. Their happy music fills the night air as they ask for alms. Other beggars wave the stump of an arm or leg as we attempt to pass, demanding payment for their infirmities by obstructing the pedestrian's path. Many ragged mothers or fathers thrust their hungry children in front of us.

Exactly as in El Salvador, there are many street children roaming unattended, irrespective of nightfall. The garbage pails behind the restaurants are obviously the main source of food for the children. They are seen tipping them over, looking for the uneaten morsel.

When we stop for coffee, I notice that the more resourceful of these ragged boys and girls enter the front door of the café along with the patrons. They skip around the tables as a little band of gypsies snatching or begging all uneaten food left on the diners' plates. The manager shows up and kicks them out, but not before the little urchins are able to grab a fistful of food, laughing gleefully as they run for the open door.

Not all employees are "loyal" to their bosses. I see a waitress slipping food to several of these hungry children, a conspiratorial wink on her pert face. I take time to reflect upon the situation here and realize with some surprise that just because I have now seen the startling poverty in Central America, makes it no more and no less a reality than before. I had thought that these social conditions existed in faraway places, in India, in Africa or Bangladesh, but not to this appalling degree in what some politicians term "our own backyard."

The next morning, as excited as I am about getting to the mountains, I am equally apprehensive about being weighted down with luggage. I learn that I am mistaken about having disposed of everything I did not need in Los Angeles.

Angela and I find our way to the main terminal, but there is absolutely no resemblance to any commuting station in my experience. A million stalls of fruits and vegetables are interspersed between millions of buses, vehicles that are parked so closely together, that moving even one would seem an impossible chore—for anyone. It must be that some particular magic, known only to the drivers of this section of the world, is at work here. The merchants continue to sell and the shoppers continue to buy, though the terminal everywhere is completely filled with mud. Guatemala, like El Salvador, is right in the middle of the rainy season. Angela and I go sloshing in and out of the fruit stalls, around gigantic piles of cabbage, skirting the stands where *atol*—a thick, sweet drink made from corn—is sold. We gulp down a cup of this delicious drink and trudge onward in our muddy journey. Just how Angela knows which of these enigmatic paths to follow is not clear, but supposedly one of these innumerable buses will eventually end up in Panajachel, our present destiny. Angela is in the lead in this maze and running along in the mud behind her are two barefoot Indian men—who with the agility of dancers manage to dodge the merchants and their wares who are also in the mud. Our luggage is strapped to the backs of these fantastic Guatemalan Indians, and I am feeling very ashamed that I am responsible for their burdens, but I am powerless. I can barely manage the electric typewriter and the two suitcases I'm dragging along. Prior to our coming here, Angela had told me that luggage is often stolen by people assisting you and I begin to wish that the thief who possesses this slippery talent would now use it and make off with just one suitcase, if indeed such a person is among us. But I know that this frazzled feeling will last no longer than this current predicament. When I am comfortable again, I'll want every blasted item I've brought with me.

I can no longer see Angela. I am certain I've met my end—here in a foreign country, among the cabbages and the squealing pigs. But as I drag myself and my cargo around another stall, there appears the procession of which I was a displaced member. The Indian men are motioning for me to hurry along while Angela points in the direction of a waiting bus surrounded by activity. I will not wander into infinity after all, here among the goats and mountains of cabbage heads. We board the bus…lots of noise and conversation accompany the process of settling us down with our luggage. The *chofer's* helper finally slings part of our suitcases on top of the bus, along with the firewood, hemp bags of corn and other foodstuffs, and we are at last on our way. I look around me and see that fellow passengers are the people I had seen at the terminal. Due to their cargo, I had somehow hoped that they would be going somewhere else.

The one luxury afforded us is but an illusion, which soon disappears—that of a seat to ourselves. Soon every inch of space is filled, seats and isles. We are all squeezed together. A very drunk Indian is leaning heavily on my shoulder. He smells awful and keeps calling me "*malo*" to a female companion—I think because I've attempted to disengage myself from him. I take a certain comfort in the thought that I can't be "malo"—that's a bad man. I would have to be "*mala*," a bad woman. I know something about Spanish. This guy's sure got his nerve

"Oh, Bōney," Angela chides from the other side of the drunk passenger, "I *nevair, evair* thought to see you on *a bos with a bonch of dronk Eendians.*" It is the charming voice I hate the most.

"Angela," I reply irritably, "I think I can handle the Indians, even this one," meaning the one leaning on me, "but what I object to is that damn squealing pig! Now try to leave me alone." The moment I've uttered these unkind words, I am immediately repentant.

The bus climbs higher and soon it begins to groan under the weight of its burden. At each village entered, passengers are let off, but this by no means indicates that the bus will be less crowded. We merely collect new passengers along the way. A mother goat and her young are added. More chickens and turkeys add their feathery wet smells to the odors of the overcrowded bus and more people board alongside the mountain with gigantic loads of firewood and avocados.

But soon the claustrophobia and all disagreeable feelings begin to dissipate. Even the hairpin curves and the high altitude of what must be at least 7,000 feet I don't notice because of the breathtaking view outside my window. The towering mountains are covered with pine, birch and stately firs, velvety in lush, rich shades of green. Delicate wildflowers sway in the gentle breeze along the banks of the mountains as we pass by. Small vine-covered cottages add their presence to the dream-like voyage. As old and timeless as the earth itself, they appear never to have been inhabited by humans, but within their walls are elves and little people waiting to communicate with the imaginative travelers. Only the little brown babies playing in nature's ample playpen bring to the forest's enchantment a realm of reality.

Beside the highway a shepherdess tends her sheep. In front of the bus, on the road ahead, two lumbering oxen, herded by one of the Indians in his colorful, native dress, moves to the side of the road as the bus moves on—chugging its way up the mountain, spitting noxious fumes…emitting sounds which do not inspire confidence in its ability to go much farther, but the impossible is being accomplished and we climb higher still. Finally we are at the apex of the upward journey. Below us there lie the azure waters of glorious Atitlán! From this height all else loses its significance—only the gladness and aroma of nature claim the senses and the spirit, heady, intoxicating.

I can see the lake in its entirety—it is immense, much bigger than I expected. It is surrounded by what looks like dollhouse villages nestled between high volcanic peaks.

Enchanting in its blueness and enclosed in the splendors of the mountains and volcanoes, the lake swells in gigantic waves, embraces the shore and rolls back into its own splendid body.

Images tucked away in the recesses of my memory come to life. I imagine the Calendar Priest reconstructing his calendar from the Preclassic Period—gauging the suns and the moons to accommodate the earth. In the thick forests of the mountains I see the Mayas hiding from the *Conquistadores*—pursued by the dreadful Pedro de Alvarado.

Beyond the limited hours of times a remnant of the Mayan culture survives. Its seed replenishes the earth down through the annals of creation.

EL LAGO ATITLAN

The bus begins to descend, perhaps about 1,000 feet, and though we are still at a very high altitude, there is a drop in the terrain down to a crater amid the mountains. We are in *Panajachel,* the main village of El Lago Atitlán, the magical land of the Mayas. Our bus, creaking and groaning, pulls onto a street, which must be the thoroughfare of the village. There smack in front of us sits a huge, comfortable-looking Greyhound bus. Across its expansive chassis are gigantic letters of one of the leading hotels in the capital. A neat-looking tour guide jauntily jumps to the ground, rubbing his shoulders and stretching luxuriously. Excited-looking tourists, all well groomed though dressed in sport clothes, follow him. Angela and I by now are no longer merely untidy. We are dirty to the point of grubbiness.

I watch in amazement as the passengers disembark from this snobbish chariot...aboard there are no huge loads of avocados, no chickens, no pigs...only people.

Over Angela's protests, I approach the tour guide. He speaks excellent English and politely he answers all my questions concerning the absurd differences in the two transportation systems. He tells me that the Pan American Highway is the route taken by the tourist buses. On the other hand the bus that brought us here belongs to the *Rebuli* buses, a company which is mainly patronized by the rural Guatemalans, the indigenous people. Oh well, I can be smug in that I am not a typical tourist, if no more! The buses of the *Maya Rebuli* reach most of the remote villages, which have no access to the modern highways. There are villages, I'm told, which have no access to any road. All their travel, from one village to another, is carried out via the waters of Atitlán.

It is immediately obvious that Panajachel is fast becoming a resort area. Along the lake shores, construction of high-rise hotels is underway.

The Naturales in this area, in addition to fluent Spanish, speak some English, further evidence of their frequent contact with many tourists. In spite of the rapidly-disappearing Indian culture, Panajachel is a village of great charm. It is a botanical paradise. Everything looks so green—from the vines that cling to the fences that enclose the gardens of pretty cottages to the tall corn still growing. Gigantic trees are laden with huge avocados. Velvety roses in pinks, yellows and reds grow abundantly in the gardens of small shops and summer homes. Bougainvillea and rhododendron add their flamboyant colors to the atmosphere.

In the rural areas of the mountains, the ugliness of the city seems far away, though a young man from the Peace Corps, the only other North American on the bus we took here, tells me that the infant mortality rate is just as devastating here as anywhere else in the country. (Survival of half the children in a family beyond the age of six is a "good average.") Unemployment and underemployment are a continuing problem. But in spite of all the dismal statistics there still seems not to exist here the same type of misery as in the capital. Perhaps this is due only to plenteous space in which to move about. The geographical beauty seems to swallow up all unpleasantness.

I see the little boys walking behind their fathers—miniature replicas in their cowboy hats, tight shirts and knee-length trousers, carrying machetes. They go to the fields to sow their seeds or to maintain their already growing crops, which, when harvested, will be taken to the public markets and sold. The money earned from this produce will buy seeds and fertilizer needed for the next season of planting. The Naturales seem to understand the order of nature and work within its pliant rhythm. Interesting, fascinating race of people. I am indeed anxious to move on to the neighboring villages. Seventeen villages surround the lake. When there were but twelve the indigenous people say they were named for the Apostles, but since five have been added in the last century, they now have other than Biblical names.

Somehow one of the villagers in Panajachel has correctly connected me with my son. The Indian man stops me and gives me a note while we meet on the path that leads to the lake. The handwriting looks dearly familiar in my son's hasty scrawl. He writes that he has an opportunity to join a caravan heading eventually for Alaska. Since he must start school in the fall he felt that he wanted to see as much of the world as possible. It is a disappointment naturally. I would have liked to have enjoyed this beautiful place with him, if only for a day or two.

At 5:00 o'clock in the morning, it is still dark and we are on the boat crossing the lake…filled with the sense of being one with nature. The tension I felt, due to the appalling poverty of El Salvador and Guatemala City leaves me. The lake at this hour is as mysterious as its immeasurable depths. Just how this magnificent spot on the globe came into existence no one knows with certainty. It is actually presumed by geologists to be a crater formed by volcanic eruptions many centuries ago. In this early hour, the lake is calm, smooth as glass. However, this is evidently only one of its moods. It is apparently as mercurial as the volcanoes from which it drew its origin. The sailors on the boat tell me that there are four winds that meet at midday in the middle of the lake and if any vessel dares to venture into their territory, in fury they dash it to pieces. In Indian language, the name for the furious winds is *Xocomil* (pronounced chocomeel). This area is greatly respected by the Naturales. Xocomil has been known to cause waves as high as the ocean's. Many legends surround this enigmatic force. A young man on the boat, a Natural in his *traje tipico*—I've by now learned the name of the native costume and early I'm reminded that the indigenous people refer to themselves as Naturales, not Indians— relates to me what is probably the most romantic of all fables about *Xocomil*. (Angela gets to translate.) The storyteller looks into space, dreamy-eyed, and says that at the lake's most profound depths are buried the departed Mayas' dreams. A dragon resides there, guarding over them. When humans dare to defile the sacred waters, the dragon, in fury, causes a storm to prevail. Vessels, both large and small, are capsized. The young man further elaborates on the story to say that a tourist boat was sunk in these waters not too long ago. (Another person, totally unrelated to the villages, and a foreigner, like myself, had told me about the boating incident first.)

While I realize that the tale goes far beyond the realm of the imagination, aside from the reality of the boating accident, I will nevertheless avoid traveling in the middle of the lake, even though the helmsman may assure me of the safety of his craft.

The darkness begins to fade. The shadowy figures of the Mayas are seen in their *cayucos*, fishing. In the distance they appear as apparitions of days gone by, before the *Conquistadores*. Silently by twos and threes they wait for the nibble at the tortillas used for bait at the end of their fishing rods. The fish supply one of their main sources of protein—frequently the only supplement to their families' diet of beans and tortillas.

In a matter of minutes the sun appears—instantly—and the earth is aglow with color. The surrounding villages awaken and come to life. The men of the villages wear their *traje tipico* for working, a garment only slightly less elegant than the one they wear for Sundays and the fiestas. Their sons of all ages follow in the rear with machetes, hoes or rakes. The mothers of the households likewise start to work—filing down to the lake with the family, wash balanced on their heads. The young ladies of the family along with the little girls join in the procession. They are all dressed in *huipiles*—a loose blouse that forms part of the native dress—and skirts that wrap around the body and are held together at the waist with a *faja*—a wide belt of hand-woven material. I am told that the traditional Maya is never seen in any other type garment. Most are barefoot—shoes are saved for special occasions and are mainly for appearance, not for working or merely walking.

The men who are not walking to the fields in their respective villages begin their labors by shoving off in the *cayucos*. Soon a lively flotilla of commerce is formed in Atitlán's waters. Apparent is the fact that time is not spent in idleness among this race of people.

The village of our intended visit is Santiago Atitlán, a pueblo directly across the lake from Panajachel. We go ashore after the boat docks. Dozens of children, dressed in native costumes, run out from nowhere, blowing on whistles and handing them to us, the tourists. "*Compra, compra,*" they demand of us; some are even saying, "Hey you! You buy, you buy from me."

Their ware consists of long strings of beads and some rather curious-looking birds, chalky and painted green. These items are of no earthly use to us, but we buy some of the beads and birds anyway to appease the children. One young man standing in the shallow water by the boat dock is saying, "If I buy this from you, do you promise to go away and not to bother me again?" They take the money he offers, but I don't hear them agreeing to any such promise!

The little people are among the most tenacious I've ever seen. They continue to follow us saying things which sounds like, "*Taka pitch, taka pitch...*" It is only when one of the tourists pulls an expensive camera out from its bag and begins taking photographs that we realize that they want their pictures taken. They know that their services as models are much in demand and the tourists will gladly pay for this valuable commodity. This tradition perhaps came about from an old mistrust of the camera's function. At one time they believed that a photograph steals their souls. Many Naturales still believe that the printed image has this "power," and I guess the kids feel that if they're going to lose their souls, they at least ought to get some money for them.

From the boat dock, there is a path that winds its way to the top over a small hill. We are told that there are rooms available along with a *comedor*—a small restaurant where we can take our meals. Since neither Angela nor I are acquainted with the village, there is little reason for us to be too selective. The rooms are shown to us by an indigenous boy whose presence at the pension, the Chi-Nim-Ya, seems to be very much rooted in the establishment. The rooms are free of any adornments and very sparsely furnished. This complex of cubicle—like dormitories, consisting of two levels—is built around a courtyard.

A corridor encircles each level and a balcony above affords an interesting view of village life. Like a painting, clusters of thatched roofs are visible against a background of coffee plants and the distant mountain slopes decorated with tall corn.

We are guided upstairs to look at the vacant rooms there. Most are merely replicas of the downstairs sleeping quarters, with the exception of one at the end of the corridor. It is large and airy, completely encased by windows and a full view of the lake comes with the room. Perfect, splendid, we grab it up, unable to believe our good fortune. From the balcony, looking down, there is a typical rural Guatemalan scene. A huge turkey is tied to a pole lying on the ground. Gobbling contentedly, it is unaware of what its fate will be when sufficiently fattened. A golden canary in a cage chants its lovely melody. Two multi-colored parrots add their monotonous squall to the sounds below: *"Como estas? Como estas? Puta, puta."*—terrible birds!

When Angela and I are in the pueblo but a day, we learn that we have chosen our quarters wisely—this is easily the best hotel in Santiago. Over a delicious and nourishing meal of vegetables and pan-fried fish fresh from the lake, we become acquainted with the pension owners. They do not resemble the majority of the inhabitants of the pueblo, but have the facial characteristics of Europeans. A handsome couple, they are polite and intelligent. They give their names, José and Francisca, and during conversation, they tell us they are not from the village, but from Quetzaltenango, Guatemala's second largest city, hence their urban air.

I decide to end my travel in Central America and settle down for the remainder of my stay here at El Lago Atitlán. Were people to ask me exactly why, I would probably tell them that I want to keep off the beaten path of tourists. Beyond that, my poetry may tell me what I at the moment do not know—that answer of course would be at the risk of sounding melodramatic. I only know at the present time I feel compelled to stay.

The pueblo, I learn, is deceptively populous for its geographical size. There are, according to Guatemala's statistics, 25,000 inhabitants in Santiago Atitlán, out of which only 1,000 are Ladinos, meaning

Spanish and Indian. There is a noticeable separation, even here in the pueblo between the two cultures. José and Francisca seem to be the only Ladinos speaking the language of the village, the Tzutuhil "*idioma.*" This language was exclusively a spoken dialect until a few years ago. A Spanish scholar who came to the pueblo translated the Mayan language to Spanish, thereby making an education available to the Tzutuhil population.

Very early in the morning, José and Francisca's general store is filled with the little Tzutuhiles doing part of the family shopping. They buy such items as a single needle, a candle, two or three pieces of "*pan dulce,*" sweet bread. Commerce here is conducted in the same efficient manner as any other reputable business. There are no complaints from the adult patrons receiving change from larger bills, nor is the smallest item given away.

At exactly noon every day, the local schoolteachers come to the comedor for lunch. It appears that they reside here at the pension during the nine months when school is in session. The teachers (two men and a woman) seem to be dedicated to their professions. Even with my meager knowledge of Spanish, I recognize their conversations to be primarily devoted to the activities of the classrooms, with emphasis on how best to help the students needing attention.

When the meal terminates and the diners disperse they murmur to each other, "Gracias." *Buen Provecho* is the invariable response. I, too, am included in this polite discourse, the latter of which I have no trouble interpreting—it means something like—at least I think— "Enjoy your meal." But why, I wonder, am I being thanked when I've not contributed monetarily or in any other way to make possible the consumption of anyone else's food? I want to ask Angela, but she looks too comfortable to answer my questions, which by now have mounted to a multitude.

Early one morning Angela engages the services of a boat and its owner. She tells me that she wants to visit the other villages at Lake Atitlán. I want desperately to accompany her, but due to a sudden onset of stomach cramps I know that the most sensible thing to do right now is stay near a bathroom. I accompany my friend to the lake's edge, no further. She climbs into the canoe with the two men dressed in the *traje* of the pueblo, and airily waves goodbye to her *gringa* friend, as the men paddle the boat through the blue waters, the sun shining on the three of them. I make some attempt to return the short-term farewell, and clutch my queasy stomach, just before the three figures in the little boat become dots in the vast waters of Atitlán.

I go back to the Chi-Nim-Ya and attempt a conversation with José and Francisca. Their vocabularies in English are almost equivalent to mine in Spanish. Among us we manage about fifty words before we terminate this tedious exchange.

As the day passes the buying and selling transactions take a different direction. The men who have been working in the fields enter the *comedor*. They have a distinctive odor, the Naturales. Their bodies smell of firewood and the out-of-doors and of the very earth itself. They brush the dust off their clothing with their hands while entering the door, and lay aside their machetes and whatever produce they may be carrying in their hemp bags, which had been strapped to their foreheads. Down comes the local moonshine from the top shelves. Several young men come in with guitars. They tune up and a "jam session" begins. Their voices are of good quality, their harmony rich and in lusty tones. The ballads of the singers, as in any other language, are songs of broken promises and unrequited love. The religious canticles are sung with the deep yearning and melancholia of the *Via Dolorosa*.

These recent patrons of the Chi-Nim-Ya are becoming quite drunk, although but an hour or so have passed. They seem to be unsteady as they order another round of drinks.

In a little while these hard-working men are dropping where they stand. Those still able to stay on their feet drag their fallen comrades to a corner where their bodies will be less obstructing and go on with their serious drinking. Presently their family members come to claim the fallen angels. One of these members is as angry as it is possible to be. She appears to be the wife of one of the *caballeros* judging from the tongue-lashing she gives to his drinking buddies. She then begins to shout at her companion, although she knows he is in a world where nothing can reach him. He makes some feeble attempt to get up, but falls back on the floor where he stays. The good woman again turns to her husband's drinking companions, shouting out her anger at them for having led her husband astray...for naught, for naught. They are, as her husband, beyond apology or repentance. Because the lady is strong from hard work, and because her adrenaline is working overtime, she is able to drag her man—in this condition—out of the Chi-Nim-Ya toward one of the huts, undoubtedly home to both of them, muttering curses all the while. She will certainly give him no peace tomorrow until he has been made aware of his gross sins.

Angela returns late in the afternoon and my first question to her is, "Do the people in the other villages speak Spanish?" She replies in the affirmative, adding, "Some of them even speak some English. They know how to say, "One dollar, two dollar, three dollar, and so on."— Who would disagree that recognizing dollars is an important phase of the person working in commerce.

At my insistence, Angela briefly narrates how she has spent the day, the highlights of each village. She tells me that she doesn't want to divulge too much all at once; like the movies there would be no surprises. From what she does relate, though, it seems that each pueblo is in some way different from the others; the clothing, though similar, has its own colors and designs. The dialects spoken also vary in each of the pueblos. Angela then inquires of the way I've spent my day and I can only tell her of the activities of the Chi-Nim-Ya. She looks slightly amused, but says that she fails to comprehend how a bunch of drunks could possibly keep anyone entertained, stating that I should have gone with her in spite of my queasy stomach.

The time passes quickly and it is time for Angela's departure. The goodbyes we say, though tearful, do not reflect real sorrow. I am happy for her that she will have an opportunity to enhance her career in the United States. There is little demand for a sociology major in El Salvador. Away from her father she can work toward healing.

Additionally, I know that if Angela and I remain together, we'll be spending most of our time talking or just hanging out, which at any other time would certainly be all right. If I were to feel that time is being wasted while just in pursuit of genuine happiness, I've come to the wrong place. Short of picking up a machete and going to the fields with the industrious Mayas, there's no work to do at present. I hope this will change. I plan to get to know the indigenous people here, to share in their culture, to write about them, to become an integrated member of their village.

Angela is gone and I'm alone. I take stock of my situation and reflect upon the days ahead. Not only am I in a strange country, unable to communicate, but also in a remote Indian village where the culture is so diverse that centuries would be required to bridge the gap.

I'm relieved about one thing. No one is able to see inside the luggage I've brought with me. Had this been possible and the word had gotten get out, I would not only have been the laughingstock among the villagers but my countrymen as well. Several pairs of high heel shoes, a store of cosmetics, even a couple of evening dresses complete my traveling wardrobe. In addition, among my belongings is a new, portable electric typewriter, which according to the salesman in the States, was the nearest thing on the market to an IBM. This may have been true where there was available electricity.

An incredulous feeling, one in which everyone is at sometimes familiar takes possession of me, that feeling which evokes the question—What am I doing here? My thoughts return to this business of communications; I can't even communicate with any degree of fluency with the Ladinos, much less the indigenous people (the Naturales of the village).

This sense of desolation does pass. I remind myself that all people, regardless of culture and appearances, can be close if they make the effort. The deficiency in the languages, too, has a cure. I'll just have to learn to speak them; lest I assign myself too rigid a task, I begin my resolve with Spanish.

Spanish, as purported, is a language rich and full, a true gourmet delight to the aspiring linguist. There are so many words from which to choose, so many ways to express just one verb, so musical and fluid a language.

The Mayan languages (Tzutuhil being the language spoken here in the pueblo) as nearly as I can ascertain are vastly different from Spanish, having a high-pitched sound in some words while others are emitted in guttural sounds. These seem to change meanings with inflections, similar to what we hear in the Asian languages. In addition to the similarities in speech, the Mayas bear a physical resemblance to the Asians. Their skin, though brown, is yellow-tinged and their dark eyes are almond-shaped.

Some archaeologists believe that the Mayan race had its beginning in China or one of the other Asian countries...but in a little book simply entitled, *The Maya*, its author, Michael Coe, completely disagrees. He writes that no relics in any of the major Mayan ruins have been found to support this theory.

I make a mental note to ask José and Francisca concerning the popular belief here in the pueblo as to the origin of the Maya.

At the moment Chico's voice interrupts my thoughts, announcing that dinner is ready. He doesn't come to the room, but calls from the dining room, "Bonnie, *la cena está lista*." I see a third budding friendship with Chico, the boy who had made up the rooms when Angela and I had arrived. He is not a Ladino, but of Tzutuhil origin; therefore his friendship seems exaggeratedly important. I notice that he is quite ambidextrous. He is able to cook, wait on tables, and wash the dishes, as if these chores were all one easy maneuver. He never seems to be irritable with this workload, but sings merrily while he performs his tasks.

The *comedor*, like the adjacent rooms, is rustic and few are its luxuries. But it seems that the table I occupy has them all—a little lace tablecloth, spotlessly white in front of me when I dine, and placed on the table is the restaurant's only coffee warmer and a glass of water with ice. Amid all the grandeur, Chico stands over me, bowing, awaiting my order. It is the stance of the waiters at the Ritz Continental, one of Guatemala's leading hotels in the capital. Above and beyond all the obvious considerations, it is Chico's smile that best tells me my affection for him is mutual, the look of gladness in his eyes when I enter the dining room. When dining these days in the *comedor*, I have a habit of saying to each of the patrons, "*Gracias*," and "*Buen Provecho*," and just to make sure of their appropriateness, I repeat the phrases many times. This way I feel a bit more Guatemalan.

José and Francisca look amused at my efforts, but not in excess of the way most citizens of every country view foreigners. They apparently have suspected that I've stayed in their village for some particular reason; my electric typewriter undoubtedly earned me the prestige as a "researcher."

The couple suggests one day soon after my arrival that I go to the Catholic church and speak with the padre there, a North American from Oklahoma. While walking uphill and over the cobblestones I notice that the pueblo is inundated with churches of every persuasion. There is a new Baptist church, and within the next two hundred feet are two Pentecostal churches. Other evangelical churches are still in construction. But the social and religious life of the pueblo still throbs through the pulse of its mother church. The main buildings of the Catholic church and its appendages occupy the space of about three city blocks. Facing the pueblo is a large courtyard, part of which has been converted to a playground for the local grade school. It is equipped with basketball courts and other equipment needed for sports activities.

A youngish priest answers my knock and invites me inside. He presents himself to me only as David, the formal title "Father" having been dropped. But I notice that the people of the pueblo performing various chores at the chapel and rectory don't address him without this respect paid to the Catholic clergy. The padre is pleasant and gregarious. Right away he begins talking about his work here in the village, and from what he tells me, the church is deeply involved with the people of the pueblo. He tells me that an Oklahoma diocese sent him here, the mission here in Santiago Atitlán having been his home for the last four years. He says he loves his work with all its ups and downs, but that he is homesick for the town of his birth in Oklahoma. The priest is not wearing vestments, but is instead dressed in Western shirt and ordinary trousers. He seems less a clergyman in this casual attire— more like any other man—more in touch with the human race around him by this identity, and certainly more comfortable than were he to wear the customary long, flowing robes.

I have the feeling that I may ask what I will and any information not already divulged by Padre David will be supplied willingly to me, not only as a one-time visitor but anytime in the future.

The padre tells me that the school is filled to capacity, but still only a small percent of the children in the pueblo attend classes. This is partly due to a lack of sufficient facilities, but the main reason is that the children's parents are too poor to spare them the time for academics. They must help their parents in the fields.

Padre David, like any priest I've met, is busy, but consistent with my initial impression of him, he invites me back.

Before leaving the grounds, I look around me and see that the structures of the church buildings bear evidence of the Spaniards who conquered in this area. It is also obvious that they had some help in the building of these colonial structures. The workmanship on the steps leading to the rectory of the church has a wide and circular effect at the bottom, which narrows gradually toward the top, having the pyramidal effect of the Maya architecture.

Venturing from the pueblo now, I begin to visit the other villages surrounding the lake, and during my voyages, I learn that the pueblos surrounding Santiago Atitlán are deeply steeped in separate cultures, separate identities. Their *traje*, though similar, is still different in design and color. Rarely does one of these Naturales ever live in another village, nor does he or she marry outside the village of their birth.

In spite of the cultural and language differences the Naturales have much in common. The ladies are all experts in the art of weaving, fashioning archaic, feminine beauty at their looms.

All the pueblos are framed against a background of the ubiquitous *milpa*, necessary for their daily bread (tortillas). People who have spent time in Southern Mexico comment that the culture closely resembles the indigenous population here, but throughout the centuries rural life has remained uniquely Guatemalan.

Between Santiago Atitlán and San Lucas Toliman (with whom Santiago has an ongoing vocal war over which pueblo has the greater beauty) lies a small village named Cerro de Oro—Hill of Gold. The

Naturales here are of the Tzutuhil tribe, the pueblo being an extension of Santiago and claim that treasures are still buried here. Whether this claim is true or merely legend, no one outside the pueblo seems to know with certainty. The Naturales, however, do not take kindly to the archaeologists who dig in this area. They merely go behind the "diggers," covering up by night what has been uncovered by day.

My limited experience with the Naturales has taught me that the handling of the "problematic archaeologists" is typical of their way of dealing with all problems, their approach diagonal, never direct. Similarly I've never heard a Natural apologize by saying he's sorry. He may right the matter with a certain act or deed, but he will never openly admit he has been in the wrong. Among this obstinate race of people, this quality is the most pronounced among the Tzutuhiles. Among all Guatemalan communities, they were the last to surrender to the invading Spaniards. Two pueblos within a short distance of Panajachel, San Jorge and Santa Catarina, are best known for their work in *petates*—these are mats made from the *tule* (rushes), which grow at Atitlán's banks.

San Lucas Toliman produces beautiful, hand-carved furniture while San Pedro La Laguna is noted for its hand-woven rugs.

San Marcos, perhaps the poorest village in Guatemala, turns out every type of rope imaginable, from the practical to the decorative.

Though none of the pueblos surrounding Lake Atitlán are in any way lacking in beauty—the lake has generously made its azure waters available to all, and each is dressed in resplendent colors of nature, Santiago Atitlán is easily the most colorful. The most talented of Guatemala's artists spring from here, one apparently having gained worldwide recognition for his art. His home, though simple in architecture, is a masterpiece of beauty because of his paintings hanging everywhere throughout the house. I had met Juan Sisay on one occasion, a no-nonsense person who seemed neither unduly conceited nor filled with false modesty. He had to have known, however, that he possessed a very unusual talent.

Among the Naturales of Santiago Atitlán are some of the most skilled stone masons and sculptors in the world. Splendorous images carved in wood and stone decorate their small shops. And their *traje*? Like everything else in the pueblo, it is exquisite. The ladies' *huipiles* are white and decorated with purple stripes, and embroidered with bright-colored flowers, while their *cortes* are ankle-length and woven from a brilliant red. Their hair, inky-black, hangs down past their waists, and on festive occasions, is dressed in multi-colored headbands. The little girls' clothing are replicas of their mothers, and the men folk dress in similar design, a Western shirt and *pantalones* in place of the *huipiles* and *cortes* Although the predominant religion throughout Guatemala is Catholicism, the superstitions brought to their shores by their Spanish ancestry, combined with the mythology of the Mayas, has resulted in a mixture of the ancient Mayan religion and Catholicism, the churches of which still exist today and where this "brand of religion" is still practiced in Guatemala's famous Chi-Chi-Castenango. Two such churches face each other. Colonial in structure, they present a dramatic appearance, nestled among the pines at 7,000 feet. As I enter one of the churches for the first time, a feeling close to awe engulfs me. What looks like a million candles burning in the vestibule, a multitude of parishioners make their supplications to a deity other than the one familiar to me. Yet their prayers seem intense and sincere. There are some Naturales among them who seem to be putting on a show for the tourists. Like all other entertainers, they want to be paid for their acting. One man stops close to me as I kneel at the altar. Dressed in the *traje* of this area, in black wool, the garment embroidered in red and purple, he asks me for five dollars, and for this amount promises me access to the wisdom of the universe. I give him the money, not because I have any faith in raffled spirituality, here or anywhere, but because he probably has nine kids at home and needs the money.

Some weeks pass before my Spanish vocabulary has reached the utterable stage. A little book, *Veinte Poemas de Amor* becomes my greatest challenge in reading. The author of this little book is the famous Chilean author, Pablo Neruda. A young man from Argentina, who had been traveling in Guatemala, gave the book to me. Though he considered himself superior to all other *Latins* by mere virtue of the fact that he hailed from Argentina, I nevertheless must admire his taste in literature. Contained in the small book are treasures of the soul, hidden music that springs to life when I am able to grasp the meaning of the music in rhyme. A small matter in which to rejoice?—perhaps—but this is rural life in Guatemala! The word I discover in Mr. Neruda's poetry is *regocjjadamente* and I adopt this lovely word for my own. It means *joyfully*, and since I've fallen in love with the word, I joyfully come to the dining room; I joyfully accept the lush, ripe fruit someone hands me to try and when José and Francisca invite me to the fiesta, I accept r*egocijadamente*.

When the big evening arrives, I consult my friends regarding proper dress for the occasion. José throws back his head in a small fit of laughter that draws a rebuke from his wife. She tells him not to make sport of me—that I'm new to the pueblo and that my questions are natural.

The three of us are ready; I take a deep breath for the trek up the hill and José jokes further about the limousine that will arrive at any moment to take us to the party in grand style. It is plain to see why José had laughed at my question. When we arrive at the downtown part of the village, its citizens are dressed in every color of the rainbow! No garment of mine even comes close to matching the brilliant hues of the *traje* worn here at the fiesta. Bright red and flaming purple dominate the designs of the Naturales' clothing. The men's trousers are decorated with hand-embroidered blue birds. These *pantalones* reach just below the knee and the outfit is completed with Western shirt and hat (similar to the cowboy hat worn in the Western part of the United States). The ladies and little girls' clothing are of similar intricate design, with the blue birds decorating the *huipil* and the *corte* (skirt) near the hem. The total dress is held together by a *faja,* that is a belt of the hand-woven material, also multi-colored. Their clothing, of course, attracts the attention of every tourist who sets foot on Guatemalan territory, but seeing the rich collage of colors deck the whole pueblo at once, startles the vision. It is obvious that the ladies have dressed more for each other than for the men; they cast peripheral glances in the direction of their friends. There is that certain looking away when they have the attention they sought in their finery.

Francisca tells me that these ladies save for an entire year for this event; undoubtedly this accounts for the disguise of the poverty at these fiestas.

The whole pueblo has turned out for the gala affair, the mothers and the dads, the grandmas and the grandpas and the children of all sizes and ages. They parade about the town in their elegance, up and down the cobblestone streets, chattering excitedly. It is here at the fiesta that the Tzutuhil population becomes visible. José tells me that the local officials estimate the population of Santiago to be higher than that which is officially reported in Sololá, the pueblo that governs the whole lake area, giving the pueblo 35,000 people rather than 25,000. The difference is attributable to the unregistered births with the government here in the pueblo.

The fiestas are apparently associated with a religious ceremony. The three of us move aside for a procession going by. The statues of the church are being pulled in carts and wagons. These are decorated with branches and flowers and are accompanied by the church's faithful who do drink to a saturation point. Soon the cobblestone streets are greatly obstructed.

Behind the statue of the Virgin and the Christ Child I see the strangest sight imaginable even in a parade. Two men are carrying a creature on their shoulders. As with the statues of the church, several people run alongside the procession, as if honor is bestowed on this personage. When the little band of people is only about six feet away I realize that this "elevated being" is not even a person but some sort of image draped in several layers of clothing. A straw hat sits loftily and on his head and in his mouth is a big cigar. But the most noteworthy feature of his appearance is the wily look on his face—it is of such extreme that one gains the impression that he enjoys playing tricks on his creators, the humans.

While I stare in awe, I cannot refrain from asking José, "What the devil is that?" My Guatemalan friend just laughs and suggests that I ask Padre David.

At about 9:00 P.M., the women and children—all the sedate party goers—begin to disperse. The small children are either asleep or fussing tiredly, leaving only the men to continue with the night's celebration. Just as they had done at the Chi-Nim-Ya they begin to drink to a saturation point. Soon the cobblestone streets are greatly obstructed with inert bodies. This worries me; a car or a truck may not see the anesthetized hombres. But I seem to be the only person here concerned about their safety. Perhaps during the fiestas caution is instilled in the minds of the *choferes* if they must drive through the pueblo during these sacred events.

The most enigmatic event in the fiesta is yet to take place. A military truck bounces over the cobblestones and stops right in the middle of town during the village celebration. The gigantic vehicle is crowded with soldiers and their weaponry. Each one is equipped with a machine gun and in their midst looms some type of canon, ominously high and warlike.

What appeared at first to be only one truck is actually two. Another one, immediately behind and overshadowed by the density of the first, is practically empty. The soldiers all jump out, as if on wartime maneuver, and there begins a chase in the night. All the young men, those still alert enough from their bouts of drinking, begin to run— shouting a warning to their comrades as they do so. Many of them tumble into the nearest ditch where they can no longer be seen, laughing uproariously; they have managed to evade their would be captors. Other young men of the village—not so lucky—are grabbed by several soldiers, handcuffed and tossed into the second truck along with other shackled youths.

I ask José and Francisca about this strange event that seems to be a ritual at the fiestas: "What crime have these young people committed?" I want to know. Francisca defers to José. His face colors as he gives me his answer. "They are not being charged with a crime," he explains, "but are merely being recruited into the military service."

In spite of the merriment of the young men in the pueblo, the presence of the military trucks seems to have cast a pall over the gaiety of the fiesta, and the masks worn by the male dancers who encircle small areas of the streets seem grotesque, resembling demons more than the angelic likenesses usually associated with religious worship. The dancers' steps quicken with an increasing tempo to the clanging of tambourines and other small musical instruments.

It seems that the Naturales have inherited not only much of their ritualistic worship from their Mayan ancestors, but from the Spaniards as well. The masks are similar to those worn by the Spanish during their holy days, alien to the rest of the Catholic world.

While I walk to the pueblo the day following the fiesta, the poverty is more noticeable. The people have changed into their workday clothes. The babies whose faces are visible now all seem to have upper respiratory infections. Neither do the tots who run along beside their mothers appear to be in the best of health. The sound of their coughs are heard throughout the pueblo and their noses run a sickening color of green mucus.

When Padre David responds to my knock, I begin right away to ask questions concerning the general state and welfare of the pueblo. He tells me that malnutrition among the Naturales is an ever-present problem. There is a high incidence of tuberculosis among the rural population also. He tells me that the church is trying to counteract the problem, which is overwhelming at times. Construction of a hospital here in the village will be underway soon. The padre also tells me that there will be a doctor along with his wife, a nurse, arriving shortly. They will begin to develop nutrition clinics and teach the ladies midwifery. Though an outsider to the village this information makes me personally happy. One of the padre's helpers, a Natural, shows me a workshop behind the main building. Several men are working over a large loom turning out the typical cloth of the village. In another room the village sculptors are carving out of wood the majestic God of Corn, the God of Childbirth and other delicate designs of the Mayan deities. The carpenters of the pueblo work busily with saw and hammers, designing furniture of less expensive, but still attractive, pinewood. The richer and more enduring pieces of furniture are shaped from conacasta, a popular hardwood in Guatemala.

The hard-working men tell me that what products they are not able to sell in Guatemala, that the priests ship to the United States—

apparently the priests at the church have connections with wholesalers in their country. Before I leave the church, I ask Padre David about the "strange object" to which tribute was paid at the fiesta.

David laughs good-naturedly and tells me that this "presence" is a bit difficult to explain. "He is not quite considered a God, but the characteristics ascribed to him are not quite human either. He is called Maximón."

Padre David, upon seeing my lips move, trying to form the enigmatic word for this strange creature, pronounces it for me again—the phonetics being mash-e-mohn.

The padre goes on to tell me that Maximón is both scorned and revered by the Naturales of the Pueblo. Having a dual personality, his function is to both bless and curse. He represents the extremes of good and evil. The recipients of his power hope that they are friend rather than foe when Maximón begins his magic. Padre David then takes me to the entrance of the church where there is a large cement porch. We look down at the hollowed-out space, which has the imprint of a head, trunk and limbs of a body. "This is the shrine of Maximón," the priest tells me. "About twenty years ago one of my predecessors grew weary of this thing being brought to the mass during the fiestas, as was then the custom. Maximón was taken from his resting place, which was and still is an elaborate casket in a shaded area isolated from the village by a mountainous terrain of thick vegetation, and with the tenderest of care, given his share of respect and adoration. Maximón is not now allowed in the church—the only change in the ritual. The enterprising priest had made a deal with the Catholics, who still adhered to the dual worship of witchcraft. Maximón could be brought as far as the entryway of the church, but no farther; he would be left in his designated home just outside. The compromise was perfect to both priest and parishioners. The shrine still remains and serves as the home for old Maximón during the fiestas." Before my "history lesson" terminates for the day, I have yet another question—the men I had seen dancing around at the fiesta, who are they? Those are members of the *Cofradia,* I'm told. "Christians who still cling to the religion of their Mayan ancestry, they also share in the governing of the pueblo, but their governing power is not recognized by the super stratum of Guatemala's government, nor given the respect paid to them by the pueblo."

Once more my visit to Padre David, my friend from Oklahoma, has proved profitable.

My days in Guatemala turn into weeks and during one such day I realize that weeks have become three months. My time is spent in either a greatly exhilarated state or a kind of purgatory, which is on the fringes of unutterable boredom. The contentment I longed for has greatly eluded me. I'm not only afflicted with the blank page syndrome writers talk about, I am plagued with the additional malady of blank thoughts. To make matters worse, I only have to look out the window and I'm reminded that El Lago Atitlán is one of the loveliest places in the world. Prior to my coming here I had imagined myself among those superior beings who can live without the theater and automobile, someone with whom I can gossip over coffee. But this favorite delusion of mine has long vanished. From my window I can see who gets off the boat. If the travelers vaguely look as if they can speak English, I lie in wait for these unsuspecting persons.

They may not know what the money exchange is in Guatemala, or they may want to know where the public market is, if it's safe to drink the water, any number of things; in these cases I can be very helpful, although a penalty is attached. They must talk to me—about anything—but they must talk!

About every week or so I have a habit of packing up and going to Panajachel or to the capital. In the city I can rent a hotel room with hot water, wear a nice dress, go to the movies.

On one such trip to the city, I come face to face with a reason for staying in Guatemala forever. While sitting in a restaurant having a cup of coffee, a voice, irresistibly sweet, seems to be addressing me from above the table… "May I sit here?"

I turn around to look into a pair of dark eyes in a very friendly, open face. His black hair is worn shoulder length, and at the moment is tied at the nape of the neck with a red kerchief, a fashion still in vogue in the United States.

During the course of the conversation, it is at once obvious that the young man is intelligent and philosophical, as his appearance suggests. There are, however, areas of vagueness in his philosophy, some elements of contradiction. He tells me he has embraced the religions of the East, although just which one he doesn't say. For some reasons Catholicism won't do—perhaps like his mode of dress, Buddhism (or whatever religion he has chosen) is more compatible with his life, its divinity allowing greater freedom than the traditional Christian Church. It occurs to me after some ten minutes that we've not exchanged names. When I offer mine he pronounces it exactly the way Angela had done—*"Boney, I am Flavio, Boney."*

Flavio speaks a lot about celibacy, as if this spiritual state in a young person so difficult to attain somehow applies to him. He persists in calling me his sister, but there is nothing in his mannerisms that suggests brotherly affection. To the contrary he looks at me now with sheer lust in those miracles called eyes.

I am able to smile at this youthful hypocrisy. (With or without the contradiction I would not have it another way!)

I tell Flavio where I'm staying and he tells me that I've made a wonderful choice. He asks my permission to visit me at the lake. It is readily given. It feels very good to have a friend with whom I can be relaxed and comfortable.

I go back to Santiago Atitlán feeling happier than when I left; this state has not gone unnoticed at the Chi-Nim-Ya. Francisca and José ask me what happened in my trip to the city. Three other very good friends wait for me in my room; they are Kahlil Gibran, John Steinbeck and Pablo Neruda. I pick up Pablo's book first. I have to translate each line before I can read it. The poems are so spiritual that they convey a similar message of a gifted priest's most eloquent sermon, and at the same time they are so erotic that they would make pale by comparison the blatant pornography sold on the "adult newsstands."

When I share my admiration of this author with the school teachers at the Chi-Nim-Ya the educators tell me that Pablo Neruda also wrote dynamic political poetry, passionate verses, expressions of deep yearning to free those living under the yoke of oppression. He sawed away with biting eloquence at the chains that enslaved the citizens of Latin American countries, including his own. These poems, of course, were considered slanderous by the dictator who came to power in Chile following the overthrow of the socialist government that resulted in the assassination of Salvador Allende, Chile's freely elected president at the time.

Although the poet didn't die from an assassin's bullet, his death was attributed to the deprivations of a refugee. He had been forced into exile and, had he remained at home, he would have had to face the same fate as countless other revolutionaries of the spirit. His hands would have been held in the chains that gripped the other "powerful *manos*" while the henchmen of the Chilean Government chopped them off*

Because of my complete fascination with Pablo Neruda's poetry, I at first don't hear Francisca calling me. Only two days since my trip to the city and it seems I have a caller from the area. I have a speech prepared for him. I am completely in agreement that we will have a great time as friends. Beyond that there's no point of his trying to pursue a relationship that can't be. I must remind him that I'll be forty-two on my next birthday, while he on the other hand can't be a day over twenty-five.

I look at myself in the mirror, trying to affect a firm expression, and of course, when I meet Flavio in the dining room, I don't say a word that resembles my rehearsed speech. He seems too happy to see me—so am I—happy to see him. He tells me that if I'm agreeable we will explore the other villages at Atitlán together. Flavio moves into the space left vacant by Angela in the large room, an arrangement doomed to failure. Very early in our conversations, he tells me that he doesn't know why North Americans are so "hung up" on people's ages. He says that I'm a woman and he's a man—beyond this obvious fact, what is there that worries me so greatly?

*On 9/23/73 Pablo died of cancer—presumably due to the unavailability of medical treatment at the time, he possibly could have had a longer life.

José and Francisca had looked upon the two of us together with some surprise, but no real disapproval. It isn't long before Flavio, too, experiences the warmth of their friendship.

Exploration of the villages with Flavio becomes a source of delight. He is familiar with the geography and culture of the pueblos. He even speaks some of the dialects of the indigenous people in the more remote areas. In spite of his small frame (he can't weigh more than 128 pounds) my Guatemalan companion drags the bulk of my heavy luggage over incredibly steep mountainous terrain without sarcasm or complaint. He never once suggests that we throw the damn suitcases over the cliffs. This is not to in any way imply that he is a saint. He can be profane at times—he knows all the swear words in English and uses them prolifically.

One day after our stay in a village called Santa Catarina, we decide to move on to another pueblo, our destination being that of San Pedro La Laguna.

We hitch a ride with a man who is transporting a pig from one village to the next in a *cayuco*. These are wonderful vehicles of travel in the water; they are dugout canoes hollowed from the trunks of large trees.

On this particular day, very typical of the season, the sky is overcast and dark. Just why we feel that we have to go through with it I don't know. There is time to turn back, but we give no thought at all to such a maneuver. But nature, lady that she is, has given us fair warning.

Rain begins pelting down on our little sea craft the moment we leave the shore. What at first appeared to be just a heavy rain turns into a full-blown deluge and for the first time I experience the other side of Atitlán's personality. The waves dash furiously against the side of the canoe. The wind blows and whistles its wrath and the waves, now gigantic like the ocean's, crash over our heads.

The two Naturales do manage to control the oars, wonderfully capable men that they are. Only when they begin to shout do I realize that we are in worse trouble than I had at first imagined.

The indigenous people are normally quite stoic and save their excitement and other demanding emotions for times like these.

One of the men produces a tarp and throws it over our heads, I think as much to prevent my seeing what's going on, as to keep out the downpour of the rain. In either case it does help considerably.

Although not exactly comfortable in the storm, I begin to feel a bit more secure, like perhaps there is some hope after all and we'll make it to shore. The men managing the boat are still holding their own.

I'm not able to enjoy my comfort for very long. There is an unmistakable odor of marijuana in our little craft, a small dot in a vast body of water. *This can't be*, I reason. *Not even Flavio would do a thing like that, on a day like this—so that fear of fire is added to our fear of drowning—wrong!* When I can steady myself sufficiently so as to look under the tarp in the direction of the smoke, there sits Flavio puffing hard, here amid the churning waters and the pouring rain. Had I thought just today I loved him? I despise him!

We do finally make it to shore The two men begin tying the feet of their glutinous passenger so that it will not run away before delivery. After all, the pig had been the main reason for the trip. Flavio and I, the paying passengers, had been incidental cargo. The Naturales seldom go anywhere without a practical purpose behind their trips.

A very gentle indigenous man, who had been waiting on the shore for the *cayuco* to arrive, greets us and remarks to me, "Yes, the journey by canoe is dangerous, but God, our Father, is always with us." In this I wholeheartedly agree, but I resolve to allow Him to test my faith in other ways in the future.

We are at San Pedro La Laguna, a neighboring village of Santiago Atitlán. The lake at San Pedro is different in character than her neighbor's. There is shallow water for two or more hundred feet. Water lilies and slender reed grown along its shores. San Pedro does not have the beautifying devices that Santiago has. The main thoroughfare, rather than the circular cobblestone streets, is little more than a dirt path.

Before we house hunt, Flavio and I visit a factory that specializes in rug making. The rugs are magnificent creations, the designs meticulous in reds and blues, greens as bright as the forest in the surrounding mountains. The God of Corn dominates the centers, while around their borders are various smaller designs, which all have some significance. One of the artists makes some attempt to explain them all to me, but the more he talks, the more confused I become. I pretend to understand.

Flavio and I decide to settle down in San Pedro for a few weeks, or for as long as it seems the thing to do. No one pesters me for money or tries to harass me to buy things I don't need. To the contrary, I'm left strictly alone, in fact ignored entirely.

However, as we inquire about a house for rent, one of the men working on the rugs graciously escorts us to an empty house, the only one available it seems, which is a cheerless affair with only one room, one window, but even when open very little light penetrates the darkness. The walls and ceilings are painted a horrendous shade of green. A cement floor is of an equally dismal color. But in contrast, there stands in the middle of the floor a table of elegant oak, obviously the work of a skilled carpenter. Our landlady proves to be the most cantankerous old lady I've ever met or hope to meet again. When I inquire about the house she offers for rent, she merely looks me up and down, and by the expression she wears, is most unimpressed by what she sees. She addresses her remarks to Flavio, not to me, as if I didn't even exist and had not been speaking to her. She and Flavio talk with each other for about five minutes. I stand aside feeling most unnecessary. Her Spanish is worse than mine. She has the accent of the pueblo's dialect, but from what I can gather from the garbled and mostly one-sided conversation, her disdain stems from my coming here to set up housekeeping so ill-equipped, nothing to cook with, no thread for weaving—nothing at all but a bag of groceries, which seems to be further cause for her scorn. She looks in its direction and sneers. As their talk continues, I believe I hear a placating tone in Flavio's voice as if he is apologizing for his *gringa* girlfriend. My new neighbor does seem somewhat appeased. She leaves, but returns in a few minutes with some household items such as cooking utensils, dishes and some daintily embroidered towels, which I think are dish towels. I begin wiping the dishes with these right away, only to have them snatched out of my hand by the lady. Flavio explains that they are for wrapping the tortillas and keeping them warm. The stove is a puzzling affair consisting of an iron grill for the top and a hollowed-out-like oven at its bottom, presumably for baking, very functional, all of it, I'm sure, but the hitch is that it's out-of-doors.

Before the lady takes her leave, I make some vain attempt to thank her for her consideration and once again she gives me no recognition, but turns to Flavio and informs him that if I break anything I'll have to pay for it. I'm getting madder by the minute and have very little optimism that relations between this lady and myself will ever improve.

I express to Flavio that, though I love the village, I don't feel comfortable in view of so much hostility and that perhaps we would be better off to move on. His response to me is maddening and self-righteous. "*Hay que tener patiencia*"—one must have patience. But then his tone softens as he tells me, "You may yet win her for a friend"—for me, far more acceptable advice.

In a moment, due to Flavio's typical efficiency, a cheery fire blazes in the stove. My companion has promised me an early tour of San Pedro. Leaving the house I put a pot of beans on the stove to simmer, taking advantage of the fire. Alas! The one ingredient necessary to cooking—salt—I had forgotten to buy in Panajachel. I think of asking our neighbor for a loan, but can't bring myself to do it. Indeed if she were to part with it, I would be in for a lecture for my carelessness.

When we return from our walk, Delfina is waiting for us. I learn her name from Flavio—I don't know how he managed to extract even this much from her. Anyway, there she is in the doorway of our rented home. She informs Flavio the moment we arrive that I have not salted the beans.

I turn to Flavio and retort, "Wouldn't you think that since she bothered to taste the beans, she would have salted them?" He merely replies in his most maddening of tones, which I'm beginning to recognize as uniquely his, "Why should she *salt your* beans?"

I repeat for him the same argument, "Because she tasted them, that's why." I can see that we've reached an impasse and think that there should be a better reason for ending a relationship than over a pot of beans, but if this argument continues, I am sure that it will lead to a breakup.

One day I actually believe that I see Delfina smile, and wonder of wonders, at me! Flavio had gone to catch some fish to compliment the meal I'm attempting to cook and would now well be on its way, but for one factor—the stove. A strong wind had come up and, as I stand blowing and coaxing, vainly trying to fan the few sparks into a flame. I sense that someone is behind me. What I at first, however, take to be a smile is actually a smirk, only partially hidden by her hands she holds over her mouth. I know what is coming next—open laughter.

I go back into the house in a huff, not wanting to be further ridiculed. I want to hit her—badly—and I think the only reason I refrain is that between the two of us, I will be the one to get the worst of it.

When my anger is considerably cooled, I am disgusted by my own pettiness. I think of what Flavio had said and think that a truce is in order.

When Flavio comes back and attends to the fire, so that cooking again becomes a possibility, I prepare a particularly appetizing dish, one of my specialties, with Delfina in mind. For really, how much had I tried to win her for a friend?

At her door, Delfina invites me inside—for the first time. The reason is all too obvious. The sudden show of hospitality is because I have something for her—but no matter.

Once in her home, I am taken quite by surprise. The members of her family, unlike her, are all refined and polite. I was never quite sure how many children Delfina had. The majority of them are married; the more fortunate ones have moved away.

One of her sons and daughter-in-law are new parents. Both are teachers in the local grade school. They thank me graciously for the food I've brought, murmuring appreciation. But if I have any thoughts that Delfina will change her attitude toward me because of this one conciliatory act, I am mistaken—badly. She merely wipes her lips of the sleeve of her *huipil* after she finishes eating and hands me an empty dish. (So much for a gift-bearing *gringa*.)

Once on my way past her house, I quite unintentionally overhear a family quarrel, one that is very one-sided. Through much verbal abuse on Delfina's part, the family members remain in subdued silence. No other route allows access to my rented home—and since the windows to Delfina's house are open—they all look in my direction; all are embarrassed but Delfina. The old tyrant is not in the least deterred as she goes on with her tirade.

She speaks half in Spanish, half in her native tongue, but obviously what she says is the message of a shrew anywhere else in the world. If she were to sit down and fold her hands like everyone else, the world would collapse; alone she bears the heavy burden of work. Her diatribe eventually narrows to include only her family. She must not only do her share in the household chores, but everyone else's as well. The cooking and cleaning fall to her, the feeding and watering of the animals, even to the chopping of the wood. When one son tries to remind her that he, too, shares in the latter responsibility, she silences him with only a growl.

Even her daughter-in-law, demure in her new role as mother, doesn't escape her acid tongue. For some reason the care she takes of the tiny infant is not adequate at all. And that is something else she must mention here and now. She, Delfina, had had nine children, and not one of them suffered the gross neglect that has befallen her grandson. "*Solo un hijito!*" she emphasizes with scorn—only a little son. On that note I slip past the house. If the members of her household are not carrying their share of the world's burdens, how much less am I?

It is here in San Pedro that I learn to appreciate Flavio. He doesn't complain. He accepts the vicissitudes of life as they are, not as he would have them. He has said not a word when Delfina has, on more than one occasion, shown herself bad tempered with us. He doesn't grumble when the one general store is consistently out of something we need to cook a meal. He cheerfully eats something else or goes without.

When I've attempted to replenish my office supplies while on our trips to the city and finding nothing I need, I've wailed bitterly. "Bonnie," on these occasions Flavio reprimands me gently, "that's no reason for you to be unhappy…you are loved. I love you and your children love you." The latter conclusion he had drawn due to my having shared my sons' and daughters' letters with him when they've caught up with me. They are always warming epistles, laced with affection and humor.

For mental exercise, Flavio, a good pupil, studies English with me as his tutor. I write verses extolling the luxurious beauty of Atitlán. My writing, however, is not accomplished only with serenity but with a large amount of accompanying frustration. Poetry, as a painting, cannot ever completely capture reality. An artist may produce a picture of absolute grandeur. Nevertheless, something is lost in its similitude, and so it is with poetry. Mere words do not describe Atitlán's loveliness and mystery.

Flavio, during these times of silence, interrupts me on occasion with questions concerning the English language.

"Why," for example—he wants to knows—"are the words wind (what you do to a clock) and wind (that blows) spelled exactly the same, but mean different things and pronounced differently?"

I have no ready answer for this and attempt to placate Flavio by responding offhandedly, "Just make sure to pronounce the words correctly, regardless of spelling."

"But how do you know the difference when you're reading?" he persists.

Though his curiosity is another of his admirable qualities, it is lost on me while I write. My trend of thought is broken.

Flavio's professed religion, one that I had regarded as little more than a current fad, proves to me after a time that it is real to him after all. One day I go to the lake's edge looking for him. Unaware that I'm nearby, he sings something very strange and very beautiful. I overhear his chanting something that sounds like "*Om…Om…*" I am moved by the mysticism here. All of nature seems to vibrate, exalting its creator. Not wishing to be irreverent, nor wanting to be in a position of exalting a strange god, I begin to sing exaltations to Christ. Do I imagine it—or is it actually happening?—that the wind and the waves pick up the praises, blend them together and send them back to us in perfect harmony. Later when I contemplate the mystery and the beauty of the moment, I begin to acknowledge that there is a certain truth in the mystics' philosophy that God is God, whatever men may choose to call Him.

Our time, Flavio's and mine, is spent enjoying the warm sunshine, swimming in the lake, in general leading an idyllic life. As in any other situation that seems to be perfect, however, a tenacious weed is growing in our Garden of Eden. In spite of Flavio's spirituality, his "earthly existence" seems less than desirable. As much as I've tried to ignore the problem, keeping in mind all his admirable qualities I find I cannot. He won't pay for anything. I might excuse him to some degree on the grounds that many people of poor countries tend to think North Americans are rich, but for one thing, Flavio was not brought up in a village. His knowledge of the world is of a sophisticated level, having been a student of the San Carlos University for three years now.

I had not wanted to deal with the irksome problem so early in our relationship and had not, therefore, intended that the subject should come up. Because on this occasion, while we are going for a walk in Atitlán's golden sunset, Flavio tells me that there is a bill at home for our firewood that must be paid to Delfina, I find myself angrily asking why he, himself, had not paid the bill...and why if he ever has any money it's always tucked away somewhere. "I'm tired of paying for everything. If there is anything fair about such an arrangement—your avoidance of financial responsibilities—I would be only too happy to hear about it!" I know that I'm very sarcastic when I'm angry; this is a fault of mine.

People with dark complexions do not blush but rather injury shows in the eyes; they darken. Flavio's are now almost black. He answers me at first in the obstinate tones one would expect from a small child—"I didn't think you were starving to death," hardly a satisfactory explanation. I become angrier as I hear his telling me that he noticed I had handed out money to total strangers on the streets. I make some vain attempt to clarify the difference between the two situations. It is one thing to give of our own free will, quite another to be manipulated into giving. I am quite cognizant that a pattern has already been established with Flavio, and it would take a great deal of concentrated effort to change this quality now. It must have existed a long time before he met me, and I alone cannot bring about the solution; this is quite obvious by his attitude. If Flavio's pride is hurt over my having spoken to him in this way, no less than mine by the necessity that brought about the argument. I am too drained to continue the subject any further and decide to end our relationship upon leaving San Pedro. I don't really feel the sole basis for our disagreement is about money, but about pride and manly ethics, which seem to be sadly lacking in him.

On the other hand, there seems to be something vulgar present when people quarrel about money, degrading, and the argument we've just had causes me to want never to see Flavio again. When I express just that to him, he begins to weep. I wish he wouldn't do that. Those tears are falling from the eyes that had drawn me to him in the first place. Tears have a way of melting angers and it is not long before I, too, am crying, no longer angry. Flavio holds out his arms to me and I feel the wetness of his cheeks blending with my own tears as if we are sorrowful for the same reasons but not knowing how to reach each other at the moment.

I make some attempt to tell Flavio that it is better this way, that some day he will want to marry, and when he does, have children. This advice is of little or no use. Flavio only tells me that he doesn't want to get married and that he wants no children.

When I think the subject is now closed he adds, "If I help to bring children into the world they may starve."—Starve! I have known poverty, known other impoverished people, but the young people were afraid of not being able to give their children nice clothes, that they would not be able to live in a fashionable neighborhood, send their children to college—never that they may starve. Any vestige of romance that might have remained has vanished. The stark reality of the situation has killed it. I shall miss Flavio, no doubt about it, but I find myself silently planning what it would be like to be free again, which of Guatemala's splendors I will next explore. Guatemala had been my home for three months before I met Flavio; I have spent an equal amount of time with him and feel that the remaining time left on my visa (three months) should be used in other pursuits.

Sensing that our damaged relationship is beyond repair, and never one for sitting still, Flavio, in a hurried manner, closes that horrid green door behind him and is gone.

I elect to return to the Chi-Nim-Ya—I hitch a ride with a truck going in that direction, and though the road is bumpy and full of potholes it still seems less hazardous than our mode of travel to San Pedro from Santa Catarina. I need to see José and Francisca.

Seated in the *comedor* of the Chi-Nim Ya, while Francisca gets up to put on the coffee, I find myself giving the most intimate description of my relationship with Flavio, along with the airing of my complaints. I tell them that I am simply tired of paying for the food, the lodging, and while in the city, the bus and taxi fares. Surely the most liberated of women should not be expected to pay beyond their share. José, seeing that my distress is genuine, comes to my side, assuming the role of a surrogate brother. Carefully he explains that there are two types of men that women in Guatemala must try to avoid. There are the *"mujeriegos"* and the *"vividores,"* the latter category in which Flavio seems to fall. I give the matter my wholehearted attention, not wanting to remain manless for the remainder of my stay in Guatemala, nor am I desirous of repeating the same mistake.

José gently tells me that I must accept part of the blame for the relationship now gone wrong because of the ease in which we had met, and that I really had demanded nothing from it. But in case he feels that he is being too harsh he further adds that there is really no cure for Flavio's condition, and that if I love him I will have to overlook this flaw in his character. (I think a woman would do well to avoid these two types of men anywhere, not just in Guatemala.)

Both types are obsessed with the same illness. Only the circumstances make them appear as separate defects.

Lest José and Francisca feel that I have been too critical of one of their countrymen, I express that perhaps I had gotten from the relationship no more than I deserved.

Getting a "vividor" (a man who lives off women) is perhaps the penalty for keeping company with someone so young. But Francisca, a true sister, will have none of this self-deprecation. She says all the comforting words everyone wants to hear during an emotional upheaval. She says that I am beautiful and kind—that the fault is not mine but his, Flavio's.

It is not long before I meet the *vividor's* counterpart, the *mujeriego*—but by the far the most attractive womanizer I could hope to meet. He comes roaring into the village along with his three friends, all on motorcycles. The four are quite drunk already, and rowdy, and they immediately begin to further enhance their drunken state. They bring several bottles with them. The village does not stock good liquor, only the local moonshine. I am very much aware of them and who would not be? They look like tall, conquering giants in their boots, tight-fitting jeans and motorcycle helmets. Dressed the way they are and tall to begin with, they could well have come from another planet, here in the pueblo where the average male is no more than five feet, three inches tall.

There's little use to pretend. I know I've been seen and it is not long before they declare their intentions and make their way to the back of the *comedor*, where I intend to be, more or less in hiding. They are, rather than the ruffians they first appeared to be, learned men from the San Carlos University. Unlike Flavio, however, a poor student, they are doctors on the faculty staff.

The man who first introduces himself is also the one I first noticed. He is very handsome, and the drunkest of the four. He begins to look for his printed business card—no easy accomplishment in his state of being—and knocks over the small table that holds the coke I'm sipping on so that both table and contents fall to the floor, the glass shattering. He then begins to pick up the pieces of glass (this act alone must mean that he is somehow a gentleman) and cuts his hand. His blood now mixes with the mess on the floor. Something tells me that this situation is far more complicated than it was intended to be.

I managed to slip past Roberto—the drunk and injured one—and over protests from all four, I make a fast exit to my room. I am just barely settled in my room, the candles blown out, when I hear the sound of halting, drunken footsteps outside my door.

I recognize the voice as Roberto's, with a confession of undying love. If I will but open the door, a thousand thrills will be mine for the asking. Aware that the door remains closed he next offers me a present—a ticket to Los Angeles, assuring me in the same breath that he not only is from Los Angeles, but that *he is* Los Angeles!

I don't know whether to laugh or cry, but shout through giggles and annoyance, "Roberto, get out of here. I already have a ticket to Los Angeles."

But it seems that he is now willing to make a supreme sacrifice. "But I'll give you my motorcycle," comes an anguished reply.

It is then that Roberto's friends, aware of what is going on at my door, come and drag him away. Amid much scuffling in the process and loud protests, they try to preserve whatever dignity that may remain with the good doctor.

The next day I have a few regrets that a friendship has ended before it has begun with the company of the night before. I've only time to lament a few moments, for there is a knock at the door. This time, however, it is sedate and self-assured. I open the door and, as I anticipate, there stands Roberto, looking handsomer by far in his improved state of sobriety. If he is embarrassed by his conduct of the previous night, he doesn't show it. He tells me that his friends are waiting for us and if I wish, we will go together to enjoy the festivities in the center of the pueblo. Independence Day is being celebrated throughout Guatemala.

We go out into the bright morning sunlight and take the cobblestone street that goes uphill to the plaza. Sober, all four men are extremely good company; in fact, they are charming and attentive. A fifth gentleman along the way joins us. Don Edgar lives in the pueblo. He is the owner of considerable property nearby, but his main interest lies in a coffee plantation just outside Santiago. I learn that his former wife, and mother of his children, also resides in Santiago and owns and manages a small restaurant. Because of the company he keeps, I begin to wonder if he, too, may be one of the *"mujeriegos"* José spoke of— this could well be the reason that the lady in the pueblo is no longer his wife, but in their estrangement, has become his ex-wife. Just as in the States where parades and celebrations are embellished with the town beauties there are young ladies from the pueblo chosen to preside over the fiesta. One is a little beauty from among the "Ladino camp" while the other is chosen from among the Naturales—the pueblo's Indians. Both are crowned Señorita Atitlán.

A group of younger girls, perhaps from the ages of six to ten years, are bedecked in frilly, organdy dresses. Marimba bands play and the sound of wind instruments start them skipping gaily around two festooned flagpoles. Their dance resembles the May Pole dance in the U.S.

Prominent members of the community deliver speeches and my friends add their oratory to these patriotic exaltations under the waving flag of Guatemala.

When the fiesta has terminated and the doctors and I walk back to the *Chi-Nim-Ya* there is a question, which has nagged me since last night, and I feel that I should approach the subject now that I had neglected yesterday. But in retrospect how was that possible?

Finally, after thinking about it for several minutes, I just blurt out, "Roberto, are your married?" "No, of course not," came the reply, indignation in his tone, but even in the process of his denial, his friends contradict in unison, "But of course he is!" I had not really expected Roberto to be single. Attractive men like him don't stay unmarried very long and also there is little likelihood his behavior would have been so aggressive were it not for the safety of marriage.

For some reason, I need to talk with him about the lie he just told me. I suspect it is only an excuse to prolong his acquaintance a bit longer. I am lonely and these interesting men have made my day. I know I should walk away without further thought, but I drop back a few paces to walk with Roberto, who is a little behind the rest of us. Beside him now, I ask him how he would react if his wife were to behave in the way he has with me, behind his back and with other men. I know this question is offensive—but then it is intended to be. His answer is no more satisfying than Flavio's had been a few days earlier. He says that his wife would never do a thing like that to him. She has women friends to keep her company—that she's no North American, a feminist, but a loyal Guatemalan wife.

I tell him that I believe that he is grossly unfair to his wife, as unfair as he intends to be with me. I say goodbye to the four of them and long for Flavio, "*vividor*" though he may be.

Back at the Chi-Nim-Ya I lie down on my bed of straw and look out at the view below me. What a comfort home is, my home away from home included.

José and Francisca have in every way proved to be my loyal friends. Chico, too, is steadfast in his affection toward me.

I've saved some of my treasured reading material for moments like these. When I feel boredom setting in or loneliness overtaking me, a good book always revitalizes my spirits, and I'm never tired of a favorite until I've memorized its passages.

I pick up John Steinbeck's, *Travels with Charley*, a thoroughly delightful little book, one in which we get to see the author in his works. He died shortly after writing this condensed autobiography. One thought he incidentally imparts to the reader is: "I can never write when hot on an event," and which seems apropos to my own present situation, "but only in retrospect—when it has had time to ferment"— wonderful words, words of salvation to the author or would-be author.

Life is good again. As I read I listen to the waves of the lake dash against the shore and grow persistent in their rhythmic force. Thus far in my reading, John Steinbeck's odyssey through the states of the U.S. has taken him only North of the Mason-Dixon line. I begin to wonder as he moves southward to the land of the Blue Grass and the Kentucky Derbies, just how he will deal with one of the most explosive decades in the history of North America—how will he handle its shame? Will he attempt to minimize the white man's sins against his black brothers?—or will he ignore entirely the events that led to the civil rights era? Mr. Steinbeck wrote *Travels with Charley—In Search of America* in the early sixties, the beginning of a decade when there were massive strikes across the nation, thousands of sympathetic whites on the march—sit-ins, lie-ins, prayers for change, clergymen coming from the North, both black and white, jailed for their convictions. A black leader crosses the barrier to the Caucasian world just for the "privilege" of sitting at a white man's lunch counter and demanding a greasy hamburger what will in a few minutes turn to lead in his stomach.

Police dogs strain at their leashes, eager to get at the job they do best. Police squads turn the water hoses on the demonstrators, blasting them off their feet. It takes some time before the opposition realizes that the burning fire in the black people's midst cannot be extinguished with water hoses or police dogs. As I turn the pages I see Mr. Steinbeck makes no effort to avoid the explosive subject, but moves right into the middle of the problem. It is here that this famous writer's truest characteristics come to the forefront. No one ever need guess again on which side of man's injustices this author stood.

There is cause for rejoicing when Mr. Steinbeck exposes the story of the "cheerleaders" and the little black girl entering an all white school for the first time. I read the account once, then reread the story, and again for the third time, laughing and crying at its triumphs and its exquisite pain. He writes that while in Texas, late in 1960, the incident most reported and pictured in the newspapers was the matriculation of two tiny Negro children in a New Orleans school. Behind the two small, dark mites were the law's majesty and the law's power to enforce—both the scales and the sword were allied with the infants—while against them were three hundred years of fear and anger in a changing world...what made the newsmen love the story so much was a group of stout, middle-aged women who gathered every day to scream invectives at the children. They became so expert that they became known as the "cheerleaders" and a crowd gathered every day to enjoy and applaud their performance.

The author says that he had to see the strange drama—it had the same attraction as a two-headed foetus or a five-legged calf—a distortion of normal life.

The show opened on time—the sound of sirens, motorcycle cops; then two black cars filled with big men in felt hats pulled up in front of the school...four big marshals got out of each car and from somewhere extracted the littlest Negro girl you ever saw...but the crowd was waiting for the white man who dared bring his white child to school...A shrill grating voice rang out...each took a turn...the crowd broke into howls and roars of whistles and applause—time to begin the real harassment!

This wonderful and lovely man, John Steinbeck, famous and beloved author, has shown us, the readers, the very best a man can be capable of. For this I shall always be grateful.

Chico calls me to lunch—in sweet and inviting tones—"Bonnie, *almuerzo*." I will always hear the echo of that voice when I remember Atitlán and José and Francisca, my Guatemalan brother and sister.

When I return to my room and turn the last page of Mr. Steinbeck's book, I read that he, at the end of his journey, is no longer seeing anything, merely looking, that he is just on his way home, lonely and longs for the familiarity of those near him. So do I. I want to see my kids again, hear their laughter, share experiences with them. I know in a short time, I'll be on a jetliner headed for home.

DISCOVERY OF THE BANANA REPUBLIC

What a fantastic feeling to be home again in the Los Angeles area and to be welcomed by my family after so long a lapse in not seeing them. They all look so good to me, so well and happy. They are all doing productive things—studying for careers.

I soon fall into the same routine as before, going to church sometimes, having dates, going to a job and returning home from the job, thankful that there is a job to go to. The doctors for whom I worked before going to Guatemala graciously accepted me back, which is something I might be reluctant to do were I in their positions. I know that when I begin to feel life's tedium once more, I'll be off again. But in the meantime, life is pleasant, a bit like starting over.

People begin to ask me questions about Guatemala—questions which I cannot always answer. I begin to explore its infrastructure followed by a period of total immersion into Guatemala's political life.

I learn that Guatemala once was governed fairly and, though it lasted but a decade—from 1944 to 1954—it was ten years of democracy. Two presidents, Juan Arévalo and Jacobo Arbenz, sided not with the small, rich minority, but with the people, a first in Guatemala.

I learn that 62% percent of all arable land has been held by a mere 2.9% of Guatemala's population, the country's elite since the

Conquistadores overthrew the Mayas (Naturales) in 1524.

Though thousands of Mayas were massacred during the Spanish Conquest, a remnant of the race survived. Driven from the valleys they fled to the highlands where they were shielded by the mountains from the invaders. Thus the rich and fertile soil of Guatemala's lowlands abandoned by the Mayas became the property of the Spaniards. The legacy of the Spanish conquerors fell to their progeny, which has lasted throughout four and one-quarter centuries, whereas the legacy of the Mayas has been one of an enslaved and subjugated race for an equal length of time.

The villages that sprang up from among the Mayan inhabitants soon became isolated from each other. There having been no means of transportation between pueblos, no link with the outside world, no roads, the Mayas were simply not aware of the activities of even their neighboring villages. They lived and died in the pueblos of their birth, never having been anywhere else.

It was in this setting that the Banana Republic, the offshoot of the United Fruit Company, was established. Since the turn of the century, the United Fruit Company has been kept alive and well on Guatemala's prime soil.

THE BANANA REPUBLIC

The United Fruit Company was formed in 1885, due to a merger of a company privately owned by Minor Keith and the Boston Fruit Company. The corporation in its infancy operated throughout Jamaica, Santo Domingo, and Cuba, but Guatemala was destined to become the nucleus of the United Fruit Empire in its first decade of existence.

Boston remained the center of the company's shipping and distribution throughout its duration. From the very beginning the company enjoyed phenomenal success. When bananas were introduced to the people of the United States through the ports of Boston and New Orleans, few North Americans had ever seen the delicious, yellow-skinned fruit, much less tasted it. Bananas rapidly became a favorite imported food and sales increased daily for the United Fruit Company. After ten years of prosperity, however, the company began to experience serious financial difficulties. The public was consuming more bananas than the Caribbean soil was producing. The analysts of United Fruit attributed the poorly tilled soil to the land's having been acquired on a land-lease basis and had not been company owned. Undoubtedly there was a certain amount of accuracy in the analysis because a banana shortage occurred, causing the company a setback, one that would have to be corrected if the company were to survive…the countries of the Caribbean could not be depended upon to pull the United Fruit out of its economic slump.

It was then that the banana world entrepreneurs turned their sights south of the border in the hopes of reviving the company's flailing economy. Their subsequent missions in Latin America were met with remarkable receptivity and their explorations proved to be, in all respects, "fruitful." The weather and soil were exactly conducive to banana growing and an abundance of land was available for the asking.

Finding the doors of welcome so invitingly open in Central America, the United Fruit Company quickly sprang into action, acquiring vast acres of property in Panama, Colombia, Nicaragua, Honduras and Guatemala. This land was purchased for so little that it would have scarcely paid the taxes on it in the United States or another major country.

As a result of these transactions, all five countries were drawn into a socio-political bond with the United Fruit Company. Always poor, their impoverishment increased. Five separate countries were reduced to one belittling title—The Banana Republic. But the country in which the real symbiotic union was formed with the United States was Guatemala. The relationship has survived to the present nuclear age.

Not only were the tropical lowlands of Guatemala generous and yielding to the banana growers but the political climate proved to be comparably pliable. The way was paved for further long-range amenities for United Fruit, allowing exercise of enormous economic control of the country.

General Manuel Estrada Cabrera was Guatemala's ruling dictator at the time United Fruit Company began to establish its kingdom in Central America. Of all Latin American countries' dictators he alone excelled in greed and corruption, characteristics which lent themselves as complimentary tools to the dynamics of the newly formed corporation in Guatemala.

The second order of business by United Fruit, after its agricultural bases had been established, was the obtaining of a contract in 1901 to carry mail from Guatemala on its ships. The commercial waters thus entered, and acquisition of the country's principal rail lines shortly followed.

Dictator Estrada, his bank account now expanded by several digits and his pockets fairly bulging with gringo dollars, granted the United

Fruit Company in 1904 a ninety-nine-year concession to finish construction begun by the Guatemalans, and the power to operate the rail lines running from the capital to the Atlantic harbor of Puerto Barrios. Monopoly of the railroads eventually led to control of Guatemala's telegraph system.

The United Fruit Company, operating ostensibly under the name of commerce only, within a short time after landing on Guatemala's soil became a powerful faction within the government—or perhaps more accurately it became a governing body itself within the government. No merchandise was left or entered the country without United Fruit's approval. There being no other means of transport available to other companies having need of importing or exporting, their products had to pass through Puerto Barrios where the United Fruit Company levied taxes and prohibited all commercial activities that might prove serious competition.

In the process of selling out his country General Estrada committed the most despicable act of all: He sold his own people into slavery— literally. "Hordes of indigenous people" facing death by starvation were driven from the rural areas in cattle trucks and then were taken to banana plantations. There they were forced to work back-breaking long hours—up to fourteen hours a day without a day of rest in the seven-day-a-week schedules. Their wages were frozen at twenty-five cents a day. Sometimes they were separated from their families.

The entire picture, however, for the peasant laborers was not all that bleak after a season for working for the North Americans. In many ways the Naturales fared better than they had under the serfdom they endured beneath their "*jefes*," the Ladinos. Recruited families were allowed to remain together. Nutritious food, medical care and adequate housing were benefits the laborers received for the first time in their lives. In some plantations schools were often erected for the Indian peasants.

But the laborers, as ignorant as they were deemed to be, first by the Guatemalan gentry and now by the "governing gringo," realized that huge profits were being extracted from their land—when in truth, they were the rightful inheritors of the country's rich resources. They knew that however benevolent the paternal relationship between the United Fruit Company and the workers, there was still no promise of freedom offered.

The workers from time to time did go on strike to protest their enslaved conditions. Rebellions occurred sporadically. But they were not skilled in the ways of violence. Their only weapons were machetes, their working tools. They were no match for machine guns. These uprisings were not considered very significant and the dissenters were dealt with quickly and efficiently when they "did get out of line." These boycotts were usually put down on the same day they occurred. This was due to the thoroughly equipped and well-maintained army of President General Estrada. The provisions made by the U.S. Government to the Guatemalan military were abundantly ample. The United Fruit had at its disposal the entire Guatemalan Army ready to do its bidding should they have run into trouble at any time.

Nevertheless, the annals of history do not exist for the ruling class alone, and it may well be that these peasant workers, who gave so much and received so little, have been a great influence on the generations to come in their struggle for freedom…but freedom was not then a reality in Guatemala; the bondage that enslaved the people outlived Manuel Estrada Cabrera and survived two successive dictators before there was any break with the past.

The feudal-like system of Guatemala's socio-political affairs continued well into the 40s. It was then that Guatemala's structure was shaken to its very foundation, producing so profound an effect on the nation that it will forever feel its impact. There emerged from the nation's greatly polarized society, without any significant awareness of the ruling class, a bourgeoisie whose cause was aligned with the poor. This group of reformists composed primarily of university students, schoolteachers, attorneys and doctors turned Guatemala upside down!

BANANA SKINS FOR THE GENERALS

A very low premium had always been placed upon the services of these intelligent Guatemalans, the country's intellectuals, particularly those of the schoolteachers. Their skills were of no benefit to the ruling class. The children of the rich were greatly segregated from this class of working people. As their parents before them, they attended only the parochial schools, long established by the hierarchy of the Catholic Church. The church, as always, represented an integral part of the existent oligarchic society. Therefore, its responsibilities included educating its youngsters of the rich and ruling class, the children who as young adults would be sent abroad for higher education.

It is difficult for North Americans to envision a society without a middle class. The overwhelming majority of our nation's populace is categorized within this broad spectrum. We are members of the upper-middle class, the lower-middle class or sometimes just placed within the sphere of the middle class itself. But such was not the case when this sector converged upon Guatemala's society. A middle class was virtually unknown.

These progressive groups toured the countryside and talked with the peasants in the fields. The peasants, experiencing for the first time an opportunity to be heard, aired their grievances readily. They expressed their frustrations and discontent with only a minimal amount of encouragement. Prior to this unusual period in history these two diverse groups had little contact with each other, but now solidarity was being formed among the urban white-collar workers and the peasants in the rural areas engaged in agriculture.

The teachers, by now sufficiently organized, held massive demonstrations. In addition to their demands on behalf of the laborers, they went on strikes to procure at least a livable wage for themselves. (Thirty-five dollars monthly was an exceptional high salary for teachers in public schools.) During one such public meeting, held in the Parque Central across the street from the Presidential Palace, President General Ubico, watching from a window, became enraged by what he saw. He ordered his cavalry to charge the group. Hundreds of teachers and students committed to the revolution were trampled to death beneath the feet of the stampeding horses. The soldiers opened machine gun fire in their midst as they attempted to flee. But the institutionalized violence rather than acting as a deterrent, added greater momentum to the revolution and impressive numbers of the populace were added to the movement daily. General Ubico fearfully realized the insurgents by now outnumbered the members of the military. When asked to vacate the Presidential Palace, he complied with very little persuasion. He made a final frantic effort to keep the military in power before complete surrender. He attempted to install (unsuccessfully) a friend of his, another general, Federico Ponce, in the presidential office. The people could not be deceived into thinking at this point that this proposed arrangement represented any change. They knew that it meant merely a transfer of dictators, not power. They would no longer be placated in this manner. They rejected General Ponce completely.

It was then that the people called a popular, much loved Guatemalan, Juan José Arevalo, who was living in Argentina. A liberal and hero to the people, he was forced to live in exile because of the strong democratic stand he had taken in former years. The telephone lines, amid the static and humming of the long distance connection, vibrated with electric optimism. The voice familiar to the Guatemalans, rich and deep, in its tones of good will and humor, was actually on the line!

"*Que es esto mis paisanos?* You want me to return to Guatemala? But they kicked me out."

The callers then explained to Juan Arévalo that the dictator, Jorge Ubico, had fallen from power—that the people wanted him, Dr. Arévalo, as the supporting candidate, in their revolution. Within just a few days after having received the surprising call from his Guatemala, Juan Arévalo was on the plane and homeward bound.

The joyful reality of actually returning to his homeland, not as he went away, lonely and desolate, but welcomed home as a vital participant in his country's revolution, prompted an outburst of spontaneous singing. His fellow passengers, upon learning the source of Dr. Arévalo's profound joy, joined in song with him. Guitars were dragged from their cases and soon the whole plane reverberated with the sound of lusty Spanish music.*

When the plane landed at the Aurora Airport, it seemed that all of Guatemala was there to meet him. His homecoming was met with so tumultuous a welcome that it was obvious his destiny was linked with Guatemala's imminent democracy.

There were some very significant world events coinciding with Juan Arévalo's return, which undoubtedly contributed support toward the democracy beginning in Guatemala. Franklin D. Roosevelt was President of the United States at the time. A strong advocate of human rights in 1933, his first year in the presidential office, Mr. Roosevelt launched his "good neighbor" campaign toward Latin America, an exact reversal of former policies when the "big stick" approach was felt throughout all Latin America. Mr. Roosevelt naturally had nothing in common with the ilk of dictators like Ubico. A Nazi sympathizer and ardent admirer of Adolph Hitler, Ubico was becoming increasingly unpopular with the United States.

*The scene in the plane existed in the imagination of the author—if the readers close their eyes they, too, can hear the music!

By the time relations between the two countries became so strained as to be practically non-existent, the revolutionary government was gaining favorable recognition by the United States during Mr. Roosevelt's administration.

Mr. Arévalo knew, however, that the egalitarian government he sought above all for his country would be a constant uphill battle. He knew that an overwhelming amount of work would have to be accomplished in a relatively short period of time. He had already been forced into hiding. Members of the old regime sought to assassinate him, but he somehow managed to elude his would-be assassins and survived the dangerous and difficult period prior to election. He was swept into the presidential office by a landslide of votes—the first president in all of Guatemala's history to be selected by the people. Thus a new day dawned for Guatemala—a budding democracy—the kind of government that, had it remained free from outside interference in order to pursue its own destiny, held promise of a full-blown democratic state, one capable of responding to its people's needs.

Guatemala is a country rich in resources. There is no need for hunger or poverty. Rainfall is plenteous. The rainy seasons last six months out of the year, generous in preparing the soil for growing a large variety of crops. Its coffee takes its place in the market as among the best in the world. The land, Juan Arévalo knew, easily had the capacity to nourish well Guatemala's citizens. During his first few months in office he devoted his energies toward eradicating hunger and poverty. Cooperatives sprang up and food was distributed to the poor.

A professor himself, among his first priorities was a better educational system for Guatemala. (Illiteracy was a very high 92%.) Among his first acts of freeing the country was the granting to San Carlos, Guatemala's principal university, complete autonomy. This vital embodiment of the country's growth and intellectual life was no longer forced to function under the control of the government.

There followed enactment of his remaining uppermost three priorities. Having profound respect for the working man, President Arévalo immediately set the peasant workers free to organize labor unions. He encouraged any and all efforts of these formerly greatly oppressed citizens to bring dignity into their contributions. Freedom of speech with the right of public assembly was rapidly set in motion. All the hard-core generals had been shipped out of the country, paving the way for honest and free elections.

Dr. Arévalo, despite the many obstacles thrown in his path, managed to serve a full six-year term in the presidential office. The dynamic and energetic president worked in frantic effort during these years toward healing the wounded Guatemala of four and a half centuries of tyranny. During the six years as president he had to contend with attempts at a coup d'étàt per year, and during the first few months after assuming office, several attempts had already been made on his life. Nevertheless, Guatemala's fledgling democracy had begun to flourish and when Juan Arévalo's successor, Jacobo Arbenz Guzman, in 1951, became the second presidential candidate as the people's choice, the country was somewhat prepared for further democratization.

Jacobo Arbenz carried the revolution to even greater extremes than had his predecessor. His inaugural speech alone was not likely to endear him to the military-industrial complex, which linked Guatemala and the U.S. together, or to the hawkish president of the United States, Harry S. Truman. (President Roosevelt had been dead for six years.) Undoubtedly this speech marked Mr. Arbenz for eventual removal from the presidential office. "…Foreign capital will always be welcome as long as it adjusts to local conditions, remains always subordinate to Guatemalan laws, cooperates with the economic development of the country and strictly abstains from intervening in the nation's social and political life…"

The fiery speech of Mr. Arbenz proved to be not just idle talk. He began early to institute an agrarian reform, an act unprecedented in Guatemala's history.

It was decided initially that only uncultivated portions of farms larger than 223 acres would be touched, but this was not enough. This land benefitted only about 100,000 peasant families. It was when his reapportionment program (387,000 acres were expropriated.) intersected the vast acres owned by the United Fruit Company that his days as president were doomed.*

*NACLA, Vo. 17. What would seem to be further proof of Mr. Arzbenz's sincerity, he gave titles of some of his own property to the Agrarian Reform Program.

BANANA REPUBLIC RECLAIMED

Although full compensation was offered for the land (the exact price the United Fruit listed as the property's worth for tax purposes) and the land had been unused for anything for several years, nevertheless this act provided the impetus needed to depose President Arbenz—an excuse to label him a Communist. It was at this time that United Fruit asked the CIA to remove Jacobo Arbenz from office. Dwight Eisenhower, President of the U.S. at the time, along with Richard Nixon, Vice-President, readily agreed that Arbenz would have to go.

When the cogs of the military machinery were oiled and set in motion and the mechanics of the anti-Communist propaganda sufficiently disseminated, the ouster of Arbenz was accomplished with relatively few problems. A new dictator for Guatemala, one that would best serve the interests of United Fruit, handpicked from several, was selected.

The overthrow of Guatemala's short-lived democracy was facilitated in the most deceptive manner possible. Two dozen small aircraft were sent to strafe Guatemala's most prominent cities, but actually only three bombers were among them. With so many planes flying low overhead, the situation appeared worse than it actually was. Had the Guatemalan president been aware of the subterfuge involved, possibly there could have been an attempt at resistance. The CIA planted boxes of rifles with conspicuous Soviet markings near Nicaragua's Pacific Coast. It was planned that the Nicaraguan Police would find these. Several bombs were dropped around the airstrip of Honduras so that it appeared that Guatemala was attacking Honduras at the orders of Jacobo Arbenz. When it became clear that the coup had been planned by the United States, not by the dissidents of his country, he realized that surrender not victory was the painful reality.

In 1954 Jacobo Arbenz, Guzman, President of Guatemala, chosen by the Guatemalans in a totally free election, was driven from his country by the Central Intelligence Agency of the United States. John E. Peurifoy, Ambassador to Guatemala, actually carried out the engineering, but the Dulles brothers, John Dulles, Secretary of State and Allen Dulles, Chief of the CIA, were the primary architects behind the overthrow of Jacobo Arbenz. During this time, Guillermo Toriello, Guatemala's Ambassador in Washington, was pleading the cause of the land reform in Guatemala—imploring the Washington officials to understand that the expropriated land benefitted the multitude of Guatemala's impoverished peasants. His pleading was, of course, to no avail. It had been decided already to depose the reformist president of Guatemala and it appeared that Toriello was the only one in Washington whose sympathies were aligned with his greatly abused country.

While the wife of John Peurifoy wrote clever little songs against Arbenz and his government—how Guatemala was free of the Commies, due to the expertise of her husband—Mr. Arbenz was leaving his homeland, dispirited, demoralized, a broken man without a country, never again to regain what he had lost. His life ended on foreign soil—the newspapers listed his death as a bathtub drowning but it is presumed, if there had not been an actual assassination, he had lost his will to live.

With the new dictator, Carlos Castillo Armas, in power, the "status quo" where in Guatemala it represents the most acute form of misery, was quickly re-established. The agrarian reform was promptly revoked and the reapportioned land given back to the wealthy landowners and the United Fruit Company. Wages again fell to the discretion of the employers under the feudal-like system. The plight of Guatemala's poor was reduced to the same unhappy state as before—without adequate food and shelter, without vote.

*Certain facts in the narrative of this chapter were taken from the book, *Bitter Fruit.*

IN THE WAKE OF THE OVERTHROW

Reflection upon the extensive involvement of the United Fruit Company compels me to dig deeper—to learn of any possible further ramifications of this period. Not surprisingly they were considerable. From 1954 to 1969 Guatemala suffered through a series of corrupt right-wing dictators. Colonel Castillo Armas, the puppet installed in office through the overthrow of Arbenz's government, was assassinated in 1957 by one of his own associates only to be replaced by another dictator. The advances made during the 1944-1954 period were turned back, all social progress blocked and all forms of free expression stifled.

In 1957, General Miguel Ydigoras Fuentes became president in fraudulent elections between two right-wing candidates. Guatemala's citizens were offended by the extreme corruption that followed, but the "final straw" appeared to have been a decision made by Ydigoras to allow Guatemala to be used as a training ground for the Bay of Pigs against Cuba.

Because of the extreme repression, it took several years for any real opposition forces to mobilize.

Brought forth from this period some significant names are recalled and appear repetitively in the archives of Latin American history. *Among them a member of the clergy comes into focus, the priest's name being Father Thomas Melville, expelled from Guatemala because of his "Liberation Theology." From the available statements

91

of his, it can only be assumed that when his "religion" came in conflict with his moral convictions, he chose the latter. Because of the controversy surrounding his ministry, he found himself in a position of having to answer to the Catholic hierarchy and responded in the following way to the many questions that came close to being interrogations "…I am a Communist only if Christ was a Communist. I did what I did and will continue to do so because of the teachings of Christ and not because of Marx or Lenin…let the world know when the war breaks out in the open, that we do it not for Russia, nor for China, nor any other country, but for Guatemala…our response in this situation is not because we have read Marx or Lenin, but because we have read the New Testament."

Otto René Castillo, Guatemalan poet, leaves behind him a legacy of the ineffable beauty that accompanies a person when he has put his ego out of the way and embarks on a course to serve the many rather than a few. He writes of his girlfriend's eyes: *They increase like nothing yet my desire to struggle, to change the world, and besides, they make me the happiest of all sad people who still live on this planet.* The military murdered the two revolutionary young lovers, a necklace of fire for each, two burning, rubber tires.

During the 60s decade a popular insurrection began at the frontlines. Two revolutionary leaders formed a guerrilla group called FAR. Interestingly, they were both former army officers. The group was divided into three leading fronts, the MR.-13, the PGT and the FGFI. They had one common goal—to change things in Guatemala—but how to go about it presented a real problem to the three leading groups.

Their ideologies and life experiences were widely varied. The MR-13 was primarily comprised of Ladino *campesinos* led by Yon Sosa, one of the original rebel army officers. The PGT was mainly formed from the intellectual community, students and workers, mostly urban-based. The FGEI encompassed sectors of the PGT cadre, Ladino *campesinos*, youth groups from prior demonstrations and some Indians from Rabinal. Luis Agosto Turcios Lima, the other leading rebel officer and an important young revolutionary, Ricardo Ramirez, headed this front.

Because of the rebels' diverse backgrounds and the wide variety of approaches introduced in their revolutionary efforts, they never did achieve any real unifying force, which greatly weakened their strongest link—the passionate desire to free Guatemala—the one link that brought them together.

During this period, one development caused the guerrilla front to "rethink" their policies. Julio Cesar Montenegro, a civilian and reformist from the popular revolutionary period of 1944-1954, was elected president in 1966. Mr. Montenegro promised a return to a period of reforms and indicated that negotiations with the guerrillas would be in order. In spite of Mr. Montenegro's intentions, he had been forced to sign away the power of the presidency to the military. The left fell prey to an army entrapment, not knowing what had transpired between the president and the army. On the eve of the election, twenty-eight members of the PGT were arrested. Their arrests were followed by torture and murder. Their bodies were dumped into the ocean. The one leader who reportedly could possibly have prevented further devastation among their organizational stronghold was unfortunately killed in an auto accident. The leader killed was Turcios Lima, on October 2, 1966. The guerrillas by this time had let down their security forces and demobilized.

Following this period there was an apparent calm; all the while the army began to change radically. Under the leadership of Colonel Arana Osorio, counterinsurgency began in earnest with the help of massive military assistance from the United States. They now went on the offensive, occupying villages and murdering those suspected of being guerrilla supporters. The guerrilla fronts were napalmed during 1966 and 1967 with the help of the U.S. Air Force. Their planes flew from Panama to Guatemala to assist in these raids.

In the fracas 8,000 people were killed while tracking down just a "handful" of guerrillas. Colonel Arana Osorio, who ordered the deaths of these people, mostly from the civilian sector of the population, was the most dedicated and most fierce of all anti-Communist leaders in the military. Because of his extreme savagery, his activities earned him the nickname of "The Butcher of Zacapa," Zacapa, being in the Eastern part of Guatemala and near the Salvadoran border, and a name that seemed to set well with all factions of the Guatemalan society, including the military!

When I lived in Guatemala, little, if anything, was ever related to me about these volatile events and the cause for this particular brand of silence remained a mystery to me. The Guatemalan people, particularly in the rural areas, ordinarily did not speak of political matters, but made practical matters of daily living their chief concerns.

Guatemala—like a person who charms and fascinates us—draws me to its side again. I hear the murmuring of the trees in the mountains, see the blue of the lake and its glorious sunset. Once again I remember the *traje tipico* of the Naturales with a fond longing. It is there that I have unfinished business. My poetry had never progressed much beyond the cerebral state and I know that I must go back and change this condition if possible.

HAIL THE BEAUTY QUEEN

The year is 1975. The big Pan American jet whose destiny is El Salvador begins to descend. The familiar message of the stewardess is heard above the roar of the engines through the microphone. She speaks in tones as soft and mellifluous as the Spanish language itself while she instructs us both in English and Spanish to fasten our seat belts and extinguish all smoking materials. I comply in a perfunctory manner for my conscious thought has turned toward Angela, who may or may not be at the airport to greet me. The prospect, however, is not nearly so frightening as it had been on my earlier visit. My son and his girlfriend, both in their twenties, are seated comfortingly beside me.

Still the excitement I would ordinarily feel by this trip—of once more traveling to a foreign country—is greatly diminished by the jarring memories of the past. I wonder if any change for the better is possible for my friend, Angela, in the relationship with her father. Coupled with this disturbing thought is the unhappy knowledge that little, if any, change could have occurred among El Salvador's impoverished citizens in this relatively short span of time; only two years have elapsed since I was in El Salvador.

El Salvador, a third-world country, so-called, had an accompanying label of being one of the world's developing nations. This is a completely misleading application, however. This conveys the impression that literacy campaigns and programs for eradicating disease and hunger are in progress, although not yet realized...the ultimate goal of democracy being pursued.

The gulf between the rich minority and the poor majority is as disparate as it was when the Spanish conquered this section of the world nearly five centuries ago, wide as the ocean that borders this hauntingly beautiful little country on the Pacific. Its attractive shopping centers and the sleek highways, presumably built with U.S. dollars, only serve to make life more pleasant for the already comfortable. They in no way serve to alleviate the plight of the poor.

I've seen San Salvador's shanty town. It is composed of row upon row of hovels constructed of paper and plastic, such materials that are available at the city dump. The houses built with good materials in the barrios of the poor are those which provide their homes with walls of tin, and wood slats complete the roof.

There is little electricity seen in these areas, no running water, no toilet facilities, no space that one person could call their own. It is from this environment that all of Gabriel's mistresses had their roots, lovely, budding flowers uprooted from a giant garbage dump, only to be discarded when more tender blossoms surface.

Just why I've come back to El Salvador for the second time I'm uncertain. I begin to wonder if I'm afflicted with a certain masochism—a propensity for seeking out misery. Though my son and daughter have insisted that we stop here in El Salvador before going on to Guatemala, I still could have said no. We could have gone on to Guatemala City from the airport, then straight to the mountains of the fascinating Mayas. We are here in El Salvador and the plane has landed. We unbuckle our seat belts and begin moving down the aisle with the other passengers. Talking over my shoulder, I begin to admonish my son and daughter to brace themselves. In San Salvador while still at the air terminal they will see the most dismal poverty they have ever encountered—nor indeed likely that they will ever see again. I begin to recount the cultural shock I had experienced on my first visit here—the assault on the eyes and the nervous system, the misery we escaped through perhaps having been born in another country, only. As we leave the plane and begin walking toward the terminal, I feel the blast of the tropical heat as it is picked up and stirred by the still-rotating jet propellers. The desolate feeling of three years ago begins to return as we enter the airport.

I look beyond the *"aduana"* to the area of the waiting room that is now partitioned off by a wall of thick mesh. Unlike the past, when no one was here to meet me and I waited alone, Angela is very much present. Her striking good looks would be difficult to miss anywhere. Her father and his mistress of three years ago are with her. Ana, the young mistress, is not wearing a schoolgirl uniform, as before. She is now a stunning young lady of eighteen and dresses accordingly. A dress of clinging silk accentuates her womanly curves.

Another look around the airport...I'm surprised a second time, pleasantly so. The crowd of destitute and hungry people does not fill the doorways obstructing the airport traffic as in the past. We are permitted to walk freely from customs to the waiting area without being intercepted once by someone begging for money. In a minute or two I experience a sensation similar to the one I felt on my first visit here. It is more an intuition than anything else, strange; everything is either wonderfully right or dreadfully wrong. It has to be either/or. There are no poor or hungry people here, no beggars. The people in the waiting area greeting the passengers are, for the most part, as in any other terminal, family or friends; there are the usual business associates, well dressed men in tailored suits, hands extended in cordial greetings.

I tell myself that once we are clear of the airport and are in the downtown section, the San Salvador of my memories will doubtless return. My bewilderment only deepens as we move toward the nucleus of the city. No desperate-looking people can be seen. To the contrary, all the pedestrians are well groomed and walk with the serenity of well-being and good health.

More puzzling still is the absence of grime and filth that once littered the streets. The commercial section of the city shines from fresh coats of paint in startling contrast with the same buildings of three years earlier when they were gray from the elements and wear.

But where are the hungry children? cries a muted voice within. *I saw them, children with spindly limbs and bellies bloated by hunger.*

The sense of strangeness I feel turns into a kind of real panic. It is as if these people existed only in the realm of my imagination—as if somehow, I'm the one out of step with the rest of the world. Everyone else is doing all right. The sensation is like those dreams we all have. Greatly frustrated, we try to warn those about us of some impending disaster—or we try to talk about some greatly disturbing situation. No one gives us their attention, not the slightest bit. Trying to speak, we are totally ignored. They go casually on their way, doing whatever they were doing before the warning. Finally, in the dream when the situation tears at us until we can stand it no longer, we are awake, and realize—gratefully—that it was only a dream. I try to convince myself that perhaps I had exaggerated the situation here in El Salvador. I was maybe comparing the small country, one of the third world, with my own, a superpower. I rationalize even further by attempting to minimize the problems between father and daughter, Angela and Gabriel. Their difficulties, after all, may not be more pernicious than the problems of any other household. In their absence from each other (Angela had returned to El Salvador just before we came to visit) there may have been a new resolve on both their parts to love and forgive. The clarity I seek amid confusion is further complicated by pangs of guilt. As a welcomed guest I had accepted Angela and Gabriel's hospitality in the past and am in the process of doing so again, not only for myself but also for my son and daughter. The thoughts I've had about the Salvadoran scene are far from charitable.

There now seems to exist an easy camaraderie between Angela and her father—among the three of them for that matter. Although Ana obviously is still an integral part of the household, Angela has seemingly accepted her. They speak with each other in the car of their plans for redecorating the house, of the latest fashions in clothes, only of feminine pleasantries. The hostilities of the past seem to have largely disappeared.

As we drive along the pleasant and wide streets in the residential area that leads to Gabriel's home, I note that my son and daughter are casting glances in each other's direction—looks of question—as if to convey that what they are seeing is not the San Salvador of my description, nor do the charming people—our hosts in Central America—seem as troublesome as I had described them. I see that my children are enthralled by the country's beauty and are responding happily to Gabriel's charm. I hope fervently that the visible picture here and now is the accurate one, not the disturbing one of the past, nauseatingly ugly.

When we enter the house, as on my first visit here, the initial sense of well-being pervades the atmosphere. The only existing clue that things are not quite as they seem…Ana, it appears has been demoted from mistress to servant in the home. The moment we had entered the house, she had immediately gone to work in the kitchen.

Another young girl emerges from the master bedroom. She stretches lazily like a kitten—obviously the latest household pet—and in sleepy tones greets Gabriel, her master and lover, and then the rest of us with a pretty voice.

It seems that Ana fell from grace when she grew to womanhood; along with her maturity came the realization that life, after all, might hold something for her other than her role as a rich man's slave, bought and paid for. In a few hours, we learn from Gabriel's present mistress—told in the strictest of confidence—that Ana took a lover while still in the company of Gabriel. The latest darling informs us that she would never do a thing like that…No, never! Ana's fate has been justly earned.

Ana is very different from the frightened and shy schoolgirl of three years ago. She no longer seems afraid; rather there is about her a self-assuredness, her beauty worn like a velvet cloak.

Though her fresh, young body undoubtedly has been violated many times, her soul seems very much intact. Her demotion in the household to that of servant appears to have had the opposite effect one would expect…rather than trapped in further bondage, Ana's personality exudes freedom.

The friendly scene, apparently a contrived performance, has been short-lived. Ana's presence in the home is no more welcome to Angela than it was three years ago, though Ana no longer occupies the feminine half of Gabriel's bedroom. The winsome Ana can do nothing right…she is in trouble with Angela for the slightest mistake, the wrong brand of cream in her shopping purchases from the market, the wrinkles she leaves while ironing the clothes, and a dress too revealing will bring a sharp rebuke. I had thought at first that the problem existed, as in the past, only between the two girls, but it becomes obvious that Gabriel, too, has only utter contempt for Ana. However, she bears the hostility directed toward her with remarkable grace.

It is quite evident as well that there is further deterioration in the relationship between Gabriel and Angela. They quarrel constantly— bitter, biting words. I see the signals loud and clear. I know that it's time to move on, lest I again become involved in the bitter scene of three years ago, and my son and daughter, too, are caught in the endless quarrels.

Even under the best of circumstances, it is not a good idea to prolong a visit, but these are not the best of circumstances. I declare my intentions to my son and daughter—that of wanting to move on—and of course they are met with objections by both of them. They have not been so close to Angela as I have been and seem not very aware of what is happening here, the emotional upheaval and unhappiness among the household members. They tell me that they want to stay at least two weeks, if not here with Angela and Gabriel, then in a hotel or in one of the *ramadas* along the beaches. I realize that it is selfish of me to deprive them of this part of their vacation, and relent to the point of agreeing to stay for another week, but under the conditions that we look for other quarters.

Angela, sensing our discomfort over the affairs of the home, invites us to spend our remaining time at the beach. The family owns a beach home in La Libertad and once again we are invited guests, only in another setting. La Libertad is exquisite, a tropical paradise of swaying palms and balmy beach air. The reflection of the moon creates magic over the Pacific at night. The fire trees shine in their brilliance. During the daytime hours the Pacific at La Libertad's beaches is warm and foamy. Frolicking in the waves is great fun. We throw the dark sand at each other and in general behave like children. Water is a wonderful antidote. It not only washes away the dross from the earth, but also cleanses the mind of cares and unhappy thoughts. Here at the beach it isn't long until I'm completely happy again. The soft music of guitars can be heard on the warm night, their melody wafted in the balmy air. I'm reminded of the travel brochures that I had been so scornful of before. The atmosphere here is one of relaxation and romance.

But even as I think these pleasant thoughts, I catch a glimpse of El Salvador's poverty that I had found so appalling in 1973. A child, completely naked, runs by me. He has all the signs of rickets, swollen belly and spindly limbs, plus the bleached out hair and skin prevalent in severe anemia. A few feet away, hidden in the thickness of the banana plants, a door opens and a parade of other malnourished and pale children dash by. They pretend not to notice the strange-looking creatures on the "*jefe's*" property, but as evidenced by their sidelong glances, they are very much aware of us.

My daughter sees the condition of the children and suggests that we all chip in and buy a cow for the family...Angela asks us not to. She says that it will only create further problems in the area; obtaining food for the animal will be an additional burden for the family—besides, one of the other peasant families will steal it. After this advice, we don't buy the cow, but something tells me that we will regret not having followed through with our initial intentions.

Before we leave the beach area, Gabriel shows up, but I can't help wishing he had stayed away, even though this is his home I'm now begrudging him. He has picked up a *mariachi* band along the way and another young girl from somewhere. Angela is sure to be upset. He proceeds to make a great show of having a great time, Latin style. He sings along with the *mariachis*, joking and talking happily with us. He turns to pinch the cheek of his recent young companion, at the same time pretending to ignore his daughter completely. But he is doing just that, pretending. He is very much aware of her. He watches her every nuance with his peripheral vision; each movement and expression are monitored. It is nothing but a maddening game and, before the day ends, I beg Angela not to play. I see her being ensnared in the net woven for her once more. Before she came here, it seems obvious she had listened to the deceptive words of the past. Gabriel had promised her peace and harmony; all would be well. There would be no more mistresses about the house—at least no more fifteen-year-olds. She, Angela, need only to return to her loving father…hope and optimism shattered repeatedly.

Angela's pain is exacerbated to the breaking point. I think if the truth were known about Gabriel, and one could see beyond this man's facade, a desperately unhappy individual would be seen. The path his life has taken in relation to women is no different from that of his father, who reportedly has sired no fewer than fifty children! Their mothers were all young women from a shanty town. Some of the children were born simultaneously with his legitimate children by a wife who was born on the right side of town. This woman's children have all enjoyed the privilege of bearing his name. When they were minors they were sheltered under his roof. The others—born of mistresses out of wedlock—are slum dwellers. This man's wife, though deceased, knew of his activities outside the home. But she was as incapable of dealing with the situation as the unrecognized children. I was once introduced to this remarkable old man and, though seventy-five, he is still cavorting with his young mistresses. I can only assume that a large part of the excitement he once felt is missing. It is no longer adultery; there is no longer any wife to deceive. In Gabriel's case, his wife divorced him. The burden falls on Angela. She fulfills the psychological role intended for his wife. To ask what Gabriel's grandfather was like would probably be a question most redundant. An account of his life, by those who knew him, would doubtlessly render a similar story to that of his son and grandson.

My better self, the one that doesn't condemn, but tries to understand, tells me that Gabriel is as much a victim as Angela. The masculine pattern of behavior set before him was far from exemplary. It may well be that Gabriel had detested his father's actions in the home and despised him for humiliating his mother. It could be the timeless story of human error. The injured one reacts to life by injuring.

The author called the most clever of all religious writers, C.S. Lewis, tells us, "I do not think that all who choose the wrong road perish, but their rescue consists in being put back on the right road. A wrong sum can be put right, but only by going back till you find the error and working it afresh from that point, never by simply going on. Evil can be undone, but it cannot develop into good. Time does not heal it."

It's time to go, time to leave El Salvador. The two weeks the three of us had planned to stay—my son, my daughter and I—have ended. Before we take leave of El Salvador completely, we visit a market, pulsating with life and local talent. We buy pretty, handmade articles, embroidered blouses and jewelry boxes, intricately carved, various and sundry items that seem to have all but disappeared from the U.S. market. This wonderful talent has been replaced in the United States by machinery.

We pass through El Centro on the way to the airport, and conditions are exactly the way they were when we had come here before. San Salvador's desperately poor are nowhere to be seen in the streets of the capital. (The caretakers and their children at the beach are proof that they still exist.) The ubiquitous army is still very much visible, a faction that seemingly never changes.

One thing, I think, that can be predicted with a fair amount of accuracy—El Salvador is headed for a revolution. It becomes clear what our charismatic President of the 60s meant when he stated, *"Those who make peaceful change impossible make violent change inevitable."* The two key words, "impossible" and "inevitable," are interwoven partners; they speak of government repression, of poverty, of despair and sickness, the condition of being trapped in a corner. Where is there to go?—Indeed, how to get out? The captors stand with steel boots inside the door.

Once settled on the plane and in the air, I unbuckle my seat belt and move toward the front of the plane. It is a small commuter plane we have boarded. I need to talk with the other passengers about this strange phenomenon, the poverty that seems swept out to sea. Knowledge of the whereabouts of these unfortunate people now strangely absent from sight becomes imperative to me.

I am selective in my "private investigation," and choose as subjects those I believe to be Salvadorans, not Guatemalans. Among the

Salvadorans, I look for those I believe to be the most sophisticated, therefore the most politically aware. Distinction between the two nationalities is often difficult, nearly impossible by physical appearance alone. But there is a difference in accent, which I'm beginning to recognize. Salvadorans usually speak much faster than Guatemalans. It is also safe to assume that if a Salvadoran has the price of an airline ticket, that person also speaks English.

I look about the plane and hesitate slightly before "conducting my interview." I hope that my questions will carry a ring of authority. I could well be told to mind my own business.

But since we will be on this plane but a short time, I must start searching now if I'm to find any satisfactory answers to the perplexing situation that causes the Salvador of 1973 and the one of 1975 to be two different places.

There is a very nice-looking lady, well dressed, and sitting in the front two rows of seats, and as I approach her, I hope I will give the impression of being a social worker whose profession always accompanies her, even when away from work. "Señora," I begin as inoffensively as the question about to be asked permits, "do you realize that your country has greatly changed in two years? When I was here three years ago, there were dozens of beggars roaming the airport— now there aren't any. Don't you think that's a bit strange?"

I ask this question of perhaps four to five other people, each time phrasing my inquiry a little differently.

"Señor, do you know what became of all the poor people in your country? All the dirty little urchins running around the streets. The airport was filled with them."

My questions are met on each occasion with much evasion, with obvious embarrassment. The passengers with window seats prefer looking at the innocuous clouds rather than talking to me. There is a sound of much throat clearing. When I realize that no one is likely to respond, I begin to supply the answers myself: "Is it then because you have initiated some recent social reforms for eradicating the extremes of poverty?"

I've asked these questions of about half the passengers on the plane, so I'm about midway, when I hear a voice, familiar in all aspects, but which seems to be coming from the other side of the world: "Mother, *sit down!* You're making a damn nuisance of yourself!"

This may well be true, but I have no intentions of abandoning my quest now and tell my son so; "Besides what have I to lose?"

"A great deal," a masculine voice informs me, "including your life if you persist in these questions." I turn around to find myself just inches away from an elegantly handsome man. He is smartly dressed and speaks impeccable English, with just the right trace of an accent to give his voice great charm. I feel a need to bring some dignity into the situation, after that hurried and immature exchange with my son. But if there is truth to be gained here, I must hurry. I may never pass this way again.

I begin to repeat the questions that I had asked of the other airline passengers. The gentleman standing next to me stops me mid-sentence, but gently. He takes his seat and invites me to share its adjacent one, which had been empty.

"In response to your comments," he tells me, "it has taken China twenty-five years to turn things around. Do you think that so great a change could take place within a span of two to three years?" He parenthetically adds that he has no way of knowing whether Communism was wrong for China, or right, only that change could not have taken place in so short a time. He emphasizes that this change had been affected only with the cooperation of all the Chinese people, and not without a revolution.

I am surprised as he continues with what seems half admonition, half information: "I will tell you what you want to know about our pitiful little nation. Then you must promise to stop asking questions like the ones I've just overheard. You're going to get yourself in trouble as others have done when traveling in this country. Some of the more curious have never been heard from again."

As far-fetched as this cloak-and-dagger story seems to be, something nevertheless tells me that I'd do well to listen and heed the advice from this handsome stranger.

He goes on to tell me, "These poor people you're asking about—

they are all dead. The military police killed them all."

"But why?" I implore, "why?"—feeling the blood drain from my head. I feel weak, but I sit up straighter in my seat. The face he turns to me is sensitive, a compassionate expression emanating from his dark eyes. He bites his bottom lip as if to stifle pain, and continues with his story. "There was a Miss Universe contest here. The whole city at that time was given a face-lift. All things unpleasant were disposed of. The Salvadoran Government wanted the dignitaries, who had come from all over the world for this spectacular event in our tiny country, to see the best of El Salvador, not its shameful truth…so the streets were swept clean of all refuse, literally."

"But how was that possible? I want to know. There were so many!"

"The police disguised themselves as civilians, as is their way in these situations, and approached these people as 'angels of mercy.' Offering food and shelter to the homeless they (the police) led them to an isolated spot and murdered them.* A few were suspicious and refused to follow their would-be-assassins. Therefore, they remained alive for a while longer. "But all beggars," my new friend explains, "are eventually killed—some sooner, some later, but none escape."

This personable and intelligent gentleman looks at me now with an expression hard to read. It is as if a book had been opened and I had been allowed a glimpse inside, but suddenly it is slammed shut. True to his promise, the conversation has ended. But his spirit had reached out to mine. I can see that he is as revolted as I. There must be some reason why he would run the risk of saying these things to me…as if perhaps he wants the world to know.

But the mask of casualness returns and he hands me a business card. I accept it and thank him for his courtesy and see he is a manager of a chain of banks that operate throughout Guatemala and El Salvador. He assures me that if I'm ever in need of money, the bank's services are at my disposal.

---

*The author learned later that this horrifying event occurred just a few weeks before her arrival to El Salvador in 1975.

I am finding it difficult to breathe. I cannot ignore what I've just heard. If I pretend this shocking situation doesn't exist, like others who fall into the trap of indifference, I, too, will become a member of the living dead.

My son and daughter are awaiting the outcome of the conversation. From their expressions I can tell they know that I've not been waved aside again, but that my questions have been met with some response.

I repeat (for them) what I've just heard. They are aghast and, when the plane lands, they are both weeping. At this moment it is appropriate to weep. Because though they weep there is yet hope.

We stay but a night in Guatemala City and in the morning early, we set out for Atitlán. I am greatly excited by the prospect of seeing this gloriously beautiful place again and anticipate showing my children around.

When we arrive in Panajachel, we look for the hotel where I sometimes stayed on my prior visit—when I needed a few luxuries to get me going again, such as a hot bath and a shampoo. My memories of the owner are that he was kind and hospitable, anxious to please his clientele. He was so enamored by the lake's atmosphere and so completely in love with the bungalows he had commissioned the Naturales to build, that mere mention of his hotel brought tears to his eyes. We find the hotel easily. The owner of the hotel, Vision Azul, welcomes me back to Guatemala.

As I introduce him to my son and daughter, he shakes my son's hand, but kisses the slim hand of my daughter.

After murmuring hello, my daughter quickly plunges into the story that was told by the bank manager to me. She repeats the story nearly verbatim.

The hotel owner's response cannot be more shocking. He calmly waits for her to finish her narrative concerning El Salvador's handling of its destitute people when he shakes his head in agreement. He is not, however, agreeing with us, our outrage.

"Guatemala, too," he nods, "…we keel all ze bad people and all ze Comunistas…no, no, don't luk like zat. It's better for ze good people—like us. Do you want to luk at zat—all zat trash on ze streets?"

My son and daughter, I can see, are trying desperately to assimilate the information that has had a further shocking effect. Until a moment ago they might have thought Guatemala political-shaky, but liberated to the point that it didn't kill its own citizens without benefit of a trial.

As we listen to these words, we soberly realize that what the hotel owner has just expressed may not be an isolated opinion, but may well be the prevailing attitude of the whole of Latin America's aristocracy.

So now we know. "Guatemala, too. They keel all the bad people and all the 'Comunistas' because it's better for all the good people...like us."

The hotel owner further defends his position by asking, "Do you theenk all ze beautiful gorls in ze beauty parade would want to luk at zat; and for zat matter, would you want to luk at zat?" meaning me.

The person I don't want to look at is him. But he exists, so I must. With clear eyes I feel I must see both him and those he wants destroyed.

Hail the beauty queen!

RETURN TO ATITLAN

5:45 in the morning—my daughter, my son and I walk rapidly down the village road that joins the "calle principal" in Panajachel and leads to the boat dock below. Three years ago this was but a well-trod path formed by the footsteps of the Mayas—and later—by the many visitors coming from all over the world.

At precisely 6:00 A.M. the boat will depart for Santiago Atitlán, the village directly across the lake. I anticipate happily the prospect of acquainting my son and daughter with the village I've talked so much about and the one I called home in 1973.

The gardens here are as lovely as I remember them from three years ago, their perfume permeating the morning air. As we hurry along, I note several new boutiques since I was here last, the clothing on display in the windows cut from the colorful "*tela tipica*," unique only to Guatemala, but designed after the fashions in the United States.

The gigantic construction projects, began a mere three years ago, have developed into two high-rise hotels at the lakeshore. Their towering structuring of cement and glass would compliment any downtown district in the city, but here their ostentatious appearances are grossly out of place. We reach the dock, walking down the short gangway, and manage to climb aboard just as the captain of the large tourist boat starts the motor and gives the orders to his helper to unloose the vessel from its anchor.

The luxurious boat, with its excited-looking passengers, glides smoothly through the waters, the rhythm of the motor blending with the lapping of the waves.

The journey across the lake requires only about one hour and some minutes in actual time, but time takes on another dimension between these two pueblos, Panajachel and Santiago Atitlán. Nature will soon haughtily display just how impressive she can be.

Her sun makes his appearance, not gradually, but instantly, and the pueblos spring to life. Fanning, golden fingers touch the wakened creation vibrating with morning freshness.

Mountains hovering over the lake frame the sky in their towering majesty. They are dressed with exquisite shades of green—tall pine, fir and stately birch grace their slopes. The volcanoes, unlike their reputations for violence, spewing hot lava in anger, are benignly beautiful. Covered with thick, lush vegetation, they do not compete in their effusive beauty, but whisper acknowledgments across the lake and canyons—respectful neighbors. I notice that the artists on the boat are taking out their drawing materials, unable to resist transferring to their talented digits what their eyes behold.

An endless blue sky stretches above—the waters lie in shimmering parallel. I lie back in the boat, my body warmed by the glad rays of the sun. Occasionally I feel the spray, deliciously cool from the lapping of the waves. I look at the faces of my son and daughter—rosy from the wind and the sun—and see that they, too, have yielded to the spell of El Lago Atitlán.

While we are some distance away, before the boat is maneuvered into the dock I see the same crowd of merchants as before, waiting for the tourist boat—the same bunch of Tzutuhil children in their "*traje tipico*," barefoot, carrying their whistles, their birds and their dangling beads—just waiting to give the tourists a "merry chase" if they refuse to buy anything. I've seen these little rascals follow a tourist for blocks, harassing the poor soul with every step he takes until he breaks down and buys something.

The captain turns off the motor and the boat glides into the pier. We disembark and I see the grassy knoll leading to the Chi-Nim-Ya has not disappeared into another world, but is still here as when I last saw it.

The excitement I feel lends itself to a sudden burst of energy, so rather than walking, I run up the slope and burst into the *tienda* of my friends, profoundly happy to see them again. José and Francisca look up from their work. They are waiting on customers as when I saw them last, but if they are surprised to see me, they don't show it. They greet me pleasantly—as if they had seen me but yesterday, rather matter-of-factly. They leave their work for a moment, embracing me warmly. Francisca, noting what must be a look of disappointment on my face, explains that their lack of surprise does not mean that they are indifferent to me. "Everyone comes back to Atitlán," she tells me.

Chico, dear Chico, is still here as well, but tells me he will soon be able to open a business of his own. Francisca tells me rather sadly that he cannot be replaced. "There is no one who works like Chico." The expression on his face is a happy one. Everyone likes to be appreciated. Chico is no exception.

Walking uphill over the cobblestones, I feel the familiar warmth of the midday sun as it beats down upon the earth. All is dearly familiar, even the moisture that forms on my upper lip and brow.

"Everyone returns to Atitlán." I ponder upon what had been stated so simply, yet which seems to be the basis for every song sung, for all prose written. Atitlán, like all lands known for their compelling beauty, is famous for drawing people back to its shores.

I begin to experience the same sensation of three years ago, the disturbance of the equilibrium—a result of the high altitude, which brings about a certain sense of giddiness. I notice that my son and daughter are also perspiring and seem a little short of breath as they talk.

Santiago Atitlán, unlike Panajachel, whose changes appear only blatantly apparent, has changed also. Some of the changes are subtle and not at once noticeable, but there is an aura of modernization about the pueblo. There are young Mormon missionaries walking about the market and thoroughfare. They are conspicuously identifiable in their uniformity—black trousers, dark tie, immaculate white shirts complete their mode of dress. There is an almost military orderliness about their appearance. Their neatly combed hair has a pronounced side part and they appear to be unruffled by the elements and by all other circumstances. A conversation, however, with any of these young men will dispel any thought that their zeal is fortified by anything other than making converts of every soul they meet. The village is already inundated with religions of nearly every persuasion, not excluding the traditional Tzutuhil, still deeply rooted in the ancient Mayan religion. (Old Maximón must find these strange goings-on troublesome as his ancient wooden frame stalks the pueblo, keeping an ever-watchful eye on his domain.) The prospect of making good Mormons of the Tzutuhiles seems rather bleak. But the reputation of the Mormons just may have followed them here—their church is one of sharing the abundance of their worldly goods with the rest of the world. Their brand of Gospel seems to go hand in hand with distributions of a generous supply of food. The poor of Atitlán are undoubtedly among the recipients of their generosity.

The rows of shops along this side of the village are exactly as I remember them. There is the *tela tipica* on display—the predominant shade of red, blending with the subtler colors of the bluebirds. The garments hang from the high windows—like gaily-colored banners blowing in the breeze from the lake just yards away…the same *tiendas*, but more of them now. I realize now why Santiago is considered the most colorful of Atitlán's villages—other than its geographic splendor, there are 35,000 people dressed in colors dominated by a brilliant red.

Interspersed among the clothing stores are two shops that I had not seen three years ago. Two cottages, side by side, now house the village sculptors. As we enter one of the shops, I immediately recognize the design and patterns as being the same as those of the workshop in the Catholic Church in 1973. The men and little boys are busily carving the likenesses of the Mayan Gods. These are of various stages of sophistication, depending on the ages of the artists.

As we wander about the shop looking at the intricate objects of art, I notice that the members of this family do not speak in the broken syllables common in the village, but the way they speak Spanish sounds fluent and clear, good pronunciation. The association between the family and church is obvious. Few people have the benefit of an education outside the influence of the church in the pueblo. Along with the recognition of the wood carving, I seem to remember the young men as being the same ones I had seen in the church workshop three years ago—now they are grown and skilled in their art. I ask the father of the household about this and he tells me that this is so. But this is not only the House of Sculptors, as the sign reads outside, it is a house of Diegos. There are three members of the household sharing the same name, the father and two sons. I wonder for the sake of identification how they can be distinguished one from another, who, for example, comes running when the mother and wife calls? If one Diego receives a letter, who opens it? There are any number of hypothetical situations that cause me perplexities about this strange situation—I make a mental note to ask this family these questions sometime when I know them better. This is not the right time for it—I'm barely acquainted with them, and from what I know about the Naturales, their heritage is regarded with sacred mystery. The majority of the landowners of the pueblos do not own businesses. Their small plot of land remains in the family for generations. It produces just enough food to ward off starvation, and only if the families have planned well their planting, adhering to good habits of agriculture. They must allow the land rest every four to five years. Sometimes just by planting vegetables, fruits or grains different from the prior season—a change from the last crop will produce the desired results. A great deal of planning is mandatory to keep the soil yielding and fertile, so that their basic food, corn for their tortillas and their black beans, can be continuous crops.

When the land produces little and is overworked, the Naturales from Atitlán, as elsewhere in the rural areas, are forced to leave their pueblos and go to work at "La Costa," which can mean anywhere between the agriculturally rich town of Escuintla to the steamy port of San José on the Pacific and beyond this point to the Salvadoran border.

The men from the pueblos leave their homes only as a last resort to go to work on the coffee, sugar and cotton plantations. The wealth in these areas holds no lucrative promise for them—to the contrary it only means a lot of hard work in the sweltering sun with little pay. They go home after months of toil without any savings for the future, many ill from overwork and malnutrition. A multitude come home to die after months of inhaling fumes from the plants that are thick with pesticides. The families in Santiago Atitlán are poor, but in general they are not so destitute as their neighbors in Santa Catarina Palopo, whose men of the Cachiquel Tribe migrate for this seasonal work by the hundreds. But this is nothing new; the story of the migrant worker is as old and timeless as poverty itself.

But what is new in the pueblo of Atitlán is a definite change for the better. There is less malnutrition now among the Tzutuhiles. They seem to enjoy an improvement in general health. The infants look cleaner. Their coughs and runny noses to a large extent have vanished. The eye infections I had seen in 1973 were horrible. The children's eyes were frequently swollen shut. They drained purulent material; blindness sometimes occurred, mainly as a result from these infections left untreated. These changes are undoubtedly due to the combined efforts of Dr. Juan and Susan and the village priests. I had met Dr. Juan and Susan just before I left for Guatemala on my last visit. Their presence is noticeable wherever they have been in a village.

I learn through my main source of information, the Chi-Nim-Ya, that they have established five nutritional clinics in and around Santiago Atitlán and are still expanding. The clinics are simple structures where the ladies of the pueblo are taught the rudiments of good nutrition, along with the necessity of washing their hands well before handling food. Midwifery is taught to the ladies with a propensity toward nursing.

Since most of the Tzutuhiles don't read and write, they are taught with pictures. Vegetables are depicted in a large pot. The right way to cook them is shown with a lot of vegetables, a little water. A big X is drawn over the picture with the wrong way of cooking, a few vegetables with a lot of water.

The padre shows us a nice new hospital, the only flaw of which is a blackened area in the hospital lobby. He explains that this is where a family cooked a meal while waiting for a new little Tzutuhil to be born.

The hospital has a surgical suite, a laboratory and an x-ray department, all outfitted with modern equipment. Although the *brujo* (witch doctor) still maintains the respect of the pueblo and old Maximón is still king of the fiestas, there is a gradual recognition of modern medicine. The parents appreciate seeing badly fractured limbs return to full function. They know when they have followed the doctor's orders, along with the treatment rendered, their babies have been restored to health following severe bouts of fever, cough, diarrhea and other maladies. Dr. Juan and Susan make it a point to visit all the new parents in the village, stressing the need for the mother to nurse her baby, rather than giving the infant canned formula. If the infant is to survive, due to the high degree of bacteria in the pueblos, breast-feeding is nearly mandatory. The antibodies the infant needs as a defense are found only in the milk of the mother. It so happens that this advice is not nearly so necessary among the Naturales as it is among the Ladino community. The ladies, however, are all accustomed to getting out of bed almost the moment their children are born and waiting on their families. Susan must be vigilant at all times to see that this doesn't happen. She oftentimes attends to the mother herself and tries to cope with the families' needs. This service is ill appreciated by an occasional father who is resistant to this arrangement. The good nurse Susan can sometimes silence him by telling him that if he wants his wife around for a long time then he must exert a little patience.

Padre David, after serving the pueblo faithfully for five years, will be leaving in a few days to go back to Oklahoma. One of the local beauties will be on the plane with him. She will, he informs us, become his wife.

His three predecessors have left the pueblo for the same reason. Among Santiago Atitlán's priestly contemporaries, only Padre Francisco remains married to the church, keeping his vows of celibacy intact.

Aside from being confronted with questions such as, "Why do all the priests who come to this village get married?" questions to which I have no answer, playing hostess to my son and daughter is great fun. I escort them to places that I had found so fascinating three years earlier. They find the twin churches at Chi-Chi-Castenango as mystical and awesome as I had on my first visit.

On our agenda are the magnificent Mayan ruins. Flights between Guatemala City and Tikal are available, although the small plane we board causes us some misgivings. In the floor of the main aisle there is a hole large enough for an adult person to fall through.

We seem to be the only North Americans on board, and the only ones who seem concerned about the situation. The motto the Guatemalans seem to live by: *Oh well, you live till you die*, seems to rub off on its visitors. So we go on with our plans. Miraculously no one is lost to the great beyond, but as we land at the small airstrip at Tikal, the wreckage from a prior plane crash occupies a large part of it, reminding us that accidents do happen, even in Guatemala!

The Tikal ruins, an entire city uncovered by the archaeologists, where history and modern culture meet, suggest to the world through their artifacts, their hieroglyphics and their complicated Mayan calendar, that theirs is a civilization immensely creative and imaginative, competing with the early Greeks in intelligence, and their towering pyramids, interestingly, resemble the architecture of the ancient Egyptians.

One day after a particularly rewarding visit to San Pedro La Laguna (which brings back certain memories to me) we realize that our vacation time has ended. But as my son and daughter prepare to leave for home, they see that I'm not doing anything but staring into space, and when they inquire as to the reason I say it's because I'm staying— that I still need to write.

At this piece of news both look a little bewildered, with my son's turning to me with slight irritation in his voice: "Whatever for? That's the reason you gave for coming here the last time—and do you really think that you've something to say that someone hasn't said already— and better?"

I don't really think I have anything to say that someone else hasn't said—and much better—but I answer in the affirmative anyway.

Upon seeing that I won't change my mind about remaining here, my son and daughter go on with their packing and, after seeing them off at the airport and saying goodbye, I begin to feel the familiar ache of being alone.

I begin to reflect on the possible reasons for my failure to write anything when I was here before—all those months. One of the reasons may have been that I had wanted to write about a family among the Naturales, the members' aspirations and dreams, their struggles and philosophies, the way they relate to the rest of the world—and what could I have written? Today I went to the market and a little indigenous girl pulled my hair. When I reacted in annoyance she pulled it again and ran away laughing. When I tried to look away, she came back and gave my hair another hard jerk just for good measure, this time eliciting the mirth of the ladies sitting on the floor selling vegetables.

Any and all attempts on my part had ended in the same way, either with total unresponsiveness or with derisive laughter. They had laughed at my clothes and they had laughed at my speech, children and adults alike.

But situations are seldom tailor-made and should I find myself in the same circumstances as before, I'll just have to be content with the friendship of the Ladinos in the pueblos. Once again, I'm grateful to José and Francisca who are perennial in their affection toward me, always courteous and helpful…and of course, I did not mention any of this to my son and daughter. I didn't tell them that things had not been all that great, that among the Naturales, aside from Chico at the *Chi-Nim-Ya*, I had failed to acquire the friendship of even one indigenous person. My staying behind is ludicrous, even to me! But I think I've learned a lesson in simple village etiquette. This possibly may be of some help to overcome the pitfalls of the past. My shopping at the public markets had been the result of necessity only—to get what I needed and to leave as soon as possible. This is wrong, not the way things are done at all in the pueblo. If a lady offers a bunch of onions for ten cents, then you must offer eight cents. The real price is nine cents. You never pay fifteen cents for a bunch of carrots. "Es mucho—es demasiado." This is too much. This perhaps seems a waste of time over so simple a matter but in the long run it's worth the effort. There comes a day when bargaining is not so tedious for the foreigner, but an acceptable part of everyday life. Anyway it is far preferable to having your hair pulled for being a snob.

One day, while walking through the pueblo, I happened upon a very strange occurrence. There was a tug of war going on between a boy and a girl. The fight seemed to have been so grossly unfair since the boy was obviously the stronger of the two. On second glance, however, the girl seemed to be holding her own. The cause for the wrestling match was a *reboso*—a shawl, very pretty and handmade, obviously belonging to the girl. From the determined expression, she did not intend to part with it if she could prevent it. She had her feet planted firmly on the ground, clutching the piece of cloth as if her life depended on it, while the boy tugged and pulled. The poor girl lost her balance on one occasion and fell to the cobblestones where she undoubtedly bruised her knees. She managed to get up from where she had fallen, with her shawl still intact.

Soon there was an audience of boys and girls—about thirty young people—but they all seemed to be cheering for the boy, and had no sympathy for the girl whatsoever.

I walked away, thinking disgustedly, *Another classic example of male chauvinism,* and turned around in time to see the girl forfeit the shawl, but a quick look at the girl's face told me that she was not in the least unhappy over having lost the *reboso*; her expression was one of triumph rather than defeat. I went straight to the rectory where I had hoped to inquire of Padre David the meaning of the altercation. "Why had the spectators taken the part of the boy, rather than the girl?"

On this occasion I had to wait before I could see the priest—he was occupied as mediator in a village squabble between a man and a woman over a cow. The woman claimed that it had been hers, but there was no remaining evidence since it had been eaten before the "court" began. The consumer claimed it had been his all along.

I never learned the outcome of the feud over the cow, but my question concerning the sparring couple was met with an amusing smile, much in the same way as when I had asked about Maximón.

"The couple you saw fighting over the shawl were in the process of becoming engaged. You've discerned correctly that she, the girl, was not unhappy over the loss of her *reboso*. With the loss she gained a husband."

The padre goes on to say that the *reboso* engagement became a tradition as a result of the pueblo's installing a municipal water supply. "The young people have had to replace their former custom of courtship."

To this story, a little mystified, a little impatient, I wonder, *What has any of this to do with getting married?* I remember quite vividly the controversy the modern utility had evoked in the pueblo. It seems that I am about to learn the reason. I had not understood how any of the Tzutuhiles, particularly the ladies, could have questioned the need for piped-in water. The ladies formerly carried the families' daily water supply in huge water jugs on their heads, many trudging over rocks and steep terrain for miles. It seems that they would have joyfully welcomed one less burden. Not so! A protest group was formed. These ladies had actually thrown rocks at the workers as they dug the trenches for installation of the water pipes.

I think I'm beginning to understand the connection. Padre David tells me now that the water jug has been substituted for the *reboso*. In the old days, before "modern technology," the girl went to the lake, seemingly oblivious to her future husband—the boy lay in wait for her, hidden in the reeds, and when she appeared with her water jug, there ensued a battle between them. If the boy succeeded in knocking the water jug off the girl's head, they kissed and went to the boy's home to announce their engagement. He almost always won these sessions. It is presumed the courtship began a long time before this formal custom took place at Atitlán's shores. It is the boy's parents who must give their approval first, since the couple soon to marry will live in the home of the boy. They must pay the parents of the bride for their son's wife according to their financial circumstances.

Sometimes the dowry consists of currency—sometimes only a piglet or a couple of chickens if the family of the groom is poor. In which case he will surely have this inadequate payment of her flung at him during their first argument—when this occurs, the honeymoon has ended.

My days in Atitlán as before are spent mainly in loneliness and aloneness. There are the occasional moments of ecstasy, but as anywhere, these have no sustaining power. Weeks have passed and I realize that outside of very superficial exchanges with the tourists on short visits to Santiago, I've not had a single conversation in English. There is a positive side to this, however, because that means a total immersion in the Spanish language. José and Francisca are beginning to comment on the improvement in the way I speak Spanish. For the star behind my name, I say, "Buena Onda!"

During my long hours of solitude—when I'm feeling only a positive effect from them—I truly see the splendors of Atitlán. A liberated feeling, free as the wind prevails, and I can reflect on the accomplishments of other people, and hopefully learn from them. Had every artist waited for the opportune moment to paint a picture, tell a story, preach a sermon, very little would ever have been accomplished. In addition to inspiration, a great deal of work is involved, unfortunately. Similarly artists do not always paint their sisters, friends or mistresses. Sometimes the subjects are little known. The beauty springs to the artist's hand from the mystery of life itself. Very often the outcome is not revealed until the work is finished…and upon reflection, I dip my pen into the saturated, dark and light fountain of the poets and begin to write, at last grateful that I am alone.

I begin to write verses of the towering volcanoes and mountains as they appear to me, benignly beautiful, infinitely tender, hovering over the pueblos protectively. Envisioning the fleeing Mayas hiding behind the rocky cliffs, the area, as fresh as a new day, takes on a dream-like quality. The scarring of the Mayan race by the sword of the Spaniards becomes the subject for rhyme. Even the sweet little houses clustered together at the foot of the hills are poetic. They are constructed from the earth itself—walls that are a combination of stone and bamboo—the stone starting from the foundation and midway joining the hollow stems of the bamboo poles. Covering each of the homes a smiling, thatched roof basks in the sun. Little brown babies play in the dirt outside their homes—never possible to know to which family these children belong. Like clusters of grapes the homes cling together, as if from the same vine. All is well. The waters of the deep blue, volcanic lake adds to the enchantment.

The abundant riches of nature have generously compensated the lack of monetary wealth in the Mayan villages. The corn grows tall and green. Its silky stalks cover the slopes of the mountains and hills, to the valleys below. Everywhere there is poetry at Atitlán. How had I possibly missed it before!

TERREMOTO

Terremoto! I've just learned its meaning. I am at the Colonial Hotel in downtown Guatemala City when it strikes. A loud bang jars the sleeping city awake—like the sound of a vast area being stuck by lightning, then the shaking. Like a giant hand it seizes the hotel building and in its tenacious, gargantuan palm will not let go. My first terrified thought is that Guatemala, all of it, is being bombed. I hear bricks falling to the pavement with a sickening thud, the sound of glass smashing on the sidewalks and what sounds like entire buildings crashing in a great roar.

I am alone, on my hands and knees, looking for a light. I have been thrown out of bed—It is pitch black—not a flicker of light. "If only I could see, I could get out of here." I crawl in the direction where I think the lamp should be, but find myself foolishly clutching a handful of clothes—I'm in the closet. I find a skirt and sweater—what luck—and begin to draw the sweater over my head when I realize that I've gone to bed in rollers. I begin to yank them frantically, thinking that if I'm going to die here, I don't want to be found with my hair in curlers. Still looking for a light, I find the night stand where the lamp had been when I went to sleep. But only the flat surface of the wood of the night stand mocks me—the lamp had been tossed somewhere else in the blast. Fumbling around, I manage to find the light switch. Another trick has been played on me—only a light switch; there's no light, nothing but total darkness. I begin to crawl in the opposite direction and, with some luck, I might find the door. I find it by being smacked in the head. I've been pitched forward; however, I have the doorknob in my hand—but when I turn it the door remains stubbornly locked. For one panicky moment I wonder why I've been locked in this room. I hear a voice crying, "God help me! Someone help me! This is an earthquake, a bad one," and I realize that the voice is none other than my own.

One moment I am praying, the next moment cursing, swearing at this terror of the night. It has by now taken on a personality, a demonic one. "Damn you anyway, did you have to lock the door on me as well?" At this very moment, as if this monster has a reasonable streak after all, it heaves one last, convulsive gasp and stops shaking. And with what seems to be the last shake, the door is flung open.

Ah freedom! Some dear person, some darling person out of nowhere shines a light on my path. I can see to descend the three flights of stairs now. The candlelight affords a view of the scene in the lobby where there is an aggregate of hotel guests. Most of them I see are as frightened as I, but others of all things, are actually laughing.

The first question I throw out to anyone who may answer me is, "Does anyone know the magnitude of this quake?"

Just why this seems important to me, I don't know. It would be like asking, "That bomb that exploded, was it wrapped in cobalt or merely consisting of nuclear fission?" But out of the dark a masculine voice answers me, "Oh about 8.5 on the Richter scale, I imagine," teasing me for my fright. He is wrong! The quake is measured at a little less than 8.2—reported by the seismologists, the strongest in Latin American history. This news is brought to us—the little group huddled in the lobby of the hotel—by a portable radio belonging to a hotel guest from Vera Cruz. Intermittently we hear the broadcast of the emergency news, then static, again nothing for a little while, then there is news of the damage suffered, but only in the city. I listen and hear Hotel El Centro mentioned—it is in the area of the Palacio Nacional, and in fact I had switched hotels just the day prior; I had come to this hotel out of anger at the management of the Hotel El Centro...I had watched the man in charge kick out a very small boy for wanting to shine the shoes of the hotel guests. I ask the owner of the radio what the commentator had said. "Did the hotel collapse?"

"Only the walls," he answers.

In a few moments we learn that all of Guatemala had been affected by the quake, extending beyond the Eastern border to El Salvador, and to the Northern tip of Mexico. The newscaster says damage is extensive—twenty-six people have been reported killed. But if I had thought that the monster was through with us, it's because I know nothing of its ferocity. It wasn't dead, but sleeping. The building begins to shake again and it seems that there is no way for the hotel to withstand the blast of another quake, but still it weathers the storm—only the china decorating the halls and the pictures and other decorations come tumbling down.

I am but a few feet from the man from Vera Cruz—between earthquakes we exchange names and personal data—and he tells me that he is in Guatemala on business from Mexico. I tell him that my purpose here in Guatemala is to write and he laughingly tells me that now I have additional experiences to add to my repertoire.

A comforting arm goes around my waist and I leave it there. I feel a great need to be close to another human. The consolation that I drew from this person, however, lasts but a moment or two, for almost simultaneously I feel a hand on my thigh. I try to push the hand away and withdraw from this "opportunist," but another hard aftershock again rocks the building, creating the necessity to choose between the lesser of the two evils.

About two and one-half hours pass. It is dawn and the gentleman from Vera Cruz has ceased being a comfort or a problem. His room is opposite mine in the hallway and he lies on his bed with his door open and in what seems to be a deep sleep. He has offered sanctuary to the small group of people crowded there together, and I see that some of them are leaning against the bed and resting on the floor with pillows beneath their heads.

The next person who "comes into my life" as the result of the quake is a North American Air Force colonel. I know that my first words to him are ludicrous and empty, but I say, "Hello, how are you?" After all how well off can anyone be at the moment? The aftershocks are still coming about three to four minutes apart—anywhere else they would be deemed full scale earthquakes. They are reported to be 6.5 on the Richter scale.

But the colonel gives me an answer anyway, "Ah'm not havin' a very good tahm here." In spite of his frustration at the moment, his voice retains the pleasant drawl, peculiar to the state of Texas. He continues with his complaints. "If I'd have known Guatemala would be like this, I wouldn't have come. The tour guide didn't show up to take me to the mountains and didn't even bother to say he wasn't comin'. Hell, ah cain't even flush muh tuhlet!"

I wonder if we are discussing the same situation that has befallen us only a few short hours ago, but I remember what had been my priorities—the hair curlers—and not only refrain from remarking, but silently I am less critical.

I tell him what I really would like to do right now is find some coffee and would he like to accompany me in my search. He tells me that he will go with me to look, but warns me that, "There ain't any."

We go out into the morning sun. The sidewalks are piled high with rubble. Broken glass, mountains of it, lies in shattered ruins. A look above tells the story. Most of the office buildings are without windows, but some lie in heaps where they had once been erect. The colonel and I go through the doors of one café, out again into another, looking for coffee. The colonel is right—there ain't any. Furthermore we find out there ain't no water, no electricity and an instant food shortage has gone into effect. The colonel goes back to the hotel and I keep walking.

I had expected to witness a complete state of panic about the city, but instead there is a death-like stillness. I notice several people lying at the periphery of the sidewalks and believe that they have abandoned their homes because they have collapsed already or out of fear of falling materials. The city officials had warned of the danger of remaining inside the weakened structures.

Walking toward the sleeping people, not wanting to disturb their exhausted sleep, but fearful for them, I try to arouse one young lady, one of the prone people. "Señorita," I tell her, standing over her, "you and your family would be safer somewhere else. Don't you want to move to the park near here? I'm going there." She doesn't answer me and I try again to talk to her—this time a little louder. "Señorita, please wake up!"

When she still does not answer me, I walk on, talking to perhaps five or six more people—when it occurs to me they are all dead! I hear my own voice saying, like a person gone mad, "Oh, I'm so sorry to disturb you."

At the corner I buy a daily newspaper—it is the latest edition—and the report of the quake lists 10,000 people dead, this high jump in casualty reports is undoubtedly due to information being brought from the pueblos.

I begin to plan my next move and realize that I have not called my children. In my last letter to them I had mentioned that I was staying at the Hotel El Centro. Since its damages had been among Guatemala's initial report, there is some possibility that the U.S. news media also carried the story.

I walk toward the *Guatel* building (Guatemala's communication center) and though but a few blocks from the Hotel Colonial, its line extends almost the same distance. I dutifully get in line, believing that when all the hopefuls are served I, too, will have a chance to call. But when I see the line is not moving at all, I inquire of the reason from a person near me. It is now that I learn something of the optimism of the Guatemalan people. There isn't any phone service, no telegraphic service; we are cut off from the rest of the world. Just now a pile of bricks tears away from the telephone building and comes tumbling down. I feel a little foolish—this is not the first time since the earthquake occurred that I'm in the process of trying to get word to my family that I'm okay here in Guatemala, but the very next moment this may no longer be true for any of us. The earth is still on the move, still shaking.

A strange phenomenon has occurred with Guatemala's balmy temperatures—the land of the eternal springtime becomes a chilly winter land. On the day of the quake—yesterday—the weather had been warm and agreeable, as always, but now the barometric pressure drops to below 40 degrees Fahrenheit. I bundle up in my winter coat and go to the park. Here I huddle together with the rest of Guatemala's refugees. The next morning I return to the Hotel Colonial, probably just to be moving more than anything else. I don't really expect that any drastic change has occurred overnight, in view of what has happened. There is still no food to be bought anywhere in the city, there's still no water or other utilities. There is no reason to believe that the Colonial has access to any of these amenities either.

What I see next I find impossible to believe. A taxicab has pulled up at the curb of the hotel. (I had tried in vain over the last fifteen hours or so to locate a cab.) But there it is, a driver with a client in the back seat, who turns out to be a youth of about seventeen or eighteen. Blond and tanned, he alights from the taxi and, dangling from one shoulder, is a leather strap enclosing several books. One of them, a how-to book, bears the title, *Guatemala on Ten Dollars a Day*. With the other hand he clutches a tennis racquet and, slung over the matching shoulder, is a new pair of white tennis shoes. I watch this spectacle in amazement as the driver removes several pieces of shiny, new luggage from the trunk of the cab.

I seem to be the only person about at the moment, so the boy addresses me pleasantly. "Do you think there are any rooms available in this hotel? It looks nice, is it?"

"Sure, lots of them, "I answer. "The management may even give you a discount!"

I expect that a bright-looking lad like this one will understand the irony of what I've just said, but instead his boyish faces dimples in a happy smile. "Well, you know—thanks a lot—that's what I like, bargains," and walks through the revolving doors of the hotel lobby, the taxi driver following in faithful attendance.

Just as the colonel wants to go home 'cause "he cain't even flush his tuhlet," this visitor is bent upon having a good time on his vacation, the ravages of the earthquake but extenuating circumstances.

"Good luck, young man," I call to him as I climb in the back seat of the taxi he came here in, and ask to be taken to the airport. On the way to the airport, I nevertheless realize that the brief encounter that I had had with the young tourist had been a respite from concentrating on the dangers of the quake. He had brought to me a sense of normalcy. I sincerely hope that someone will help him should he need it.

Before I leave Guatemala, perhaps forever, there is something I must do…someone I must know about. I instruct the taxi driver to please turn around and take me to an address in Zona V. An ironic, little smile tugs at the corner of his mouth.

"Señorita," he tells me, you may be asking the impossible. That zone was hit very hard. Many people there have been killed. Oh well, it's your quetzal. "

When we arrive at the zone in question, the taxi cannot enter because of the massive destruction; blocks of debris block our path. There is no longer any road so that location of an address is not a possibility.

I ask the driver to wait for me, and I get out of the cab, not knowing exactly what the results will be. I walk about one hundred feet, dusk now settling over the ravaged city, and there, as an apparition, climbing over the rubble is Flavio.

He calls to me in English, "Boney, is that you?"

"Si, Flavio, *soy yo,*" calling back in Spanish.

As always, when you know someone well, there is no need for much conversation, but Flavio tells me that his entire family, including his mother who is frail and elderly, escaped injury from the quake. I explain that I really must go, that the taxi is waiting, but that I am happy indeed that he and his family escaped injury and death.

He holds me for a moment and tells me, "I never do forget you, B ney. God go with you and pray for our poor Guatemala. Tell your friends to come and help us—who knows, someday maybe we help the gringos."

When we reach the air terminal I ask the driver to again wait for me, in case I'm unable to get a plane out of here—there are no flights available, neither to the United States or elsewhere.

I buy a newspaper before going back to the hotel and see that the death toll has taken a quantum leap—a shocking 20,000, and over a thousand people are homeless. I notice that the zones hardest hit by the quake are in the poorest areas, sections of Zona I and II, but the most devastated area of all being Zona VI, a residential area already afflicted by poverty of the direst nature. I learn that in the less affluent areas, the homes are constructed from adobe, the most collapsible of all building materials in an earthquake.

I am by now hungry. And what wouldn't I give for a cup of coffee—oh just to be able to splash some water on my face. I go outside the hotel again, only for some fresh air, and thinking perhaps there will be someone to talk with, if just for a few minutes.

A camper pulls up alongside me and the young man on the passenger side of the vehicle, having a French accent, calls to me, asking if I know the street that leads to the San Carlos University. I tell him and continue standing in the same spot, thinking wistfully that they at least have some mobility while I have not. In amazement, I watch them make a U-turn and return to the spot where I stand. The two young men, driver and passenger, want to know if I want to go with them. "There is an open field at the university where we can be safe from falling objects."

This is easily the best offer I've had since the earthquake. They help me collect my things and we are on our way—two wonderful French Canadians, and I, an American woman who had wanted adventure for her writing!

We pick up other passengers along the way. They are not tourists—they have all gone home—but are travelers in a foreign country. Each one has something to contribute to our journey to safety, a loaf of bread, a jug of water, six oranges. The only thing I have is money and I realize that nothing can be bought.

I begin to think of the times when the kids were little and money had at times been very scarce. My marriage had ended and so did, as is so often the case, the financial security. Now the situation is ironically reversed. I have all the money I need right now and there is nothing to buy! However, this does not seem to be a problem at the moment. Everyone shares generously and I, too, am included in this wonderful recently formed community of sharing. Wonder of wonders, there is even a stove in this vehicle of rescue.

The young people have chosen wisely; the grounds of the university do indeed have large areas with no buildings, nothing but wide-open spaces, and many where green lawns flourish.

We explore what might be available to us in the way of facilities and discover, to our complete delight, a bathroom with running water. Not completely deserted after all, there is a band of young people sitting on the lawn. They appear to be university students since they all have books and writing materials, and despite the devastating effects of the earthquake, and indeed the danger still not having passed, they all seem to be enjoying themselves, chatting and joking with each other. I wonder what the particular joke among one little band can possibly be…curiosity wins. I am told that they are Salvadorans, not Guatemalans, and they had come here to hear a lecture. A seismologist was to have been the speaker! Since the Salvadorean students were gone in a short while, I can only guess that they had been waiting for help when our group saw them, and that they were heading back home, having had demonstrated to them first hand a lesson in seismology!

While we take turns using the bathroom, a young man, his girlfriend and I begin to talk about the current disaster. This seems to be common ground for almost everyone these days. I express a fear to them that we may be in for further quakes. Just why I believe myself to be a authority on the subject is not known. But I had been in the Los Angeles quake a few years ago and this concern was expressed, mainly by the news media. At any rate, the young man, a hirsute youth, begins to berate me for my fear. He tells me that now is the time to think positively, and the world, unfortunately, is filled with negative thinkers—obviously implying that I am one of those. When he takes his turn to use the bathroom, I remark to his lady friend, "I seem to be the only one here who's afraid."

The young woman tells me then, a look of knowing in her bright eyes, that her boyfriend is probably more frightened than anyone among us. "That's the way he always copes with things—through bravado. He's totally stressed out!" Evening falls and we all bed down for the night. Some of us take the bed in the camper and others camp out under the stars on the expansive green lawn.

The last voice I hear belongs to the owner of the camper. I have learned his name, which is Andre, and he says, "Oh, this is good, this is nice here." I drift into a very pleasant sleep. It had been a long day.

The next morning I awaken refreshed. While I yawn and stretch, I remark that I am so relieved that we may have seen the last of the quakes. A European girl smiles at me, the way she might at her mother, at once lovingly and condescendingly, and tells me that a report, brought over the radio but an hour ago, gave account of more than a thousand aftershocks, which occurred during the night! I realize, however, that my olfactory sense, at least, is very much intact. There is a delicious aroma of brewing coffee about the camper. Andre hands me a cup and, while greedily gulping it down, I think I hear a familiar voice from the past, blended in with the conversations of the young people. The voice belongs to Roberto, the doctor who teaches at the San Carlos University, and my nocturnal visitor of 1973. By his side is a replica of himself, only smaller, but not for long by the looks of things. The lad appears to be about twelve, tall for his age, particularly noticeable here in Guatemala. Like his father, he is quite charming. We are introduced and he says in English, just slightly tinged with a Spanish accent, "I am so happy to make your acquaintance," extending a hand gentle and warm as he takes mine.

Roberto tells us that he has come to investigate the ravages of the earthquake upon the university and mentions he is surprised that it is not worse. It is true; the worst damage to the building just on superficial assessment seems to be broken windows.

Roberto takes the time to show me the laboratory and the classrooms where he spends his time teaching. As we enter one of the larger structures, it begins to sway and that terrible noise, like the whole world crashing down, again occurs. Roberto takes the hand of his son and my hand and goes running with the both of us out of the brick building toward the open grounds. Roberto makes no show of remaining unaffected. Like I am, like most of us, he is terribly afraid. With him is a very good reason for his fear. Who would want to leave fatherless a boy like this one, or would want something to happen to him?

When we go back to the camper, there is another one of the doctors I had met way back then, with Roberto at Atitlán. He is talking with the young people and, after our greeting each other, he tells us that people other than residents of Guatemala are encouraged to leave, that a food and water shortage has gone into effect. (The truth of the latter part of the statement we had surmised already.)

They say goodbye to me as they leave in separate automobiles, the doctors both with a son, and our little group makes plans to disperse. Some of the young people elect to go north, heading toward Mexico, There had been reports that large sections of the Guatemalan-Mexican roads had been destroyed. I tell the young people that I really do not feel that the plan to go to Mexico is such a good idea, but they decide to take their chances anyway. Others say that they want to go back to the city and there they may be able to find out some information that will be the deciding factor for their course of action. I ask to be taken to the airport, still having hopes of flying out of here to the U.S.

I say goodbye to the dear young people who have been so kind and generous to me and say a prayer for their safety.

When I go inside the air terminals I learn that there are no flights available to the United States—not even to Mexico is it possible to flee.

I ask the ticket agent if any flight at all is available to anywhere. He says that there is a flight to Costa Rica, but the plane is ready to take off, in seven minutes to be exact.

"Costa Rica is fine," I tell him, at once thinking, *Anywhere other than here—this inferno of fear, death and destruction.*

The airline agent hastily begins writing out a ticket for me to Costa Rica, and since it is too late now even for a baggage check, he informs me that I must carry my bags on board.

I am handed my ticket and the polite gentleman calls after me, "*Buena suerte.*" I think I need all the luck I can get!

The porter and I go running, slipping and sliding over the polished marble floors of the main terminal, reaching the area where the passengers and luggage are checked for weapons and other contraband. This procedure takes but a moment and we are running again. I am the only passenger left behind. The others are all on the plane. Tearing down the corridor, the agent checks my face against my passport as we run.

The jet is still on the ground, but the propellers are in fast motion and it will soon join the other planes in the "friendly, blue skies."

It's too late, I think dejectedly. *All this running for nothing. Since I can't leave here, maybe I can just wait in the terminal until another flight is available—to somewhere.*

The porter, still running toward the plane, throws up an arm as if signaling a plane is the same as hailing a taxi. But how is that going to help? This is the airlines. They wait for no one. Only we, the passengers, are kept waiting. Come hell or high water...or earthquakes, once they're ready to take off, up, up and away they go or so I've always thought. "But what pray is this?" The steps are being lowered from the door of the plane to the runway below. A blue-uniformed flight attendant comes down the steps, taking two at a time, and runs toward the porter. Scooping up my luggage as the porter sets it down he waves for me to follow him. I again start running, the bags I'm left with banging against my shins and knees, this time toward the waiting plane. Wonderful, resourceful, haphazard Latin America! Where else would this be happening?

I had wanted to visit Costa Rica for a very long time. The opportunity now has presented itself. The flight to San Jose, Costa Rica's capital, is relaxing and pleasant. The fear and destruction of Guatemala now seems far away as we the passengers are served one appetizing dish after another. All the while dulcet Latin music is heard in the background, soft and non-obtrusive.

I look out the window as we fly over Managua, and from the air the city looks like an aggregate of Quonset huts—the earthquake it suffered four years prior had taken a terrible toll on the country, both in terms of lives and structures. Now Guatemala suffers the same fate.

When the plane lands in San Jose, Costa Rica, and we are outside the terminal, as in Guatemala, I depend on the taxi driver for the recommendations of a hotel. The one he takes me to is a rather elaborate high-rise, and I'm given a room on the eleventh floor. Settled in my room I am determined to rest after calling my children. My call this time is put through right away, and once my children are satisfied that I'm really fine—that I've not perished the way they thought everyone in Guatemala had—they want to know why I've not called before, allowing them to worry constantly for these two days. At this I smile a little and reply, "I'll tell you sometime in the near future. The call is long-distance and you're paying for it. I'll see you soon. I love you."

They don't know the extent of what I have just said, nor did I until the earthquake in Guatemala jarred loose any complacency I might still possess. I thought there was some possibility I might never see them again—now that there is some chance barring some unforeseen event that I will—I'm thankful already.

I lie down, thinking I'll sleep right away, but in spite of my weariness and a comfort at my disposal, sleep is far from me.

I decide to take a stroll about the city, and at first, San Jose seems a little strange to me—here there are no people walking about in their "*traje tipico*"—the ambience is one instead of European influence—that certain flavor—difficult to describe, but once Western Europe is visited, it is at once recognizable. Costa Rica too is beautiful in its own way. The city is clean and orderly, although every inch of space seems to be utilized for shops, banks and office buildings. There is a sense of spaciousness along with the feeling of freedom. Although it is the time of morning when banks open their doors, I've not seen a single policeman with a machine gun, and I do not feel in the least afraid. I realize suddenly that this is what sets Costa Rica apart from her neighbors; there is an absence of fear and that heavy, prevailing sense of oppression—there's a sense of lightness about the city, as if humanity is approved of rather than condemned.

During my walk, the bit of exercise and the sun have made me sleepy; I return to the hotel room feeling relaxed and relieved that the earthquakes are a nightmare now passed. When I return to the room, I begin to feel the whole building sway, not a very different sensation than the hard aftershocks in Guatemala. I again walk down to the lobby, feeling apprehensive in so high a building, and begin a conversation with the young lady who is the receptionist in the lobby of the hotel.

She explains to me that it is not unusual for survivors of a severe earthquake to suffer a type of neurosis—to the point where they feel the earth to be moving for as long as a year afterward—that the swaying sensation I had just experienced was due to the heavy traffic going by.

I'm very grateful for these comforting words; they seem logical.

After again returning to my room and resting, a maid comes to check on me, inquiring if I need anything. We chat for a few minutes and she tells me a little about herself—that she is a college student and works part-time at the hotel to supplement the family income while going to school. That she doesn't see herself as a servant is easily discernable. She seems to have a healthy measure of self-esteem.

At about 2:00 in the afternoon, while crossing the lobby to the restaurant I notice a little boy carrying a huge stack of papers, and when I ask him for one, I notice that the headlines are glaring and menacing while looking for the right number of coins for the price of the newspaper:

OTRO TERREMOTO EN GUATEMALA. It had occurred exactly at 12:00 o'clock midday—coinciding with the very minute I had "imagined" that Costa Rica, too, was trembling. Poor, poor Guatemala—the magnitude of the second quake must have been on par with the first in order to have been felt four countries away.

I spend but two days in charming Costa Rica. I decide that the place I really want to be is home. The plane flying to the United States lands in Guatemala and we the passengers must transfer to another flight. Most of the main part of the terminal and the waiting room where I had thought to stay while waiting for a flight (just two days ago?) is blocked off by dark, massive canvas curtains. In a moment I learn the reason for this unbecoming addition. A large part of the terminal has been destroyed by the second quake. This is the second time since the earthquakes began that I've escaped a possible accidental death by unwittingly moving on—first at the Hotel El Centro and now here at the airport. I take time to ponder the meaning of life—that the inevitable end is death—and wonder why I was spared and others were not. It is not that God loves the ones who perished any less than he loves us who escaped. In my case it may be that I've been given another chance to live my life to a fuller potential. Perhaps I will be given the divine privilege of serving others.

I learn that the effects from the second quake have indeed been as devastating as the first. Antigua, the lovely colonial city, once

Guatemala's capital, suffered heavy damages, destroying at least half of the town entirely. Because of the hour, being midday when the quake occurred, a greater number of people were killed in the second quake than the first. Building structures already weakened had crashed to the ground, crushing the victims underneath tons of cement.

The moment I arrive at the San Francisco Airport, I hear my name being called, and when I answer the page I am asked to go to the White Courtesy telephone booth. It is my daughter on the other end of the line, asking that I take a helicopter to Santa Rosa—she and her husband are visiting friends and will be waiting for me. I wish there had been someone to meet me as I got off the plane. I realize, though, I am on the last leg of my journey—only twenty minutes or so and the nightmare will come to an end.

Through all this—the long hours of the earthquake and its aftermath—I had managed to remain in a state of dry-eyed silence, but the catalyst for the release of a flood of tears is, of course, much less traumatic than what I had been through in Guatemala. The porter at the Pan Am Air Terminal had refused to assist me with my luggage at the terminal to the helicopter service a few buildings away. In addition, the ticket agents would not allow me to leave part of my luggage with them, while I myself made the trip to the end terminal in two trips. I realize in retrospect that no one in the airport was truly as mean as they had seemed. The porter earns his living not from a single passenger transferring to another airline, but from the bulk of the passengers disembarking from the Pan Am flights. The rest of the airport personnel undoubtedly have their rules regarding responsibilities, which do not include management of luggage of the airline passengers. Nevertheless, I begin to cry brokenly, abandoned, as I carry, kick and shove all six pieces of my luggage toward the terminal of the helicopters. I do not realize that what I am actually crying from is hysteria. The passenger beside me in the helicopter, a dignified and well-dressed man, about my age perhaps, seems thoroughly annoyed, his annoyance conveyed quite clearly through the glance he casts in my direction, as if to say, *Woman, have you nothing to do but cry like a baby? Where on earth is your adult dignity?*

I don't at this time have any dignity. Furthermore I don't even care—I am beyond the point of caring what someone else thinks. I may cry for the rest of my life.

Back in the States and settled down once more, I find that I am a celebrity of sorts. Everyone is interested in talking to someone who has lived through a major catastrophe. People with whom I'm acquainted begin to call me and a teacher from the local high school in Mill Valley asks me to speak with his students. After all, Guatemala's disaster is headline news. A reporter from the San Francisco Chronicle is taking pictures and interviewing the North Americans who were in Guatemala at the time of the quake. When it was my turn to be interviewed and the story printed, the title read: *My God, this is an earthquake!* He never did publish my picture, however. I think of the silly grin I had forced on my face and I am far less critical than I had been in the past when I have thought someone insincere because of his or her smile.

Even our family physician, a very good doctor, is more interested in my experiences in Guatemala, than the salmonella I brought back with me. "How many of my patients," he asks, "are the survivors of an 8.2 earthquake?"

Guatemala's disaster is published far and wide and there is an expression now being used among the columnists and news broadcasters: "Guatemala's earthquakes have put the little country on the map!"

My daughter, Rita, traveling with her husband of a few months, learned of the disaster while in Greece. After having been isolated on a small island for two weeks, the pair arrived in Athens in time to see the screaming headlines: *BLOODIEST EARTHQUAKE IN GUATEMALA'S HISTORY.*

Just as I had been indifferent to my surroundings on the helicopter, apparently my daughter had given no thought to hers either. They had been on one of the busiest streets in Athens (so goes the story) when my eldest daughter and her husband saw the headlines of the newspaper. My daughter began to scream, "My mother's in Guatemala—my mother's in Guatemala…my mother, my mom!" "For God's sake, stop screaming," Jeff implored. "People will think I'm beating you. There's a good chance that your mother is still alive." Jeff had logically pointed out that there are 7.2 million people in Guatemala—26,000 people were reported dead.

These statistics, however, unfortunately, are in no way in keeping with the actual facts. *Guatemala lost at least 50,000 people through the disaster. More than one million were left homeless.

(Teremoto: A Guatemalan publication covering the events of the earthquake.)

The discrepancies between the international news coverage and the actual deaths that occurred in the ravaged Guatemala can probably be attributed to the very large faction of the indigenous population. When the babies of the Naturales are born, more often than not, their births are never officially recorded, making difficult, if not impossible, any records of death.

People in the United States are now aware of the country's identity. Many people confess to each other that they had believed Guatemala to be a part of Mexico or El Salvador, and some thought the country a part of South America. But due to the widespread coverage in the news media, the public has been made aware of the Central American country, its illiteracy and poverty, the hunger, the diseases, all made worse by the earthquake.

The TV viewers see the mothers on the television screen going to work in the fields along with the men, sometimes pulling a plow when the family is too poor to buy a horse or a mule. The mother's back also bears her children, cradled in a shawl—very close to her body. I watch these mothers posing for the cameras on the television screen, knowing the child she holds may die before reaching his first birthday. On an emotional level the children of the Naturales, the segment called "Indians," are gently nurtured. Always these children are carried close to their mothers until they are old enough to walk. On a physical level the families live far below the realm of ordinary poverty. Their dark eyes haunt me when I close my eyes at night. Like the Texas colonel I met during the earthquake, the man who was not having a very good time in Guatemala, I'm not having a very good time in the United States. I was able to leave the ravaged land and return to safety where there is plenty to eat and drink, pretty shops with elegant clothes to buy. The *Guatemaltecos* can't leave. Unless we help them how then can their plight be changed?

My family and I talk over how we can best serve the Guatemalan people—each according to our own abilities. One of my sons-in-law cannot leave the States; he is a member of a popular band about to perform in one of their many concerts, in which case he and my daughter, Jeannette, offer a generous contribution of money toward the cause of the suffering people.

My other son-in-law, Jeff, and my daughter, Rita, follow suit.

My two sons load up two rented campers full of medicine, food and clothing and take off for Guatemala. These supplies are donations from the people in the California Bay area working with the Guatemalan Relief Committee, an organization that sprang into action just days after the earthquake.

I call some friends, a doctor and his wife, a nurse, and ask them if they would be willing to give me a crash course in caring for the injured—that is, procedures that would not endanger anyone through my not having gone through the regular channels of learning. My friends readily agree and will happily comply with my request if those are my wishes, but want to know why I want to return to Guatemala, when I was lucky enough to have gotten out. The doctor's wife compares the situation with escaping from a burning building, only to go running back inside. But this is not the first time I've acted a little foolishly and begin to learn some simple rudiments of medicine, how to apply casts, to give injections intramuscularly, taking of blood pressure; bed pans I can empty without instructions.

One day one of my sons calls from Guatemala, greatly distressed. He tells me that the Guatemalan authorities had confiscated all the emergency supplies he had taken to the victims of the earthquakes—all the food, all the medicine and clothes—locked up, and he was not able to find anyone who could help him get them released. On the verge of tears, he tells me the poor are receiving no benefit whatever from all the donations coming from the States. My sons, in addition, had been checked at regular intervals wherever there were law enforcement agents while traveling in Mexico and Northern Guatemala, having to prove on each occasion the intentions were honorable—only to have their journey end in emptiness. I am ready to cry from despair also. At times it seems easier to do something bad than to do something good.

I, however, refrain from comment; the call could well be monitored.

A lady of Guatemalan origin, with whom I had come in contact, had written an article that had been published on the front page of the San Francisco Chronicle. She had admonished people to use discretion in their donations to the earthquake victims. In her article she criticized the Guatemalan Government, stating quite simply that the poor ordinarily never benefit from donations, as the authorities steal everything designated for them. Following the publishing of the articles a bomb went off outside her bedroom window. She subsequently received a number of menacing phone calls and letters of threat in her mailbox—all this in the United States!

When my sons arrive home, after having been in Guatemala for six weeks, obvious is the fact that they, too, have had their experiences. They say that Guatemala is still shaking and for this reason they were relieved to have had to sleep out in the open under the stars.

In spite of their having been stripped of the bulk of their supplies, they were able to be of assistance to the suffering Guatemalan people. They offered themselves as ambulance drivers to the U.S. medical team in the agricultural area of *Comalapa*. An emergency hospital had been erected and my sons' rented vans provided transportation for the wounded. They tell us, while looking for victims rendered helpless by the quake, they stumbled upon an entire family whose every member was sightless, presumably blinded by injuries from the quake. Suffering from great deprivations when my sons found them, my sons were able to help them without their supplies. They had about five thousand dollars, which were contributions from our friends in the United States, and they were able to hide the money. They admitted they had fears that the money would be confiscated as had been the supplies, and they would have therefore been rendered totally helpless to aid the poor. They went on a buying spree with the money they had, sometimes buying out an entire *"tienda"*—the local store.

I return to Guatemala three months after the quake. I am greatly surprised, shocked in fact, at the change in the country. Despite my having been there when the quake occurred and having known its damages had been extensive, I am unprepared for the devastating effects left behind.

Whole villages have been wiped out—some areas resembling ghost towns, huge black hollows surrounded by rubble, where homes and offices have been. At least half of Antigua lies in ruins.

The ruins of the past great earthquake—in the early 1900s—are once again ruins of the 1976 quakes. Two lovely old churches, built by the priests in the early days of the Conquest, now lie in two gigantic, forlorn heaps of rubbish, their magnificent altars inlaid in gold buried somewhere beneath the ruins. Many churches in the capital suffered the same amount of destruction.

Only the pueblos surrounding Atitlán escaped with minimal damage; there were no deaths and no severe injuries reported. Presumably, as reported by the seismologists, and the assessment of the indigenous people as well, the lake absorbs the shock of the seismic activity, but during the quake it receded several dozen feet, however, giving rise to some worry that it could disappear in the same manner that it came into existence.

I spend about a week or two between the capital and Antigua and go to the hospital after this to see if I can put into practice some of my newly acquired medical knowledge. The hospital in Comalapa, a very hard-hit town, suffered extensive destruction, and its citizens—many deaths and injuries. It is here that I learn something about myself that I never knew before. I am a horrible nurse!

Among my "first patients" is a man brought to the hospital during the early days of the quake. I learn from him that my sons had brought him here. They had been great buddies, telling jokes and playing the guitar, singing songs and admiring the girls. But when he pulls up the leg of his pajamas and unwinds the bandage over a large portion of his leg, a gaping, suppurating wound is exposed. At the sight of it I let out a loud shriek, which brings one of the nurses running to our side. When she learns the reason for my expression of horror she berates me severely, and tells me that she never wants to hear an outburst like that again. I feel thoroughly ashamed and among the lowliest of beings.

What the nurse doesn't know, and I'll certainly never tell her, is that I had committed another error—if they had to be measured—worse than my horror in seeing the open wound. I had been asked to give a man a vitamin shot. I was proud of my knowing the right places to give intra-muscular injections, the right needles to use, etc. My patient, an out-patient and employee of the hospital, trustingly lay on the bed before me. It was when I asked him where he wanted the injection, "In the *brazo* or the *culo*?" that he sat straight up from the bed, looking alarmed. Oh dear, oh dear, what had I done, or said, that caused my patient to fear me?

One of the men who was also of the crew assisting the maintenance of the hospital began to laugh; then the whole crew was in a state of hilarity, and that only further increased my bewilderment.

I begin to defend what I now gather was the offending word, by stating, "In Spain, even the doctors use the word culo: it doesn't mean anything except 'your bottom.'"

One of the crew explained, "With all due respect, Señorita, that isn't what it means in Guatemala. It either refers to your genitals or your anal area." Small wonder the man who was to receive his vitamins had leaped away from me!

The next patient, however, who comes to the hospital affords an opportunity for a measure of my self-esteem to be regained. I diagnose the case as "acute alcoholic gastritis," and according to the visiting doctor, this assessment of the situation is absolutely correct. The patient, an elderly woman, does admit to having drunk a bottle or two of gin by herself; she also tells us in a voice numb with grief that she has lost every member of her family to the earthquake.

I don't stay at the hospital very long—three weeks or so, because its function has nearly ended. Most of the emergency patients have been treated and sent home. I know that I can be of better service elsewhere, though the work may be considered less dramatic.

I go back to the capital and rent a shabby apartment—the kitchen, sleeping quarters and living room are all combined. A maid working at the apartment complex tells me that she lives in Zona VI, now a typical shanty town, where there are rows of shacks constructed of makeshift materials such as tiny pieces of scrap wood and cardboard. About a thousand families are crowded together in this area, without running water, without electricity and toilet facilities. Many suffer from epidemic diseases left by the deprivation of the earthquake.

The maid's name, I learn, is Maria, and together we begin to devise ways to help her family and neighbors. (My contribution is so small while Guatemala's needs are so staggering.) During a sleepless night I remember something I once read. The author in one passage had stated—and perhaps it is applicable here—something to the effect that, "it is not what society has to offer en masse to mankind that makes a difference, but that which counts is what each person contributes to a whole." I think of the many people I had seen from all over the world here, helping to rebuild Guatemala; everywhere these good people were alleviating its sufferings. Suppose they had, each one, stayed at home? On that note I fall asleep, exonerated for the smallness of my efforts.

The next morning I resume cooking my pot of black beans and beef-vegetable stew that Maria will carry to Zona VI.

GUATEMALA ESTA EN MARCHA

Construction of the country has begun. The healthy sound reverberates throughout the capital, millions of nails driven by thousands of hammers. And for once the scanty work the carpenters sought now becomes plentiful. People from many nations donate their time and energies toward the rebuilding of Guatemala. In the countryside, North Americans, Italians, Frenchmen, Englishmen and a few hearty women work side by side with the Naturales and *campesinos*, replacing their homes destroyed by the quake. Many families of the poor actually fare a little better, where homes are concerned, than they did before the disaster. The adobe huts are being replaced with sturdier materials of wood. The bricks, fashioned from the earth, have returned to dust and now lie in forlorn heaps away from the construction sites, wounded, and not able to serve their inhabitants any longer.

The signs, *Guatemala está en Marcha*, are everywhere. This message can be seen along the highways that lead to and from the city, in all the government buildings, decorating the walls of the police station and the post-office. Valiant words, words of hope and encouragement—Guatemala is on the march.

During its period of recovery there seems to be something other than the structures new to the country. There is an aura of freshness, a feeling of strength and solidarity among the classes that was not present before. The line of division between the rich and the poor is less visible and for the first time in this era, bigotry and envy recede, making way for tolerance to be exercised among the polarized classes of society. It is as if they intuitively know that…"A house divided against itself cannot stand"…and although the poor undeniably suffered greater losses than the rich in the traumatized nation, the wealthy in the disaster had not gone scot-free either. Building materials in their homes withstood against the shock of the quakes; the frailness of their bodies did not. Many of the elderly died from strokes and heart attacks. Sleeplessness and nervous disorders were common *sequelae* among their children.

There is something else conspicuous in its absence. Before the earthquakes shattered Guatemala, its intentions seemed quite clear toward its neighbor, Belize. It had been impossible to pass through the frontiers of Mexico, Honduras or El Salvador and miss seeing the ubiquitous message, *Belize es de Guatemala*; that was later substituted to read, *Belize es Guatemala*, which means their prior claim that Belize belonged to Guatemala was changed to mean that Belize is part of Guatemala. The pronouncement immediately had followed England's intentions to free Belize from British rule, giving the country its independence.

Guatemala's intentions toward the country of Belize, not yet having achieved independence, were more apparent. If Belize did not surrender peacefully, then military force was imminent; the evidence of Guatemala's resolve to conquer Belize has disappeared—a respite from the threat of war and internal conflict.

One morning I awaken to the incessant sound of knocking and, when I open the door, it seems obvious that the couple standing in the doorway have come to the wrong place, so conspicuous are they in the shabby apartment building where I now reside. I'm sure that I must present a suspicious appearance as I gawk at the pair in their finery. They both smile at me in a friendly and amused manner, simultaneously extending their hands to me. The pretty lady with her man by her side explains that they are with the Guatemalan Relief Committee in San Francisco and that we had spoken together on the phone while in the U.S. during the early days of Guatemala's earthquake.

They are both acquainted with my sons and, over coffee that I've made from the rich coffee beans from Antigua, only now do I realize what a linguistic fast I've been on. Just as it had been difficult for me at one time to converse in Spanish, I now find English a bit strange. It so happens that there is not a problem in either case, the couple being fluent in both languages. So we settle in unspoken agreement on English. They tell me that they were born in the United States, but are both of Guatemalan origin. I am happy to note they've not forfeited their culture by abandoning their ancestral language. They both have vibrant mannerisms, that effusiveness common to Latin personalities and that strained silence so often present among new acquaintances is not a problem here. I learn their names, not by way of introduction, but by their address to each other; Leah and Marcelino, handsome names for a handsome pair. They tell me that they must cut short their visit. Two important matters await their attention while they are in Guatemala. They need to visit the medical personnel at *Comalapa*, the place where the patient's gaping wounds had proved that nursing is not my forte and where my sons had been ambulance drivers. The second order of business, they say, is getting the supplies that my sons had brought to Guatemala released. Marcelino says that I may be able to help in this area. It seems a bit mystifying, as well as irksome, that donated goods need some kind of release procedure.

Apparently an airline pilot, bringing donations from the U.S., had been forced to forfeit the plane's supplies to the Guatemalan bureaucracy.

I am rapturous to have company again and to emerge from my intrinsic wilderness. But not unlike so many other experiences I've had in Guatemala, my happiness is marred by the disappearance of the food and clothes intended for the poor.

Marcelino and Leah ask me if I will accompany them to wherever the supplies presumably are locked up and, if I wish, we'll make a day of it, going to *Comalapa* afterward.

On the outskirts of the capital, en route to *Comalapa*, Marcelino stops unexpectedly on the grounds of a large building, which appears

146

to be someone's residence. It has a large tree in its front yard with branches covering most of the small garden, its profusion of green leaves offer the friendship of shade to those accepting its hospitality. But this building with its pervasive expansion of nature is as deceptive as many other things in Guatemala. It is not a residence at all, but a heavily guarded government building. Surrounding this benign-appearing structure are young soldiers with machine guns.

Marcelino begins talking with the guards right away, attempting to learn of the whereabouts of the authority who can release these donated goods that have now become government property. The young soldiers are silent and evasive as they lean on their machine guns, turning away while they shake their heads in defiance. After a few minutes of this exchange, a young officer appears with a key and unlocks a door that can readily be seen as a warehouse. Only at this moment do I realize that Marcelino and the soldiers have been bickering over the supplies my sons brought to Guatemala from the United States. There tumbles forth from opened door huge quantities of black beans from rotted gunny sacks. Gigantic piles of canned goods coated with rust are added to the heap of nothing but rubbish. I recognize garments of clothing, clotted mildew, as being the once fashionable dresses and shirts of my friends and family. While we view this mess—the end result of much toil and good intentions—the three of us just stare at the other, greatly discouraged.

Marcelino sits beneath the huge, friendly tree, his head buried in his arms and a more dejected picture in so vital personality I've seldom seen.

The food and medicine that had been flown here from San Francisco lie rotting also, along with the donated goods my sons had brought.

I at first don't realize the magnitude of the treachery involved at the time, and presumably it is because of the innocence of my question that I get away with asking, "Señor," I address a uniformed guard, "what is the purpose of this waste when there are so many hungry people?"

The soldier shrugs his shoulders, affecting at once both an arrogant and helplessly indifferent attitude. "There's no one to distribute the supplies."

I mumble, more to myself than to him, "With the whole army at your disposal, there's no one to help?"—but I say aloud, "My sons are young and healthy and would have been happy to have been of assistance. They've come a long way only to have their efforts end like this."

The guard with whom I'm speaking only shrugs and walks away. I notice that Marcelino makes no attempt at employing simple logic. He tells me that questions like these (in English, of course) go hopelessly unanswered in "normal times" in Guatemala—much less likely to hope for sensible exchange with the country in turmoil and the military involved. The trip back to the city affords some continuity of thought, something that my scattered and disjointed perception of the present events was incapable of back there among the heavily armed soliders. A refreshing breeze blows through the windows of Marcelino's van. The three of us are seated comfortably in the front seat—and the freshness of the countryside undoubtedly is responsible for my sudden clarity of thought…I realize that the most disturbing factor of all is not that these donated goods were confiscated, stolen, but the unbearable truth manifested here is that it is a case of the poor robbing the even poorer, and the helpless.

The merchandise is seen across the counters from the capital to the rural areas of the countryside. New *tiendas* have sprung up everywhere en route to *Comalapa*. In one of these country stores, among rows of canned goods with labels in English, saucy, high heel shoes and dozens of frilly dresses on display—there is even a bright red wig!

Marcelino and Leah have come and gone. They seem to have accomplished half their mission—and for Guatemala a good average—having put aside their disappointment of the ruined goods and busied themselves elsewhere with the task at hand…investigating the needs of the people and responding appropriately with personnel and supplies still available.

I go for a stroll in the city, but as always when there has been good company to enjoy and suddenly removed, a sense of loneliness settles around me. My visa is about to expire and I realize that I will soon have to make a choice. What will it be for me—Guatemala or the United States? If I decide to stay, I need to arrange with an attorney a more lengthy immigration status than I have at present. The thought of seeking the help of an attorney tells me something of my decision. I'm staying in Guatemala.

As always the city depresses me. In addition to the poverty and grime about the central part, there are so many people walking about the streets talking in loud and angry voices, as if they are surrounded by people giving them a great deal of trouble. They are quite alone. Undoubtedly they are shouting at the demons of disregard and indifference.

Just a bus ride away, there lives a good friend. Her name is Marina; she is very good-looking and intelligent, a schoolteacher. While boarding the bus and seating myself, I think of her great sense of humor, her liveliness, and these qualities are exactly what prompted my visit.

Marina goes on weekly raids through her sons' closets, extracting their shirts and trousers, which she carries to the destitute students in her classroom. Her sons—when they catch her—protest loudly, but she only laughs and snatches another garment from its hanger.

My friend, Marina, is partially an enigma to me. She and her family do not seem to be lacking in material wealth—her husband is a rancher—and yet she has compassion for those less fortunate than herself, for the poor. One of her friends had told me that she had a humble beginning and that her marriage had saved her from a life of poverty. If this is so, this would explain her affinity for the downtrodden.

Now planted on her doorsteps she opens the door with a smile of welcome. "Bonnie, *buenos dias. Pase adelante.*"

As troubled and depressed as I was but a half hour ago, I find my depression leaving, and in its place, a sense of joy and warm feelings.

"*Marina, como estas? La familia?*"

"*Bien, bien.*"—We are well...

"*Y tus estudiantes?*"

"*Chingados!*"—a very vulgar and excessive word in Spanish.

She says that the bigger of the male students bring mirrors to school with the express purpose of looking up her dress. They approach her desk with the pretext of seeking help with their studies. She tells me that she made this discovery when one boy, never too studious, made frequent trips to ask for help with his lessons.

There are two maids in the home, Greta and Sofía, both of whom have been nicknamed by Marina. Greta is called "*Ingrata,*" but one only need to look at this modest little maiden of fourteen to realize the joke. She has a long, dark braid that falls gracefully to her waist and apparently comes from a family of some gentility—nothing that could possibly convey that she is in any way ungrateful. Due to the death and illness of her parents and grandparents, she is now working as a maid in the home. She bears her nickname with good graces and smiles.

Sofía is a young woman of twenty-three, nicknamed by Marina Sofía Loren, and is not at all pretty. Furthermore, she has none of the feminine mystique that alludes to prettiness and charm. Mention of the beautiful actress seems to make her aware of her own plainness and peasant background.

While Marina and I are engaged in feminine and frivolous gossip, which can be great fun when no men are about, and Marina's husband is not home but away at work, we are interrupted by the sound of loud crying. The sound seems to be coming from "Sofía Loren's" room.

"Marina," I ask, "what can be the matter?" She only jokes and tells me the part Sofía wanted in the film was given to another actress.

"But surely," I persist, "there's something dreadfully wrong. Shouldn't we try to find out what the problem is?"

Still joking, Marina retorts, "Oh, she just has not received the attention she feels she deserves."

And on that note I tell her, "If that's all she wants I think I have that to give." The moment I enter Sofía's room, she looks up startled and the face she lifts streams with tears.

While she still lies on the bed, I ask her, "Sofía, whatever is the matter?" My concern is met with only a fresh outburst of sobs.

"Okay, okay; it's all right if you don't want to tell me…just thought I'd ask."

Sofía looks at me again and, still sniffling, tells me that she has totally forgotten why she was crying, that it is the first time in her whole life that anyone has ever asked her why she was crying, and begins to cry again, though this time her sobs are intermingled with laughter. That face that had seemed so plain only a few minutes ago becomes greatly transformed. It is suddenly beautiful. She has a lovely smile; she is now smiling, holding out her arms for me to hold her.

I never did learn the source of Sofia's deep distress, but I did learn a fresh lesson in human behavior. Sofia is not talking to herself like the people on the streets, nor am I. We are both listening, hugging each other.

A CASA IN ATITLAN

No longer a stranger and wayfarer, in the year of 1978, I have a home in Atitlán. It is a darling little house and the walls are fashioned with stone and bamboo, in keeping with the decor of the pueblo. The floors are done in floral pattern of multicolored tile. The pattern was to have been interspersed with plain blocks, thus adding Contrast to the design. But the warehouse in Guatemala City had sent only the floral patterns and the workers finished laying the tile on the floor while I was away. I decided at the time to leave it the way it was. Getting the tile from the capital to the pueblo had been no easy accomplishment.

The early part of any construction, I learned the hard way, is deceptive in its smoothness. If the stone and bamboo are not on the builder's property, they are easily acquired. But when the walls are erected and it looks as if construction is progressing nicely, the real headaches begin. Abandoned construction in Guatemala's villages is a common part of the landscape. When I found myself with four walls, I understood the reason for this oft-repeated phenomenon. The plumbing fixtures, the wood and the roofing materials—everything needed to complete a modernized home has to be shipped from the capital or other places of industry. It was while I was on these buying expeditions that I ran into the most trouble. At the beginning of the construction, I had welcomed the buying expertise of the contractors. When the contractors returned, however, the receipts were invariably altered. Many scrawled letters, childish and laborious, covered the original price, so that it was not possible to know what I was paying for. At this rate, I would soon be broke and the house I had started would be abandoned with all the other unfinished projects about the lake area. My assuming the responsibility for buying the materials, however, was to no avail either, and it seemed that there was no way I could win.

On one particular buying excursion, I had driven into the middle of a massive demonstration in the capital. Dozens of municipal buses had been set ablaze and were burning to the ground. Undoubtedly the activities of the riot were fueled by a unified power, but the most amazing part of the protest was that the demonstrators were between the ages of twelve and fifteen. In spite of there having been millions of dollars in property damage, few injuries were reported. The *choferes* and the passengers had been allowed to leave before the vehicles were set ablaze. The rioters killed no one intentionally. There were two accidental deaths in the furor.

A hike in bus fares from five to ten cents had precipitated the demonstration. At the time I thought this was a strange reason for actions so extreme. But a friend of mine, a Guatemalan lady, not a poor one, had pointed out that a family of nine in Guatemala is not an unusually large household. If all are taking buses twice a day or more, then riding buses costs half of the family income.

On the other side of the spectrum, the company's side, oil prices had skyrocketed, making a five-cent bus fare unprofitable. It would seem that the most reasonable solution for all concerned would be to raise the workers' wages so that a ten-cent bus fare would not be out of reach. There seems to be no immediate solutions, however, and the matter a very complex problem for some time.

After one such day I arrive back at Atitlán, thankful that the problems of the capital have not affected the villages very greatly. When I go out to look over the house I'm having constructed, I realize that easily half of the materials on the property have been stolen. I am greatly discouraged and vow to get to the bottom of the stolen supplies. At first I try bribery. I offer money to the worker who will tell me the name of the person doing all the stealing. "In this way," I explain, "I won't have to sack all of you, just the thief." But this devious method accomplishes exactly nothing—it only makes matters worse—for me. The collaborator takes the money and quickly makes up another story the moment we confront the culprit he names.

I vow I'll fire the whole damn bunch of them, but my threats are of little use; the workers know as well as I that whatever crew I can find to replace them will only repeat the same offense.

I begin to accuse all the workers of being thieves, but am aware that generalization is never fair. (One of the workers may have been absent the day the materials were stolen!) This is about as fair as I can be at the moment.

Seeing that I won't be put off, they all begin to accuse each other, and pointing skyward, declare piously, "God loves me, but this hombre he doesn't love." A long and vociferous argument then ensues as to whom does God favor the most.

When I reach the limit of my exasperation, I shout, "Be quiet, all of you! God doesn't have anything to do with this!"(I am beginning to question if *either God or I* have anything to do with this!)

A burly worker, one of the best stone masons in Santiago whose name is also Santiago, declares himself the spokesman for the group. He begins to reprimand me severely for my last statement in the argument. Seeing that he now has the backing of his companions, which makes me greatly outnumbered, he tells me that it is only because I'm a gringa that I would say a thing like that. "God doesn't have anything to do with this? God's in everything!" How terrible he thinks it is that I'm a pagan and not a worthy Christian like the people in Santiago Atitlán.

Seeing that nothing can be accomplished, I turn around and start to leave. I loose my footing and begin to slip around in the mud. I try to regain my balance, but to no avail. I fall flat and slide on my backside all the way to the bottom of the hill. I am not even spared the humility of being seen. I turn to face my tormentors once I can get to my feet, and they are all laughing uproariously.

When the various stages of rage have passed, I am in a much less argumentative state. Calm has returned and, along with it, reason. I realize in the first place I have crossed over the barrier of a woman's world in the pueblo and have intruded in the inadmissible world of the men—not easily tolerated here in the pueblo where the separation of the sexes is even wider than in the Ladino world.

When José and Francisca learn of my difficulties, they advise me not to be so upset, but rather regard the stolen materials as the bonus I had intended to give the workers when the construction is finished. As sound as this advice may be, it would seem that trust and respect are desired entities anywhere in the world, and when found, are to be greatly treasured.

Nothing can last forever, although it had seemed the construction of my house would outlive me. Before the building is completely finished, a new member is added. I don't think he is a person exactly!—but an angel perhaps sent down from Heaven to soothe my spirits. He neither steals from me nor does he seem to lie about anything. He is in every way sincere and in no way does he try to irritate me. I wonder how it is possible that he remains in good standing with the rest of the workers when he obviously became my favorite from the beginning. Aside from a little teasing from the rest of the gang, he suffers from little discomfiture. I never do learn the secret of his diplomatic success. There is much about him to appreciate other than his honesty.

Before long he is my surrogate son, my little love. Since he joined the crew, I no longer worry over stolen materials. Often when I come home after a buying trip from the city, the house I still rent is cleaner than when I left it and there are often fresh flowers decorating the kitchen table. I have no idea where these came from. The Tzutuhiles don't grow things as frivolous as flowers—nothing that isn't food.

To make matters worse, in the rare moment when they decide to be respectful (usually on payday) they persist on calling me Señora Bono. When finally I can't stand this unflattering name any longer,I tell them loudly, "Will you stop calling me Señora Bono! Bono is a member of the mafiosa." My shouting avails me exactly nothing, Si, Señora, Bono.

One day my home is at last finished. I move in and survey my surroundings. There is a cleverly designed bookcase built into the stonewall. (The workers know that I love books and always have a few dozen lying around.) Even though the day is hot, there is a cool feeling about the house. The sofa and bamboo-hanging chair in the living room are decorated with the colorful *tela tipica* of the pueblo. I have two bedrooms—one is separated from the rest of the house and will be occupied by the guardian, a job which, of course, goes to my Tzutuhil son, Nicolas. He tells me that the house still needs some touch-ups, which he wants to work on. In the kitchen there is a table that has already become a conversation piece. It is fashioned from a huge stone that had been embedded in the earth where the kitchen now stands. We had decided to leave it for its novelty effect.

Shortly after the house is finished, I decide to throw a bash, a housewarming and birthday party combined. I have a birthday coming up, so does Santiago, my archenemy of a few weeks ago. We have a little get-together, a kind of pre-fiesta celebration, (this is, after all, Guatemala) so that we can make plans for the real party. I make a huge pot of coffee and for dessert, strawberry crepes. The workers at first approach these delicate little pancakes with some trepidation, but do admit after tasting them that they are good and want to know how many they can have. While we are in the process of discussing plans for the party—who will play the marimbas, who will sing, strum the guitar, the kind of food we'll serve—I have a visitor. My company is an aristocratic lady and at the moment a horrified one.

"My God, Bonnie," the lady exclaims, "with good reason you've had problems with the workers. You not only have them in your house, but you're waiting on them!" She says this while she is still on the steps of the front porch, making no effort to lower her voice—the workers are easily visible as they sit around the kitchen table talking and drinking coffee. I do not intend that they should be further insulted by holding a conversation in their presence about them, but I tell Gloria, the name of my visitor, that we will talk about it later. She assents to this and I am, not for the first time, invited to visit her home and spend the night or the weekend should I wish.

Gloria and I had become acquainted as neighbors at the lake. She was in the stage of construction of her vacation home where I had been a year ago. Because she had assumed the construction was progressing at a faster pace than it was, she had been without a place to spend the night, and without kitchen facilities, her permanent address being the capital. She and her daughter-in-law, a charming North American young woman with two little boys, came to my door and told me that they were temporarily stranded next door. Gloria explained that her husband was to have picked them up in the family helicopter, but must have been detained. I offered them lodging for the night and, among the three of us, we had made an appetizing meal over my new gas range.

My house has the better of two worlds. In spite of all the problems with construction, the workers have done a beautiful job. The men in the village are excellent carpenters and stonemasons. I am gratified to say these days, "*Mi casa es su casa.*"

In the interim, between our casual meeting and the visit to Gloria's home, the Naturales begin to question my friendship with this lady and one man said to me in whispers that she is one of the richest ladies in Guatemala—that her husband owns hundreds of acres in the agriculturally rich area of Retalhuleu, that he is said to be both rancher and farmer. I had thought the family to be merely well off, not immensely wealthy.

On the first evening of my visit to Gloria's homes I see that it is very tastefully furnished, lovely in appearances but not ostentatious, and certainly not by anyone's standards, a mansion.

Gloria has the same number of children as I—four—three of whom are married with the family's blessings, their eldest daughter and two sons, but the youngest daughter, always somewhat the black sheep, has disgraced the family.

She is married to a commoner, an ordinary young man who works for a living. I'm shown some photographs in expensive frames of the three weddings that were obviously approved by both Gloria, and the man who can only be her husband, standing beside the six young people in their wedding finery. There are only snapshots of the youngest daughter at her wedding, and these are handed to me with gestures as if something hot is being handled. Gloria calls the young man in the photograph—the one who had the nerve to marry her daughter—a "*mozo,*" a laborer, and asks if I agree that her daughter looks dreadfully unhappy. No such assessment can be made from the photos presented to me since they are small and not at all clear, but if I were to make any kind of judgment as to the state of her daughter's emotional welfare, I would have to disagree with her. When I inquire as to the type of work he does, Gloria tells me he's a pilot.

"But a pilot, Gloria? That's a much-respected position in the United States. Isn't it the same in Guatemala?"

She says he is in the employ of the family—a *chofer* for their privately-owned helicopter. His other duties include crop-dusting along with the other pilot employees.

This seems as good a time as any to continue the discussion we had at the lake (when she saw the workers in my house). Gloria doesn't wait for me to open the conversation, but tells me in a belittling manner that she had noticed that my workers all call me "Bonnie."

I know what she's getting at, but I shrug and say, "That's my name."

But Gloria is determined that I hear her out. "My workers would not think of calling me other than Doña Gloria. What this unequivocally means, on her part, is that she has the respect of her workers, while I on the other hand do not. (She really doesn't know about half of the problems I've had with the construction workers or her criticisms would be more accusing than they are, more severe.)

I begin to feel uncomfortable and wonder just what I'm doing in someone's home whose residents feel themselves above their countrymen because of their class or "inferior financial status." In my own country, it's not that I would not be found in their homes, but I would have never had anything in common with them to begin with.

As if Gloria reads my mind, she further defends her position by saying, "In Latin America, we are prejudiced because of class. Your prejudices in the U.S. are involved with color." Pursuit of this argument is useless; that's clear. But just as I am willing to let the matter drop, at least verbally, Gloria points out in further defense of her attitudes that none of her servants have ever left her. To myself I say scornfully, "But where would a slave go?" I must admit, however, in all fairness, that her servants do not look miserable, but content. An elderly lady, stooped and barefoot, works in the kitchen, turning out dozens of tortillas that she pats rapidly between work-worn hands. I notice that among her tasks are the piles of dishes that we have used during dinner. She addresses her mistress with the utmost respect, but what is more with a certain fondness that undoubtedly stems from years of service to a household where she has been treated well.

I awaken during the night with a slight start, having the feeling that something or someone is in the room where I am sleeping. I look into a double pair of the most ominous eyes I've ever seen. Two black animals are standing over me—and to say that they are mean is inaccurate. Meanness has a certain stupidity about it. These dogs are not stupid, but they have a look about them, the message of which is quite clear: *One false move and you've had it.* I want to go to the bathroom, but I decide against it. I suppose that this is an entirely unreasonable request without their checking with their mistress, and so with a bladder full to the point of bursting, I remain in bed until sunrise. (I can only hope that Gloria is an early riser.)

In spite of my nervousness, sometime during the night (or early morning) I fall asleep and awake to the pleasant aroma of coffee.

Gloria comes into the room and announces that breakfast is ready. She is fresh and pretty in her negligee and a more charming hostess never existed. It is as if the conversation of last night had never taken place. Over cups of coffee, I am shown the blueprints of the home she and her husband plan to build in Florida in the United States. She tells me that the dogs are never a worry—"unless someone goes near me unexpectedly or from orders that only I have given them. They were trained by the United States military. They respond to only three commands: alert, attack and kill…"

I feel greatly comforted that, under these conditions, I am entirely safe, thankful that I am not nor have ever been a sleepwalker!

While traveling back to Atitlán, as I pass through the pueblos in my jeep, I observe the green stalks of corn with their healthy golden ears and the leafy green vegetables that have sprung up from symmetrical furrows. Always I watch in amazement the indigenous people with their machetes planting their *"milpa,"* and harvesting on incredibly steep mountain slopes. Each time I am impressed afresh of how frugal the Naturales are—that nothing is wasted—not even a plot of ground that the average farmer would consider non-arable.

Back at Atitlán, I carefully climb the steps of the huge stones that, like stairs, form an upward journey to the high cliffs overlooking the pueblo. I sit down on a large, flat rock and here at the outskirts of the village, the panorama of the area comes into exquisite focus; the lake, a shimmering, lovely body of water, laps peacefully at the shores. The ladies and their little girls, dozens of feminine beings, like an aggregate of birds in theirs reds and blues, dip their equally bright apparel into the lake water, while others dash their men folks' garments, containing stubborn stains from mother earth, against the huge stones in the shallow water.

The men seen working in the fields gather their immense yellow squash, bright red tomatoes and string beans in brimming straw baskets. These crops are loaded into wheelbarrows while they return for the next batch. The mountains covered with tall green corn stalks form a collage of colors blending with the "*traje tipico*" weaving in out. This is Indian life at its fullest—splendid, industrious Mayas.

On the road below, now hot and dusty, the rainy season long been past, a Tzutuhil walks along with his son a few paces behind. They both carry machetes. Small clouds of dust form about their footsteps as they hurry along. The little boy is a replica of his father—from the cowboy hat he wears to the sandal-shod feet. Just like his dad's, the miniature Maya wears the *pantalones* made from the hand-woven and embroidered cloth, reaching just below the knee. A Western shirt and *faja* completes the outfit. The *faja* has a cummerbund effect, wrapped around the body several times, the overall costume as flashy as a Spanish dancer's.

It occurs to me that this is like a theater—as if the clothing worn by father and son were fashioned by some famous designer and the little boy dressed for the role he is to play with his stage father.

I devise new ways, invent new phrases to extol the splendors of Atitlán. I am actually able to laugh a little at all the agonizing hours spent staring at the blank page of paper I inserted into the roller of the typewriter. My book of verses has swollen to include over a hundred pages. During hours of intense frustration—working at something that will not happen—it is difficult to realize that all accomplishments are born out of great yearning and frustration. Only when the determination of the artist has been tested to the limits of extreme is there anything created with lasting beauty.

I am reminded of an old Pentecostal preacher I once knew. Every Sunday he preached interminably long and boring sermons to a small, disinterested congregation. My family and I had sat through many agonizing hours in which we were chastised for sins committed by other people. He always condemned to hell the people who didn't show up for church on Sunday. (There were times when I had considered taking my chances if going to Heaven meant listening to him.) It was only because each invitation of his was presented in such a way that the world would end if we failed to attend his church, and it was because we loved him that we endured this Sunday torture. We were not even members of his church!

It was always difficult to glean meaning from this long, drawn-out monologue. Sometimes he left the content of his sermon entirely and talked about something else. But he never failed to screech at us sometime during his sermon, "If you do your part then God'll do his!"

These could have been the only words of his that made sense. If so, it is a pity that the good reverend can't see me now. I'm doing my part. Whether my poetry is publishable, or more importantly—after publication—is edifying to anyone, remains to be proven. But neither publication nor reading is possible with only unwritten ideas.

I no longer feel alone and isolated, as before, here in the pueblo. The sense of belonging I had hoped for among the people of Atitlán is at last a reality. The young women no longer pull my hair in the marketplace but greet me instead. The children do not make those awful faces at me with their mothers' laughing approval. I do not believe the shift in the attitude of the pueblo toward me is due to any sudden surge of affection or that I have gradually earned their respect. I still don't possess any of the dexterous skills of the Tzutuhil ladies. I don't weave fine cloth nor embroider the way they do. I don't even know how to make tortillas. I think what has happened instead is that their harassment of me has lost its appeal; I've become a permanent fixture.

There are a lot of newcomers to the village. They are mainly North Americans and Europeans. Nearly all the men are bearded and all, both men and women, have long, flowing tresses, the style of the sixties not having faded from vogue. Every day can be a field day for the village hair pullers! The young people add further color to the pueblo already dipped in brilliance. There is a young man whose eyes are not merely blue—they are faultlessly blue, like the color of the lake reflected by the sky on a cloudless day. He is quite naturally "Roberto Azul."

His friend, also named Robert, has carrot-red hair—he is, of course, "Roberto Rojo." There is Stanley who sells peanut butter. He is quite appropriately named, "Stan, the peanut butter man."

There is a young woman who eats no meat. She inherits the title of "Macrobiotic Mama," although still a young and slim woman. Then there is "Sausage Michael" and I had dreamed that the two would marry, giving rise to further irony, but who, when he does wed, he takes the hand of a translucent-skinned, white-haired from birth, Scandinavian young woman dubbed "The Snow Queen."

Then there are the daring young men who live on the slopes on the far side of the lake—they've earned the title they have given themselves, "The Slopers." They transport by canoe the houses they build in Atitlán's more remote shores...and there is "Banana Bette." We mustn't forget about Banana Bette. She makes a mean Banana bread. There is "John, the Tallest Indian." He wears the *traje tipico* of the pueblo. This garb only partly covers his tall, skinny frame.

I feel a little left out that I'm not interesting enough to be tagged something in the pueblo. On second thought, perhaps I have been and it may be that I'm better off to remain in blissful ignorance!

There is a girl, very blonde, who has begun to speak English like the Tzutuhiles in the pueblo were their language translated to English. Once she invited some friends of mine visiting the pueblo to her house for dinner. This she did by holding her fingers to her mouth in a gesture of eating—the way the people in the pueblo do—and with a primitive grace extended the invitation, "You come, I cook, we eat."

Santiago Atitlán over the last few years has changed drastically. Due to the labors of Dr. Juan and Susan, the changes they have affected have been greatly positive. Thirteen medical clinics, the primary focus of which is to improve nutrition, are scattered about the village and surrounding areas. The Tzutuhiles can now receive medical cares including prenatal visits of the pregnant mothers at these clinics at minimal cost (or at no cost) depending on the family incomes. The medical history of the reveals that four out of every five children suffer from malnutrition. Perhaps these statistics are now lower since Dr. Juan and Susan began their work in the village. The citizens of Atitlán do look healthier and cleaner.

I hear many young members of the "hip generation" criticizing work carried out by the medical personnel and the Catholic Church in rural Guatemala, heaping scorn on the efforts of the people here in the village who seek to lessen the misery of the villagers. It is the old story—"The ancient culture of the Mayas' heritage is being destroyed and replaced by the civilization of the Western World." But reason tells me that poverty, disease, malnutrition and illiteracy are no more a part of the Mayas' heritage than the English language, cheeseburgers and nylon clothes. Archaeologists' studies of the ancient Maya culture reveal that the Mayas were among the most intelligent people in the history of humankind. One has only to visit the magnificence of Tikal's pyramids or wander among the archaeological remains of any site of Mayan ruins to have this theory eloquently substantiated.

In the village of Santiago Atitlán today, there is a widening dichotomy of a very strange nature. In contrast with the grandeur of the ancient Mayas, there is a very ugly element infiltrating the pueblo.

The medical personnel and the Catholic Church continue to work for the Tzutuhiles of the village, alleviating the hunger and the ill health among them. They are, however, for the first time, having to treat the men and boys of the village for syphilis and gonorrhea. Imported prostitution from El Salvador, along with jukeboxes and slot machines, invade the pueblos. Large carnival tents are erected during the fiestas; the tinny music blaring away in the night competes with the clinking sound of the hard-earned *centavos* dropped in the voracious machines. It is as if a nefarious plot has been hatched among these innocent people, designed to corrupt and subvert.

There is talk among the villagers that there will soon be a floating casino with ports based on Atitlán's waters. Exact information as to who are the financiers of this planned million-dollar project is a little vague, but the corporation is said to be a part of the Guatemalan Government. People are seen in the village these days whose appearances are grossly out of place. They come to Atitlán in Mercedes Benzes, complete with *choferes*. When they do get out of the cars, as occasionally happens, one can see at a glance that their suits are expensive, sleek, and that guns bulge from their tight-fitting trousers.

One might ask, "What in the world is happening?"—here in the pueblo where the Mayas are engaging in what they have always done, planting and reaping, preparing the soil for the next season.

GUATEMALA AND THE COLD WAR

The year is 1979—the end of a decade that is to mark the beginning of change in Latin American politics. The structures that have tenaciously held Latin America together along with the Caribbean countries are beginning to crack and threaten to give way. The People's Revolutionary Party in tiny Grenada under the leadership of Maurice Bishop overturns the oppressive regime of Eric (Uncle Gairy). The thirty-seven-year-old, corrupt dictatorship of the Somoza gang is toppled by the Sandinistas. Somoza himself is on a plane bound for Florida and the Sandinistas come riding into Managua, triumphant, sitting atop the tanks captured from Anastasio Somoza's army. There is singing and dancing in the streets of Nicaragua. For the Nicaraguans it is a year of victory and rejoicing. For the people of Guatemala and El Salvador it is the year of renewed determination and the beginning of sorrows. A coup is staged in El Salvador close on the heels of Nicaragua's victory. A junta composed of both civilians and members of the military come to power. But lacking the solidarity that holds the Sandinista's government together, dissension of the junta members soon matches that of the parties they seek to represent. The government is unable to affect even the slightest conciliatory measures between the aristocracy and the poor. The rich minority is unwilling to concede to even the bare minimum of reforms on behalf of the poor. The "power-sharing-junta" soon deteriorated and all semblance of order evaporates. The tiny country already shaken by political violence erupts into a bloody civil war. Many of the unarmed populace flee across the border to Guatemala and Honduras. What begins at this point can only be termed as "extermination" of the Salvadoran citizens by the military government that comes to power when the junta is dissolved A full-scale war is waged against its own people.

Many Guatemalans are beginning to express concern that they, too, will be caught up in the volatile situation that is becoming not a conflict of its neighboring country, but a regional war.

Although here at Atitlán the impending war is but a dramatic event far away, the young men of the village begin to talk among themselves over what course of action they will take. They gather in my kitchen in the evening after their work for the day is finished, and a long discussion, similar to the one they've had the day before, begins. The *guerrilleros,* they know, are regrouping and getting ready for the "big fight." The young Tzutuhiles speak of these guerrilla bands with admiration and exhilaration.

One boy says, his eyes dancing with excitement, I will go to the mountains and ask to be admitted to this band of daredevils."

Another young man says, "I don't want be a *comunista* and will, therefore, join the regular army—not running away as I have done in the past when the soldiers came to the village."

One of the members present at my table, serious and thoughtful, states, "I do not believe that the guerrillas are Communists, but are fighting a valiant war against oppression and are in truth the army of the poor."

He has had the benefit of a formal education, having studied at the Catholic school here at Atitlán. But whatever their particular loyalties, they believe as I do, that neutrality is a choice.

My little Nicolas says that he wants to be neither a member of General Lucas' army nor does he want to join the *guerrilleros*—he wants to continue his peaceful life in the pueblo, neither shooting nor being shot at.

At this point I feel it is time for "my two cents."

"Look, guys, there will always be wars—they are the result of greed and hatred of the other person. Let the people who started them do the fighting. Each of you here, just remain neutral and stay out of the conflict as much as you can. There's no way you can help in the pueblo when you're in your graves. Besides," I say with emphasis, "think of the sorrow you will each bring to your mother if you die."

I know that this statement is shamefully manipulative, but will have an impact on their consciousness where nothing else will. Every Latin male I've met loves his mother almost to the point of idolatry.

In other areas of Guatemala, the politically shaky climate is such that not only is widespread civil strife looked upon as a possibility, it is thought to be inevitable. The violence of the sixties that claimed thousand of lives revisits the capital. This underlying fear, always present, is greatly accentuated by the assassinations of two respected opposition leaders. Alberto Fuentes Mohr, a former Foreign Minister, the head of the Democratic Socialist Party, and a member of Congress is murdered on January 25 while driving his car on the streets of Guatemala City. Manuel Colom Argueta, a former mayor of Guatemala City, is murdered on the streets on March 22, 1979, exactly one week after his liberal party—the Social Democrats United Revolutionary Front is legalized. It had taken six years for him to come this far—working against a growing tide of opposition, and a statement he made to the press, "There are no political prisoners in Guatemala, just dead politicians," could have been his epitaph.

I arrive in the capital from my home in Atitlán in time for the funeral of Señor Colom Argueta. I am immediately caught up in a giant traffic jam on the outskirts of town. I believe when I see a throng of people that there is a celebration of some type going on—one of Guatemala's many fiestas. When I can go no further and am forced to come to a complete stop, I begin to wonder how I can escape these crowds that I had at first thought to be "merrymakers." But they are far from happy—they are all mourners, as evidenced by their sad countenances when I am close enough to see.

A lady walks by my car and I call to her, asking what the problem is.

She is dressed in black and wears a veil. The face she lifts streams with tears and I realize—all too late—that this is not an opportune time to be asking questions. There is so much grief, so much sorrow here. But in spite of the pain the lady obviously feels over the loss of this person who has died, she takes the time to answer me. "Our beloved countryman, the former mayor, Sr. Manuel Argueta has died. This is his funeral."

Another person, a man, also a mourner, tells me that this greatly loved Guatemalan and former mayor had died not from natural causes, but had met with a violent death. The henchmen of the ruling government (Romeo Lucas) had gunned him down. This is the second year of General Lucas' presidency.

Although I did not know this man, Señor Manuel Colom Argueta, I, too, wept. With profound regret, I lamented that he had not been a friend of mine, he who inspired so much love and devotion in the Guatemalan people, to such extent that they themselves risk death in order to follow his lifeless body to the cemetery.

Following the death and the subsequent mourning of these two popular politicians, Alberto Fuentes and Manuel Argueta, the equilibrium of Guatemala's capital appears quickly restored. As one would expect, there were no gross uprisings, no massive outcries.

From all outward appearances Guatemala is in a state of calm. One would think that all is well, but this seemingly peaceful ambience is but a mirage, as soon will be proven. No, all is not well in Guatemala.

Early in the conflict overtaking Guatemala, it is obvious that the military is not the only faction exercising control over the country. They have their orders.

Guatemala has great interest for the CIA as well. This knowledge about their presence in Guatemala found its way into my consciousness quite by accident. I had found a comfortable hotel in the city when I come here from Atitlán, times when I've not wanted to wear out my welcome at the home of Gloria or Marina. The hotel is downtown, but on a quiet street, a few blocks from the city's central section. Rather nondescript, it really has none of the charm of the colonial hotels in the capital, alive with color; it offers little but cleanliness and economic accommodations.

As is often the case in Guatemala, the hotel is not only occupied with overnight guests, but residents, mainly those with jobs in the city. One young man with whom I had become acquainted works in a local bank. From what he tells me, and others have corroborated the story, his parents are extremely wealthy, his father being an owner of the bank that employs his son. Apparently the job is supposed to play the role of a therapist for the man, having caused his family the problems that plague many parents of the well-to-do in Guatemala—drinking problems, reckless driving, the keeping of "objectionable company," having no particular purpose for their lives.

One day I check into the hotel and the young man—the same one—has a new friend, a North American. The gentleman is tall and blond, Anglo-Saxon from head to foot. I am introduced to him and soon, in our conversations, some questions come to the forefront of my thinking. He has a working knowledge of Spanish, knows something of Guatemala's culture, converses intelligently and presents a general show of interest. It is soon recognized, however, that his interest is on a very superficial level. There is a lack of real concern about the country's welfare. He carries a briefcase, but he has no office, as nearly as I can ascertain, and if his boss is who I think he is, he is not getting paid to care about the people.

During the course of a conversation with this gentleman, the Guatemalan young man interrupts us, saying that he has something very important to tell us—something to show us. He leads us to the back of the hotel, a deserted spot, and there pulls out an impressive-sized pouch of marijuana. I decline the invitation to join them in a joint, and there leave the two of them in the shaded alleyway.

Later I have occasion to run into the Guatemalan man again and draw him aside. "Alberto," I warn, "Don't smoke marijuana anymore in the presence of that man you introduced me to. He's a CIA agent."

Alberto, not wanting to believe that this is true, begins pointing out his observances that would negate such a suspicion of mine—that he speaks good Spanish, knows all the dance steps and night spots and loves the Guatemalan women."

"Alberto," I override, "all that may be true, but cuidado!"—be careful. Indeed, The young man, Alberto, already seems to have his brains scrambled by too many mind-altering drugs.

A black young man from Panama had accused Alberto of stealing his watches and other jewelry from his room that he had come to sell in Guatemala. After the altercation had ended, Alberto expressed a sentiment that was hard for me to handle: When he returns to Panama, he won't be returning to Guatemala again; someone will be waiting for him! His father will make sure of that.

On my next trip to the city, while I attempt to check into the same hotel I find it is taken over by the North American in question, apparently a complete delight to its owner who had grown tired of its demands on her time. She had wanted to go shopping, attend matinees, and lunch with her women friends.

When I ask the new "manager" for a room he clears his throat and says he will have to check the books to see if there are any vacancies. Frowning, he looks at the guest registry, turning many pages, as if faced with a very difficult task. The doors of the rooms are still ajar, indicating that there are many vacant rooms. (This is not now the tourist season.) Finally at the end of the gentleman's investigation, I am led to a room in the attic. Right away I hear a knocking sound and realize it is the furnace room. There is a small bed in the room, presumably occupied at one time by a servant. The door is closed soundly, and as I survey my surroundings, I see that the room I'm expected to pay for is full of cobwebs. I find that I also have a roommate. A rat appears from somewhere and stands looking at me, the intruder from the big world outside.

I go downstairs and ask for the owner and the real manager, irate, demanding another room. It is of course given. I have patronized this hotel frequently. Surely I deserve something better, in spite of the surrounding circumstances.

Interestingly, I had blown this particular agent's cover quite by accident. Like all of us, when we discover that a few careless words prove to have a greater impact than intended, I am more surprised than anyone that my offhand and compulsive remarks have been exactly accurate! Needless to say, I don't go back to the hotel.

The man now running the hotel is there for a reason. He, too, has his orders!

THE WAR COMES TO THE WEST

For Guatemala the year 1980 is a year of crises—a year destined to change the course of its history, perhaps irreversibly. At the beginning of the year, January 31, 11:00 A.M., the Spanish Embassy is bombed and thirty-nine people perish in the flames. Spain immediately severs all ties with Guatemala. It is the beginning of a decade when the Naturales cry, "Never again," and begin to take up arms. They begin to collaborate with the Ladino guerrillas in their struggle against repression. It is the year when massive resistance begins. The most active guerrilla bands—The Armed Rebel Forces (FAR), The Guerrilla Army of the Poor (EGP), The Guatemala Worker's Party (PGT), The Committee of Campesino Unity (CUC), and the newly organized group, The Revolutionary Organization of the People in Arms (ORPA) lay aside their differences and unite.

In the middle of January, a group of Naturales from a *Quiché* province comes to Guatemala City. The capital, as any other city, is not an environment where the rural Indians feel at home. But because of the gravity of their mission, the little band has agreed that the trip is mandatory. Tired and hungry, the Naturales arrive at the Palacio Nacional to protest a wave of murders among their people in their town of Uspantán. They claim that the government soldiers are capturing and shooting the population of the Naturales in a massive spree. But only deaf ears are turned to their pleas for justice.

The more persistent of the group of Indian representatives are threatened with serious reprisal should they pursue the matter further. Not to be dissuaded, the Naturales look for help elsewhere and find it. The liberal students from San Carlos University, having long been the champions for the Naturales and otherwise oppressed, come to their aid. Together these unlikely appearing collaborators, the students in their modern, sleek clothing and the indigenous men in their *"traje tipico"* converge upon the Spanish Embassy. Trouble is, of course, anticipated. Students who have dared to speak out against governmental abuses have been targets of murder since the overthrow of Jacobo Arbenz in 1954. Therefore, fifteen of the embassy workers are taken hostage. There is no intent to harm any of the hostages by the students and the Naturales—they are only buying time so that they can be heard; the unsolved problem of an entire nation hangs in the balance like a heavy, crushing weight.

The Spanish Ambassador, Maximo Cejal y Lopez, realizing the seriousness of the situation at hand and the justness of the complaints of the Quiché Naturales and their sympathizers, agrees to negotiate. He immediately telephones the Foreign Minister, asking that there be no intervention on the part of the Guatemalan Government until further word is sent. "The meeting," he states, "is progressing peacefully with a solution in sight concerning the problems of the Quichés." The call is totally ignored—the security forces have by now surrounded the embassy and have climbed onto the roof and are scaling the walls. As they begin to break down the door, shooting as they enter, the Ambassador again puts through another frantic call to the office of the Foreign Minister, pleading that the security forces be withdrawn. The second call is no more heeded than the first and amid the shootings the invaders throw a Molotov cocktail, when they are at a safe distance. The whole building goes up in flames and everyone inside is burned to death with the exception of the Ambassador and a visiting dignitary. They miraculously escape through an open window.

A small group of Naturales outside the embassy, mainly comprised of the wives and children of the men who have burned to death—trapped inside the building—look on in horror at the tragedy.

This is not the first time the Naturales have come to the ruling

Ladinos seeking peace, but it is the last time. They will not make themselves vulnerable again—this is the turning point. Rather than the strangled silence that followed the murders of Alberto Fuentes Mohr and Manuel Colom Argueta, three thousand demonstrators take to the streets in protest of the mass murder of the embassy victims. From among the protestors, two university students are shot in the streets as they march with others, denouncing the outrage.

A wave of kidnappings and arrests begin in the capital. (Sporadic killings again started in Guatemala with the election of General Romeo Lucas Garcia in 1978, due to a massive resistance movement.) Many students and professionals are grabbed off the street—most are never seen nor heard from again. There are bullet-ridden bodies every morning found lying beside the highway to El Salvador. Some of these people have been tortured beyond recognition. For those still having recognizable identities, they are reported by the government press as "victims of accidents"—a young man fatally shot by a jealous rival in a bar room brawl—motorists killed while falling asleep at the wheel— hundreds of students from the San Carlos University pursued by enemies among their peers—a multitude of sleepy motorists going over the cliffs.

Guatemala has historically suffered from the "Conspiracy of Silence" that has afflicted Argentina—the family and friends of murdered victims also eliminated so that there could be no one to tell, the deeds of the government criminals snuffed out for long periods of time and hidden from the world—but the spell of silence is being broken. For every false report concerning the victim, there is a newspaper reporter willing to print the truth or a television station denouncing the government's atrocities...no coincidence that their newspaper offices and television stations are being attacked—raided by the "*desconocidos.*"

Many deaths occur during these raids.

The families of the victims begin to accuse the government too openly of its atrocities. At this point, everyone is suspect; no one is safe. In spite of the widespread insurgency, there is still the majority of citizens completely innocent of any act connected with subversion, but they may know someone actively involved in the revolutionary front. Their names may appear in someone's address book, or they may have been seen in the company of a person on the "wanted list." If this were the case, their names are also distributed among the assassins working for the government. Some Guatemalans at this point become traitors. They think that by turning in their fellow citizens that they, themselves, will be safe. (Santiago Atitlán is a pueblo of unity and local pride. For the time being, traitors in their midst are not among their worries.)

The traitors are merely buying time. When they have outlived their usefulness, they, too, become victims of assassination. They have seen too much of the government's operation to be allowed to remain alive.

At Atitlán, there seems to be a growing awareness of the political climate of the country. The Naturales believe that they, too, will be caught up in the violence sweeping the country. Since the Spanish Embassy crisis, the villagers sense that the war is no longer confined to the East, but is moving westward at a rapidly accelerated pace. There is a choice to be made, one that involves their very lives. They must choose between the government of Romeo Lucas Garcia or cast their lot with the revolutionaries. A middle of the road position—they know in some vague way—is no longer an option. The leaders of the centrist parties are being gunned down right along with the "leftists" and the guerrilla.

One bright October day a band of about forty men, heavily armed, march into the pueblo. They come from the direction of San Pedro La Laguna, Santiago Atitlán's neighbor to the west. They gather at the plaza, discharging bullets in the air. About six of them unfurl a banner and stretch it across the street from the plaza. (This complex of buildings includes the police station and the mayor's office.) Soon a group of Tzutuhiles surrounds these exciting rebels. It is obvious that they, the Naturales, are awestruck

"We're from ORPA—your Revolutionary Organization of the People in Arms," the leader announces. "How many of you have heard of us? Let me see your hands—ah bueno, bueno!"

Nearly every hand has been raised here at the plaza, but if the truth were known, very few people of the pueblo know who these men are.

They just don't want to disappoint their entertainers.

Since the crowd is becoming larger, the leader begins to talk through a bullhorn: "We come to tell you that Romeo Lucas, our bloody dictator, will soon be overthrown."

There is wild cheering, hands waving in the air forming the "V" for victory sign.

The glances of the revolutionaries search the faces of their awestruck audience, but the rhetoric is primarily directed at the group forming an inner circle about them—the Tzutuhiles in their prime of youth.

"How many of you are property owners?" They again ask for a show of hands. A few go up. "When we win the war all of you will be property owners." There are further shouts of approval, whistling and stamping of feet. "Everyone will have enough to eat, good clothes to wear and the leisure to enjoy good things. We are for the Agrarian Reform." Nearly all are acquainted with these words, their meaning has been carried over from the days of the popular Jacobo Arbenz.

The revolutionaries begin to ask for volunteers from among their audience held in rapt attention. Several young men move forward, submitting their names to the ORPA leader. These are recorded in an enrollment book by a secretary of records. The *guerrilleros*—warriors—spend the day walking about the pueblo, commenting on its beauty, buying food and soft drinks at the small *tiendas*, being friendly with the owners. They even bed down for the night at the three *pensiones* available in the pueblo.

When I retire for the night, sleep eludes me. There is an aura of falseness about the events of the day. The golden promises of the *guerrilleros* have been too effusive—they've not told their recruits of the hazardous and hunted lives of the revolutionaries; these men bear no resemblance to the ragtag band of guerrillas I had once seen in the mountains. Those thirty-nine men and one frail girl were hungry and desperate-looking. These men are well-fed, robust in appearance: they've not come to the village surreptitiously but freely walk about. Their *compañera* is muscular, almost masculine in appearance. Even though the guerrillas have begun to unite and have grown in numbers during the recent months, the army continues too overwhelmingly strong to allow this to happen. "Where was the police?" There was a rumor circulating about the pueblo that the policemen had disappeared two days before the revolutionaries came to the village.

Before I fall asleep I keep thinking of the clean-shaven faces and the recently cut hair—impossible grooming for men living in the mountains, but the most disturbing factor of all points to the freedom they enjoy. They feel secure enough in an unknown pueblo to spend the night; my guess is that these men are not guerrillas at all, but agents of the military police. (The group of guerrillas, ORPA, had been to the pueblo at an earlier date, and with a lot less fanfare.)

It is morning and for me, at last. The day is as bright and warm as the day before. I stroll through the pueblo, trying to conceal the residual anxiety from the night before. I note the "friendly guerrillas" are still busy collecting signatures and the sixty-one recruits are willing to follow them right now, but this is forbidden at present.

The exciting band departs at midday, admonishing the young Tzutuhiles to be ever vigilant in their struggle against the government. They say that they will be back and the leader pats the enrollment book with the sixty-one signatures. These young men may have just autographed their death warrants, unaware!

After the departure of the "guerrillas" some semblance of normalcy is restored to the pueblo. The mayor removes the colorful *bandera* from the law office buildings, the police return to the pueblo from hiding and the Tzutuhil men return to their fields. But there is a subtle feeling of unrest, a certain uneasiness like a dark cloud hovering over the pueblo. It feels menacing, as if it is ready to strike. People begin to talk in whispers.

A certain young man, Pedro by name, boasts to his friends that he receives notes at the post office from the guerrillas. Each evening, he says, he meets with them at the cemetery. Everyone in the pueblo knows that Pedro and his father guarded the flag the whole night for the visiting guerrilla band.

In a matter of weeks Pedro is yanked off the streets in Panajachel in the presence of his terrified and helpless father. Father and son had gone to Sololá on business and while walking on the sidewalk beside the government buildings, it is told that marijuana was planted in Pedro's shirt pocket by the Hacienda guards, a branch of the military police. Pedro is beaten for having possession of this "deadly weed" and thrown in jail. According to Pedro's father he had not had any drug at all in his possession—nothing. Pedro's father comes back to the village alone and the next morning when he goes to Sololá to bring his son home, he finds that his injuries from the beating are severe enough to warrant attention from a doctor. They take a bus together to Panajachel and just outside the doctor's office a jeep pulls alongside the pair. "Papa, Papa, here they come—the men who beat me up," Pedro cries out. But he is again grabbed and carried away. His family knows that they will never hear from Pedro again—for that matter so does the whole pueblo.

I go to his grieving father—and we both know that nothing will bring back his son—but I tell him that at least I might be able to obtain some information concerning his whereabouts. "I have a few friends, well connected, who may know something about Pedro."

When I reach San Lucas, the town en route to Panajachel and Sololá, it is completely surrounded by army troops. An officer stops me at the entrance of the village—in a very polite voice he says that he is sorry, but he must search the car. Finding nothing, he orders the men around him to put my car back in order and smiles at me. I have only two bananas in the car that can be offered as a sign of peace—I hope these are sufficient compensation for his not having killed me. I see that the officer is devouring them hungrily and I realize that in the early stages of a war-like schizophrenia there is a realm of sanity—it becomes madness when left unchecked.

A family, good friends of mine, live in San Lucas. The father and husband, Don Carlos, is a well-known, respected businessman in the whole area, and I ask him if he would be willing to accompany me to Sololá, explaining my mission. (I know that he and the governor are good friends.)

When we reach the governor's office, my friend is greeted warmly, but I am entirely ignored. Thinking he possibly may have forgotten me,

I remind him of our acquaintance. I am thinking of the times when he had exuded nothing but charm, calling me "guapa" (beautiful woman), saying that if there was anything I should need at any time, he was completely at my disposal.

When I state the purpose of my visit at the urging of my friend, Don Carlos, I am stunned by the governor's reaction. He mumbles and looks at the floor, totally evasive. I try to make him look at me by eye contact but it doesn't work. I eventually ask him outright, "Will you help me?"

Any vestige of goodwill he may have had toward me when I entered the door to his office, evaporates entirely. There is instead a menacing look in his eyes when he finally does look at me and I know the interview is over before I've had an opportunity to explain fully why I've come.

Don Carlos and I get back into the jeep parked outside the governor's office. The town of Sololá is completely occupied by battalions of soldiers...machine guns are the hardware of the day. We drive down the steep, mountainous road to the bottom where Panajachel begins. Don Carlos tells me he has another friend, an army colonel, who may be able to help me since the governor will not.

The colonel, retired, is the owner of a very pretty hotel close to the lakeshore. He invites us to have lunch with him and I am again encouraged by Don Carlos to tell the distressing story. He is not in the least evasive, but listens attentively. When I am through he tells me as casually as though we were talking about the weather that Pedro had been picked up by the military police. He adds that he had been seen with the guerrillas.

Unable to assimilate this news on a moment's notice, I ask in a state of panic, "But is he still alive?"

"Now that I can't tell you," the colonel replies calmly. "There are sixty others in the village of Santiago Atitlán who will be picked up in the near future. They, too, are guerrilla sympathizers."

My worst fears of the guerrilla band that had visited the pueblo are at this moment confirmed. I am beginning to understand something of the system here. If there are no available Communists then some are created. In its grip are players, and in the ultimate outcome, they are as helpless as the victims marked at the outset.

My sandwich turns to lead in my stomach, but I comment, "That's the only way to do things—Kill all the Communists to save the country from turning red."

Back in Santiago Atitlán I burst in the door of the *Chi-Nim-Ya*—I must talk with José and Francisca. It must be that my appearance is startling, for Francisca asks me, alarmed, "Bonnie, *que te pasa*?" (What is the matter?) Unable to speak at the moment, I merely sob, and then hysterically I give my answer.

"Someone please help me, help me! Death is coming to the village. Sixty people are going to be killed...I don't know who they are. How can they be warned?"

José offers me a chair and pulls up a seat for himself facing me. Our knees are not quite touching, but the chill of my fear is warmed in his presence—as dear as any brother.

"Look at me, Bonnie," José tells me. "Look at me and listen, carefully. You have just said that you don't know who the sixty people are—furthermore you don't even know whom you can trust. If you say anything at all—to anyone—you will be number sixty-one."

I leave the *Chi-Nim-Ya* greatly comforted by the tenderness of my friends, but still troubled, weighted down.

In bed at night, when saying my evening prayers, I make the sign of the Cross, saying, "Father, Son, and Holy Spirit," but begin conversation with the human one. "Jesus," I say, "first I want to ask your forgiveness for my cowardice. These people marked for death are no less important to you than I. Please give me strength for whatever needs to be done." It is well know in Christian circles that nothing can ever be accomplished until we become willing channels. I then take a sort of inventory of my life, trying to stand back a little so that I can be objective. No one can live forever. The moment we are born, death awaits right around the corner. And really what difference does it make whether I die now or at a decrepit old age? I see myself in a convalescent home, dutifully swallowing Thorazine so that I'll not make so much noise. At least now I have full function of all my limbs, no gross abnormalities of sight or hearing, and most people who know me would agree that my mental faculties are at least partially intact! I'm actually able to fall asleep—I've made a decision. It is clear what I must do.

In the early morning I stand at the door of the mayor's office before it is yet open. (I had to come early before I changed my mind.) When the mayor shows up at his office, I am grateful to see that he is not a Ladino—he is newly elected to the post and I've not seen him before. What I have to say to him concerns his people. I tell him that I must speak with him and he beckons me to follow him past the outer offices to his private office in the rear of the building. I close the door behind us, but when I begin to launch into my "tale of warning," he calls his entire office staff into the room. I cannot be more upset by this action—but seeing that I cannot speak freely, I begin telling of a dynamic black man in the United States. *His name was Martin Luther King. Perhaps you've heard of him. Liberation of his people had become the primary goal of his life.*

Behind this man were God and his Angels; behind the Southerners was a legacy of fear and prejudices—three hundred years of it. There is no force anywhere in the world that can be overturned without paying a terrible price."

I look for signs of interest in the mayor's face. I need to know if he has any idea at all why I'm talking this way. I see that his eyes are watchful, alert.

"The good man won," I say, determined that he should hear me out. "Mr. King started the wheels of justice turning in our country for the black people, but he paid with his life. He told his wife just before someone shot him that he would probably die from an assassin's bullet."

At this point the mayor pretends he doesn't understand me—by now I'm aware of this subterfuge—when the person who pretends not to understand it's usually because he doesn't want to understand.

I've been in Guatemala now a total of six years and I know that my Spanish is not that bad. I also know that the interview, as with the governor and the colonel, is over. I'm escorted to the door without even being allowed to say what I've come for. I leave his office more frustrated than when I had come. The mayor in the pueblo here had been the one person I had counted on to show some concern for the Tzutuhiles, and there had been some hope. There seems to be little difference between the reactions among the three—the mayor and the first two I tried to talk with, the governor and the colonel. The man in Sololá ordered the murders, an observation that by now seems obvious; the colonel is a collaborator and the man here in pueblo is concurring by high refusal to intervene.

On the way from the mayor's office I run into Diego and Nicolas—literally. My head is bent forward and suddenly—thud! They both tell me that I behave as if I am carrying the burden of the whole world on my shoulders. "No," I answer, "just sixty people."

All merriment ceases and they are immediately soberly concerned, stunned by the news I've just imparted. I notice that Diego has changed his *traje tipico* for blue jeans and boots, so that he could easily blend in with the Ladino camp. They agree with José and Francisca, however, that nothing can be done. "Even if we knew who the sixty men were, there's no chance to warn them. They would have to leave their families behind, in which case what would become of them?" The implications seem rather clear; if the victims are no longer around, then their families take their places.

After Pedro's kidnapping, the village seems to know a brief respite from worry, perhaps two or three weeks, but no more. But this is merely due to the fierceness of the storm venting its fury elsewhere. Santiago Atitlán is by no means a forgotten village. In the second week of October, on a Sunday, complete terror strikes; at 11:00 A.M. the army invades. Six military trucks roll over the cobblestones through the pueblo carrying their deadly cargo in front of the pueblo's frightened eyes. Each gigantic truck carries at least one hundred men; this means that six to eight hundred machine guns are aimed at the defenseless pueblo.

Because of a little knoll between my house and the lake (I'm lying on the beach) I at first only hear the commotion, and don't see its cause until I stand up. There they are—these are my new neighbors! I find myself doing something so idiotic, it isn't even rational. I run toward the governmental exported truckloads and begin waving at the soldiers, calling loudly, "Bienvenidos" (this means welcome) but there is nothing rational about fear; it is a paralyzing emotion. Both Diego, a 21-year-old wood sculptor in the pueblo, and Nicolas, my trusted friend, intuitively knowing that they are most certainly not any more welcome to me than they are to the rest of the pueblo, come running toward me from the lake, shouting, "For God's sake, Bonnie, don't let them see you—run and hide."

But as in nightmares I've had when I have tried to run and cannot because of a weight pulling me down, I am not able to move now. Like the rest of the pueblo, when they had been returning home from church with their families, I am rendered totally immobile.

A wave of terror such as the pueblo has never known before now begins. After three or four days of the army's occupation, the radio operators are shot and killed. The father and a son of one Tzutuhil family are dragged from their beds in the middle of the night and carried away.

I awaken to the bright sunlight and to the sound of knocking on the door. My dreams are a continuous nightmare of forced entry and death, but unlike most nightmares these do not go away when daylight appears.

I open the door cautiously and see that it is Nicolas, his young face lined with worry. He asks me if I know what happened last night.

I tell him that news like that travels quickly. By killing the radio operators, the message is quite clear. The government doesn't want its atrocities broadcasted. Yesterday, having been a Sunday, the radio programs consisted of Christian sermons and Bible readings; these men were killed while preaching the Gospel of Christ.

I do not think that I can face another night alone in this house. I ask Nicolas if he can sleep in the spare bedroom and he says that he must ask his parents first, but I have an idea they will let him, not only because I need a male presence, but because they think he, too, might be safer in the home of a North American; so a lonely vigil is kept by a team of a woman and a boy—hardly an impressive defense against six to eight hundred murderers.

How dreadful are the nights since "they" came. Each night I hear footsteps about the property, but unlike the past when I could laugh at my fears—when the noises had been nothing more than a horse or a cow enjoying my grass—my worst suspicions are now confirmed. When I get up and look out the window, the soldiers with machine guns are stalking the property. Each time this happens, I go to the bedroom where Nicolas sleeps. Shaking him, my teeth chattering, I say, "Nicolas, get up. The soldiers are back!" Together we go to the window and look out, watching, waiting…dreadful, not glamorous and exciting like the intrigue on the movie screen.

Each morning Nicolas gets up early, goes home to check on his family and then returns. What had been once a source of joy to me, I now look upon Nicolas' visits with dread. Every morning when I find him standing on the front porch, I know that there will be a new report of death: "Bonnie, did you know that they wiped out the whole Lopez family last night, no sign of human existence in the house, only a dog and a cat and a lot of broken furniture."

On the fourth morning after the army's occupation, Nicolas relates that three homes had been raided. All the family members were killed except one of the children who was sleeping at a relative's house.

One night when the soldiers are on the prowl, I go to Nicolas' bedroom. The moonlight floods through the window falling on his face, childish in sleep. The tears that I've not shed begin to fall, softly and then in a torrent—this person lying here is no more than a boy— still in his teens—so many heavy burdens. He is at the age when most boys in the States begin smoking marijuana, rebelling against their parents, getting in trouble over hard drugs, racing fast cars—not this boy—he has to worry about how to keep himself, his family and his pueblo from getting killed.

I do not want to awaken him again, but my fear, still the strongest of my feelings, compels me to do so. When I shake him, he tells me sleepily, "Bonnie, can't you leave me alone for just a few hours. I can't work for you if I'm to be kept awake all night." (He has been doing some carpentry about the house.)

"But what if they come and kill us," I ask, still shaking, "while you sleep?"

"Well then," he says reasonably, "if they kill us we die. But in the meantime I must sleep."

Such a casual approach to the thought of death would make no sense whatever to most people. But here in the village death is as much a part of living as being alive. Nearly half of all children never make it to the age of six because of disease and malnutrition.

With each passing day a new group of families joins the mourners of the day before over the loss of their dead. There is a sound of wailing throughout the pueblo these days. The small processions carry the casket up the hill, over the pueblo to the cemetery. After the funeral all is deathly still.

There seems to be few people who are not in some way affected by the army's occupation of the pueblos. Two more families have been added to the death toll of last night.

I meet Edgar Bauer, rancher and conservationist in the pueblo, one day. I had not seen him since the army came to town. In truth I had worried about him. He is the same man I met way back then—in 1973—a friend of the doctors from the San Carlos University. We stop to chat for a few minutes and he tells me he, too, has lived under pressure from constant threats these days, that he has been receiving notes of extortion under his door at his home and at the office, at his *finca*—a coffee plantation. Though they bear a signature of the leader of an opposition leader, he does not believe that the threats are from guerrillas, but from the army ranks. He states reasonably that it is rather obvious who brings this harassment to the pueblo these days.

"Nothing like this ever took place until *they* came."

Since the citizens of the pueblo begin to unite, the church has opened its doors to the village, making the Catholic Church at Santiago Atitlán among the first of the Guatemalan sanctuaries since the civil strife began. The villagers sleep in the church every night in large numbers. It is, therefore, no surprise to Padre Francisco or anyone in the pueblo, when the army comes to call. Those present at the time say that no braver man ever existed than their good Padre.

The military band, heavily armed, surrounds the church, the soldiers shouting for the priest to come out. Complying with their demand, Padre Francisco comes out of the parish house, meeting them head on. "Is anything wrong?" he asks mildly. In reply, the commanding officer tells him to cease from these activities, or else...Padre Francisco, through it all, according to the account given to me by Nicolas and others, reacts calmly. Typical of his temperament, he merely responds to the threat by the "*comandante*," backed—by an entire army patrol, that the people sleeping in the church are afraid to stay in their homes at night, since the occupation of the village by the army.

"They feel a bit safer here together—and really, what do you expect?"

Having delivered the last word, the padre turns his back on the killers and walks back into the rectory. Underneath the benign and chaste robes, there is fire and passion, the willingness to defend to death his little flock over which he is shepherd.

The community of young North Americans, in general, is a disappointment. They mainly behave as if nothing different is happening, and on the rare occasion when they admit there is some violence, many of them say that this is not their problem but Guatemala's. This attitude, however, does not exist in every young person from the U.S.—one girl who had been living in neighboring San Marcos told me that she would die for these people—that they truly are her brothers and sisters. In the village of San Marcos, one of the poorest of Atitlán, another young person like the brave girl talking with me, did lose his life. He was machine gunned to death in a classroom, while teaching the Naturales agriculture, hardly a subversive subject anywhere else in the world. Four thugs entered the classroom and shot him in the presence of the terrified students. The teacher, a North American young man, had expressed his fear only a few days before he had met with his violent death.

One day I happen to be at the plaza and, meeting the girl nicknamed Banana Bette, I tell her I am so distressed. This is in response to her telling me that I look like death warmed over. "But, Bette," I exclaim, "haven't you heard? They killed another family last night, maybe more."

She answers me as if I had just been complaining about the lack of strawberries in the village.

"Well, if you're so distressed, why don't you just go home?"

"Thanks a lot, Bette, your bread is better than your advice!"

Every day there are new developments in the pueblo. Nicolas tells me that some Tzutuhiles are now betraying their own people. Lists are being submitted to the army with the names of the *Comunistas*. For these names they collect the equivalent of one hundred and fifty dollars per month.

After two weeks of this death and destruction when homes are raided every night, the murders seem to have stopped. Some of the military trucks begin to pull out with their paid assassins. But their leaving does not end the surprises—one of a different nature comes through the pueblo where I at the moment happen to be checking my mail. There are carts and wagons, decorated with leaves and flowers, the young men of the pueblo aloft with guitars, tambourines and bullhorns; the sound of music and gaiety are heard throughout the pueblo. A young girl rides on top of one of the wagons filled with hay and flowers, her black hair shining in the sun. Three men take turns shouting to the pueblo that a grand fiesta is taking place. But of course this is not a fiesta; these amazing people are calling the pueblo together, organizing a support group.

At this point the telegraph operator asks me, "Why don't you go home?" Greatly disheartened I begin to turn around and leave. I have been in the pueblo all this time, and still I'm not trusted. I feel that I want to be a part of helping to protect the pueblo in their valiant efforts. Interrupting my thoughts, a loud burst of machine gun fire blasts the pueblo. Just across the street there are lines of people dropping dead; still others are waiting to be shot.

"Oh my God," I cry, held to the scene in stupefied horror.

One would be led to believe that these people being executed were capable of the most heinous of crimes, and indeed had already committed them—traitors and the like. As nearly as I can ascertain, judging from the threats of those still alive, they have done nothing other than try to make things a little better for the poor and the oppressed. (Not all the victims were from the pueblo of Atitlán but brought here for execution from other areas of Guatemala.)

Two West German men working in the villages had both been declared undesirables by the Guatemalan authorities. Both men had married women among the Naturales. One barely escaped with his life, having boarded a plane just minutes before the Guatemalan soldiers came looking for him, after he had been run out of the village of Patzun. His only crime seems to have been that he was installing a potable water system in the pueblo. The other man had not been so lucky. He was shot while trying to escape. The homes of both had been burned to the ground. No one knows exactly how many members of his or her families were trapped inside.

Elsewhere violence takes its toll in a public market. An attorney, a mother of two young children, is shot to death while buying vegetables. An elderly lady, talking with her at the time, screams and she, too, is gunned down. The attorney's aunt tells me tearfully that she does not know why anyone would want to shoot a person like her niece, that she is very kind and good, a noble woman, that she spent most of her time helping others. (I can only guess that the kind lady had been a friend of the poor, as evidenced by her fate in the violent conflict.)

Early one morning I hear something like the sound of footsteps outside my window. I open the curtains only slightly and look out, hoping the same is true now as in the past, when the noise and rustling were nothing more than a cow or horse coming to make a meal on my grass or plants. As I draw the curtains aside, slightly, I realize that my worst fears are not my imagination as I had hoped. There they are! Judging by their height and military elegance, they are most probably officers. They are tall and fair-skinned. The machine gun they individually carry looks as if it has the capacity to blow away any number of Guatemala's "undesirables."

Not knowing quite what to do nor how to still the rapid pounding of my heart, I open the door. (The villagers have warned me that "they" seldom come to your door unless they intend to kill you.") Perhaps there's a solution here before I surrender myself to the unknown.

"Do you want some coffee?" I ask of any of the four, and indeed, they all look interested. So far, so good! I had just put on a full pot of the delicious Guatemalan brew, being a coffee lover myself. I scurry back inside my house and into the kitchen. I throw together some biscuits and pastries onto a plate and pour out four cups of coffee with sugar and cream into the largest mugs I own. When I again open the door and hand them the treats prepared for their coffee break, the four look grateful and gulp the coffee while they seem also to be appreciating the snacks.

They set down their coffee cups and seem ready to leave when, suddenly, something quite unexpected happens, a turn of events that causes more surprise than the officers' initial appearances at my door. Yes, they begin to tremble—violently—as if they are in far worse danger than I.

I then ask the four, "Do you want to see the rest of the property."

Still shaking, one replies, "*No, no, me quedo, me quedo!*" That means something like, "No, no, I stay right here."

This time the militarists really do leave—in a hurry, to escape any hidden danger that may befall them!

I feel as if I don't leave here, I'll go completely mad. If someone fails to shoot me, I'll die anyway—from nervousness. I need to get away from here, at least for a few hours. I decide to take my chances by boat. While all the roads are patrolled in Guatemala, as far as I know, the lake is not; the tourist's boats are still running.

I hastily pack a few clothes and some cosmetics in a small suitcase and am now ready to go—somewhere—anywhere. I go to Nicolas' home and tell his family that I'm going to Panajachel and they are, of course, welcome to stay in my house should they feel safer there. There is really no safe place—no one knows at this point when they will be next. There is an oft-repeated phrase these days: "If I die, hopefully it will be without torture."

The tourist boat is filled with laughing, chatting tourists. Most are North Americans and there are a few Europeans. "Is it possible that they don't know what is going on here!" This seems incredible, although I suppose it is possible that the atrocities are to reappear when they have gone. The happy-looking visitors look through their binoculars at the scenes around them, taking photographs, commenting on Atitlán's beauty. Guatemala is flawlessly beautiful.

In Panajachel I walk along the path, incongruous in its pleasantness—the roses are as lovely as any other time—grateful for the reprieve from fear. A beauty salon looms into view among the row of shops along the main street—a welcome addition to almost any woman and for me, "just what the guru ordered!"

My hair is dark with some streaks of gray in it, but generally in good condition. Due to the dust and the neglect lately, I decide it could use a lift. I ask the beautician to liven it up with a little auburn color, but to please leave its color dark. When she is through with me, I have a smart Cleopatra haircut, but when I am given a mirror, I see that I am also a flaming redhead! I leave the beauty salon, trying to disguise my disappointment. The stylist had been too ecstatic over her artistry and the damage had been done. I walk about two blocks or more and I am conscious of being followed. Four men in a jeep are following alongside me. They are dressed in civilian clothes, but are, I suspect, members of the military. This phenomenon is hard to explain, but once you've seen through this disguise of theirs, you learn to recognize them, in or out of uniform. As if my suspicions are confirmed, I see that their vehicle has no license plates. I quicken my steps, my heart beating faster with each step. They continue to follow me until I am in front of a restaurant. It has a large garden in the front and a gate with a latch on it. I fumble nervously for a moment with the latch, but it opens and I quickly walk toward the door of the restaurant, attempting to assume a casual air as I hurry. One of the men gets out of the jeep and follows me inside. He comes to the table where I have already seated myself, giving me a long, hard stare. After looking me up and down a number of times, it is apparent that he is satisfied that I'm not the person he's looking for. As he leaves, I breathe a sigh of relief, thankful that I'm not on anyone's list yet. Those assassins, however, want some poor woman. They will undoubtedly rape her or kill her, or both. And then it hits me right smack in the solar plexus! Due to lack of sleep and worry, I've lost about twenty pounds, a cause for rejoicing at any time, but this weight reduction has helped to save my life. The brutes were asked to pick up a small but substantially built brunette, not a skinny little redhead. I don't know what I did to have made the "hit list," but I know that I, too, have been labeled an enemy of Guatemala. Again the words of John Steinbeck leap from their pages of wisdom in my thoughts. In his search of America with Charley, his dog, his journey taking him through the troubled South, he writes: *Beyond my failings as a racist, I knew I was not wanted in the South. When people are engaged in something they are not proud of, they do not welcome witnesses. In fact, they come to believe the witness causes the trouble.*

Herein may lie the answer. I may not be accused of anything at all, but I know about the atrocities committed by the Guatemalan Government. Naturally the top authorities do not want people like me returning to the States with this kind of news to spread to countrymen. It cannot set well in any democratic society to hear that the government they support is comprised of murderers.

When I return home from Panajachel further surprises await me. My home is in shambles. There is blood everywhere. The curtains are torn from the windows. All my dishes have been taken from their shelves and thrown on the floor. My books are torn and thrown everywhere about the house.

My dog, which has just had ten puppies, is going absolutely crazy. She whines and moans and runs about the house, in a highly emotional state. Beyond the pain and trauma from the multiple births, there seems to be something else the matter with her. She jumps on the bed and now I see that part of the problem is not gestational, but blood is also pouring from a wound in her side—stabbed.

I can offer the poor little creature very little comfort at the moment. Not only am I labeled a "*Comunista*," but my dog, too, is a Communist! I am too discouraged and ill for further fear…to think that the government of our country—our powerful nation—trained the leaders of these soldiers.

In a short while Nicolas makes his nightly rounds, bringing me the death reports of the pueblo—more homes entered, more men and boys dragged away. Everyone in Guatemala has to be aware that the army's presence means torture and murder, not protection.

Nicolas helps me clean up the mess. Tears are streaming down my face now, tears of remorse, of sorrow for the whole human race. Nicolas and I kneel together to pray, asking for courage, for faith and hope.

As if our prayers in some mystical way have drawn others, there is a knock on the door, then another caller. Soon there is a prayer meeting in session and the house is alive with supplications. There are requests in English, supplications in Spanish and the unlearned language of the Holy Spirit. Most of these prayers are petitions for the safety of loved ones. Nicolas has an uncle who has been threatened by the military; his brother-in-law, Martin, a North American who embraced the culture and religion of the Naturales and who helped the pueblo in many areas is now in grave danger, having to hide from the military in someone's closet while the henchmen hunted him to kill him.

Softened by the nearness of what we feel to be God's Holy Presence, we are able to pray for the murderers just outside the door. Their multitudes can be seen near the lake, children themselves, bearing weapons of war. Our better selves tell us that they, too, are victims, having been taken from their homes at a tender age and forced into the army. Their indoctrination has included denouncing their families, their origin—turning them into children of hell like their "mentors."

In the midst of our intense praying, wonder of wonders, another knock on the door brings us Gloria, bless her aristocratic little heart. I had forgotten she existed, but I can't seem to feel too remorseful about this. I am sure that she forgot me first until now. But there she stands in all her finery, appearing as unaffected by the country's violence as the tourists on the boat a short while ago. While asking her in, the family's helicopter can be seen at the edge of the lake. I see this helicopter as a possible way out of here and know that it depends on the passenger load, nothing more.

If Gloria's cheerfulness contains even a shred of falseness, her demeanor is at least an impressive facade. She joins us in prayer, remarking that I am a good example for the pueblo. (This is not exactly what I had in mind when we began our frantic supplications.)

When the others have disbursed, Gloria asks me if I know Vinicio Cerezo. "Gloria," I respond, "everyone knows Vinicio Cerezo." (The Cerezos are a very prominent family here in Guatemala.) Gloria informs me that Vinicio, his children and his father had been waiting next door at the gasoline station for half the day.

"Were they not then waiting for you to return?"

I cannot be more disappointed in having missed them until I remember what the state of my house was in when they came—hardly ready to receive visitors. Their visit coincides with the breaking and entry of the soldiers, smashing my home and stabbing my dog.

Once in the past I had found myself with distressing legal problems, my helplessness greatly exaggerated I am sure due to my being a resident of a foreign country. The stolen materials during the building of my house and the harassment that ensued made it necessary to seek the aid of an attorney. The worker who had stolen the most money was suing me for more even though I had decided to drop the matter if he would. Vinicio Cerezo was the thief's representing attorney!

Mr. Cerezo and I met, and hearing "my side" of the story, he quickly realized that the story had been reversed, that the person stealing was the worker. It was not long before the matter was resolved, as well as it could be, and without injury to the worker or me. There was enough reason in itself to feel gratitude and respect, but I had a better reason, one that did not concern me.

The moment that I had entered Mr. Cerezo's office, which also served as the political headquarters for the Christian Democratic Political Party, it had been immediately apparent that there was something very different about the aura in the office. Their secretaries were young women who spoke and acted with the intelligence and reasoning afforded by authority.

I noticed something else about their offices that was very different from the average place of business in Guatemala. The little boys coming in from the street were not thrown out, but their wares of jam and honey were bought by someone in the office, and a foot of the younger *Cerezo* extended for a shoe shine that was never intended for polish to begin with.

One little boy had snuggled against the elder Cerezo; undoubtedly this child was comfortably acquainted with him for some time. Perhaps these are among the early supporters of the emerging, popular Christian Democratic Party of which Vinicio is said to be the preferred candidate for the presidency. The liberal party does seem to offer some hope to the country's volatile political state of affairs and certainly an alternative to the growing unrest—but how quickly can change be affected in a nation of repression that dates back four and three quarter centuries? A question I surmise remains presently unanswerable.

Just a few steps away from my house the "alternative's leader" waited and at the very hour my home was ravaged. Whether the target was the potential president or I, an unknown in the world by comparison, is anyone's guess. The difference is not really so great when machine guns have been placed in the hands of trigger-happy children.

Gloria's soft voice breaks through the barrier of my ruminating state to tell me that there is room for me in the helicopter, as if this is the purpose of her visit, but that I must be ready by noon-time tomorrow.

I am preparing for bed when I have yet another visitor, a pale and shaken Nurse Susan. She comes on foot, explaining that she had left her van down the street for fear of jeopardizing my safety. I keep to myself the fact that I, too, am already a suspect, that my house just today had been ransacked. I say only that I will be gone tomorrow.

I put the water on to boil and, while waiting for coffee, I listen to Susan tell me that all the clinics in Atitlán's pueblos have been destroyed—all the medicines, the instruments, everything—smashed to bits. Already known about town is the fact that Susan and her husband are the ones who went to the American Embassy to report the violent death of the young schoolteacher in San Marcos...a very strange set of circumstances already, but in addition, there had been something mysterious surrounding the whereabouts of the Ambassador at the time of his disappearance had left room for further speculation. I don't, however, ask Susan about this. It seems that she has enough to think about already without my questions adding to her burdens.

I am amazed at the grace with which Susan accepts her own personal tragedy. The loss of their clinics must be causing her a great deal of pain. Susan and Dr. Juan love the Tzutuhiles. They have worked tirelessly for them. They were never seen spending hours in the local restaurants like some of the rest of us, talking and whiling away their time. They were always busy, taking care of the children, establishing new clinics, training the young ladies in the pueblos to become midwives. The army's ruthlessness had destroyed in a few minutes what had taken them years to build.

Susan further tells me, while I listen aghast, that there is a common burial ground, a gigantic hole, just outside Santiago Atitlán, where the soldiers are throwing the bodies of their victims. She says that people from other villages are being brought here to Atitlán and shot in the plaza. (The latter part of her horrible tale I knew already.)

Susan and I hold each other, but we do not cry. The unshed tears will have to wait until we can afford their luxury. The difference between life and death now hangs in the balance by a tenuous thread for all of us.

Suddenly I realize how much I love Susan, how profound my respect is for both her and her husband—they whose company I had never sought out before, and vow if the opportunity ever presents itself in the future, I will certainly try to amend the situation.

In the morning I feel my arms and legs and examine the rest of my body, just to make sure I'm still around. I am amazed that I could actually have slept through the entire night. Then I remember the reason. I'm going home!

I put on the morning coffee and open the door to my faithful Nicolas. I tell him of my plans and he responds in a soft voice with undertones of sadness, "*Si, tienes razón.*" (Yes. I don't blame you.) "If I lived somewhere else, that is exactly what I would be doing."

Nicolas tells me that a meeting was held recently in the pueblo to seek a solution to the country's problems as it affects all the people in it. He says that my name was mentioned.

I experience a sense of anoxia, of which I have lately become acquainted since the onset of the political turmoil, and find his words now cause me a fresh wave of anxiety.

I begin to wonder for the first time how I must appear to the people of the pueblo, the Naturales…with a civil war going on, do they think I am a part of the polarized segment who hates them? This particular fear is soon put to rest. The pueblo's only request of me is that I spread the news—tell my friends and my government's officials what the Guatemalans are faced with. Both petitioner and listener are ready to cry. I feel it is my country, too—I have known right along with them that the Guatemalan Government is comprised of little but a bunch of murderers.

Nicolas and I are still talking when there is a knock on the door. I had thought before that my being able to leave, just like that, was too easy, and indeed, my superstitious thoughts are justified. There at the door stand two local policemen. They are new to Atitlán, their predecessors having obviously been transferred elsewhere; the policemen these days hold their posts for just a short time. Again, this seems to be another example of the system's perverted logic. Emotional attachments to the people of the pueblos cannot occur easily if they keep their law enforcement personnel in constant transit. There is less chance that they, too, will become sympathizers of the rural residents—a point well substantiated at the moment.

The law and order men need a favor. They have come not to apprehend but to investigate. The owner of a coffee plantation, a woman of considerable means, had filed a complaint yesterday with the local police station. Four of her employees had disappeared—been kidnapped, and she wants them found.

The policemen, having no automobile at their disposal, ask me to drive them to the ranch where the workers were abducted.

My way out of here lies just next door. I go there to verify our time of departure. Gloria tells me that there is time to go with the policemen but that I must hurry. We must leave at noon sharp, as planned.

The men say that they must go back to the station before leaving, that they have to advise the town of their whereabouts, but they are probably going back to the police station after their guns, since none are to be seen on them right now.

While driving though the pueblo, the girl who speaks English with an Indian accent peeks out of the doorway and shudders, then closes the door. What a pity it is that she does not know the men are on a mission of mercy, and that I am merely providing the transportation. It seems incredible to me that people are willing to blame almost anyone for the world's ills, rather than trying to recognize the real source of danger in perilous times like these.

I begin to have some misgivings as I leave the pueblo with the two officers and turn the jeep to the left at the crossroads. They could be leading me to an isolated spot where I will meet with death as so many others have in the pueblo. My intuition, however, the most reliable source I have right now, tells me that their concern is genuine and I have nothing to fear from them. We bump along the road that is a hazard at any time for motorists. It is seldom repaired and each rainy season leaves new potholes in addition to the ones already left behind by prior rainy seasons. They are six or seven feet deep, gulleys really. Twice the jeep falls into the potholes and the men have to lift the back wheels while I gun the motor in order to move on. At one point, there is a steep incline in the road. The terrain is thick with selva—forest vegetation. It is an effort to control the vehicle, increasingly difficult to just hold the wheel. Neither of the officers drive or I would gladly turn over the job to them.

At first I don't see what lies ahead and the jeep goes down with a thickening thud; the mud begins to suck the tires quickly into its tenacious mire...and there below, just as Susan had described, that hideous thing, the communal grave—and if one were to look below, I'm sure, limbs askew, bodies of all sizes and shapes piled as refuse on top of one another, could be witnessed.

I swallow the vomit welling up in my throat. My hands are shaking so badly that I am rendered helpless. If the vehicle had not been stopped against our wishes, it would have gone no further anyway. Paralyzing fear has seized the driver. I see that my two companions are badly shaken.

The jeep sinks further down into the tons of mud left by the heavy rains and begins to claim its potential victim. Right now we must play a game of pretend. At this very moment an army officer, along with his subordinates, climbs over the bank and walks in our direction, stylish in his uniform and expensive boots. The soldiers' primary job seems to be one of guarding the hole in the ground where there are only dead people.

The commander checks our identification papers while the guards hold machine guns on us. The platoon officer addresses me first, demanding to know what I'm doing here. I tell him that I've come looking for my husband. He is a colonel and I need him because our daughter is home gravely ill. I had been told that he works here in this area, but perhaps I'm mistaken about the direction, surprised that I can lie so glibly, but more surprised that he seems to believe me. I look at the faces of the two policemen seated beside me and there seems to be not a trace of denial as they look straight ahead, even further embellishing on the story I've just told, saying sorrowfully how distressed I am, the poor *señora*, looking for her husband on this terrible road. It is not the first time I've admired the Guatemalans for their theatrics—especially remarkable without the benefit of acting lessons!

Satisfied that we are who we are purported to be, the commander tells us we can go. With this simple and liberating statement, he has brought a little comic relief...all of us laugh a little. Obvious is the fact that we can go no farther without some help. The jeep won't budge an inch. The officer whistles to the men below and a dozen or so "enlisted men" come running, jumping over the embankment and spill onto the road. The commanding officer barks an order and as easily as lifting a toy, the jeep is pulled out of its fixed position and set erect on the road. We are ready to resume our journey. I realize how lucky we have been, all three of us. This deadly phalange would have summarily executed the three of us had they known that one of us was a spy—me. Naturally I do not belong to an espionage ring, but I am a spy nevertheless. I have seen, and I intend to tell.

After what seems like a hundred miles of bumping along over the horrendous path, passed off as a road, we arrive at the plantation. Upon arrival we learn that the workers were set free—allowed to return home...three among a multitude who did not come back. The two policemen appear very happy that the workers have returned home unharmed, their expressions of anxiety replaced with smiles. They thank me all the way home for having driven them here. (We are allowed to return without being stopped again.) They call me noble of heart and many flowery, flattering things. Whatever Guatemaltecos may lack, it is never a loss for words. I love it!

When I drop the two men off at the police station and return to my home, Gloria is waiting for me and says that I must hurry. She tells me that I have just a half hour to get ready. I throw a few things, the best I have, in a suitcase, and hastily pack the rest away.

The helicopter, I see, has landed on the small strip of land at the lakeshore. I close the door of my house for the last time, giving Nicolas the key. I tell him that it can be used as a center of refuge like the church, if anyone should have need of it.

The dog follows me out of the house, wagging her tail. It is as if she's in some way asking to be taken along. I see that her hair is still matted with dried blood from the stabbing by the soldiers who broke into my house.

Crowded around the helicopter there is a congregation of a hundred or more people. I think that they are here merely to watch the big bird take off in the air, but I am wrong. This is my *despedida*—my farewell. There is a spokesman chosen from among the group who delivers a speech. I begin to cry brokenly—I had thought myself friendless at one time in the pueblo. The speaker says that I must return one day to help rebuild the pueblo. I understand him; he isn't speaking about the architectural state of the village, but the brokenness of its people. These are among the dearest words ever spoken to me. At the same time I explain that I am not important as a U.S. citizen in the overall scheme of things—that I have no direct line to the White House, but that they have my solemn promise that I will try to do my share.

"*Vaya con Dios,*" they call to me as the door of the helicopter closes and we begin to be lifted into the air. The dog standing there tears at my heart. I realize that not one single living thing is untouched by the war. Nicolas had told me that he fears a famine in the village. "The people are afraid to leave their homes and go to the fields." Reports from San

Marcos, the neighbor to Santiago Atitlán, where the North American schoolteacher was killed, are brought to Santiago.

The men are being killed in the fields, the women raped and subsequently killed while taking their husbands their lunches, or they themselves are working with their husbands in the field.

Seated in the helicopter is a young lady. In a few minutes I realize in our introduction that this is the "black sheep," the daughter who dared to defy convention and marry the young man of her choice, rather than the one her family chose to be her husband. I am glad for her company—she is interesting and vital.

As we are about to land in Guatemala City, I see that in my haste I've taken the wrong suitcases. I not only have left my best clothes behind, but all my writing—my poetry. There seems to be no remedy for this just now. Perhaps it can be reconstructed from memory. I am at this point dissatisfied with the poems anyway. They tell of Guatemala's beauty, without mention of its ugliness, extol its glorious history without depicting its misery and pain.

All my thoughts run together, separate, and then come back together. A myriad of emotions settles about me. For the last three weeks I've been terrified, and still I would not trade the experience for safety. As we traveled by helicopter, I think of what the ground looked like below; every valley and canyon nestled between the mountains were clearly visible. While thinking, *How beautiful*, I was also very much aware of how necessary helicopters are to a country engaged in "guerrilla welfare."

We land at the airstrip of which Gloria and her husband seem to be owners. The "peasant pilot" who married Gloria's daughter is waiting for his wife as we land. He lifts her to the ground from the helicopter and, setting her down, gives her a long and passionate kiss. She responds to his embrace with obvious delight and I notice that he is quite handsome…so this is the brute who ruined her daughter's life!

Lying on one of Gloria's beds in her home, I am conscious that I am comfortable and feel safe for the first time in four weeks since the army came to Santiago Atitlán. The military does not raid rich people's homes, unless of course the rich are sympathizers with the persecuted masses. I listen to the sounds of the night, the rustling of the leaves, the mother birds singing as they bed down for the night with their young, the crickets chirping—all lovely sounds, those of peace and promise. I fall asleep immediately, forgetting the differences between this hospitable lady and myself that had so disturbed me before when I was a guest in her home—and the black dogs—I forget that they had been a source of fear before.

At about 2:00 o'clock in the morning Gloria is shaking me awake, and as I open my eyes, still sleepy but trying to become alert, she tells me to please pray for her husband. A messenger has brought word that the guerrillas are at the ranch and with her husband right now.

When I am fully awake we hold hands and I honor her request to pray, but I also preface the words I speak aloud by a statement that the guerrillas are not known to kill people at random—possessions with them is not a reason. This is true. I know of only one instance since the civil strife began in Guatemala—at least in the Western rural region—when the guerrillas have killed someone.

It was when the labor union of the *campesinos* (CUC) had begun a campaign to have their wages raised from seventy-five cents a day to three dollars and fifty cents a day, minimum. Their efforts had been met with success, but a hundred and fifty of them had lost their lives in the process—killed by the government. One rancher drew a gun when the guerrillas had come to call and he was shot to death in the doorway. I think Gloria's husband far too wise for this kind of action. My guess is that he will be home by daybreak.

Gloria's husband does come home—unshaven and tired, but unharmed.

After breakfast, Gloria drives me to a travel agency and I am able to book passage for home. There had been talk that travel agencies now have instructions to report departing passengers' names to the police…only this particular agency that I now go to has not begun this practice as of yet. I have no way of knowing if this is true, but certainly a reason for being selective.

While I'm in the city seeing to my plane reservations, and buying my ticket, being in the capital affords me the opportunity to look at the newspapers. I buy a stack of them, as in the "old days" when I was trying to learn Spanish, and find myself a table at a McDonald's restaurant.

The local newspapers in the past had been somewhat dull. Now they are alive with stories of violence and opposing views.

Peace, liberty and justice are words infiltrating the newspapers, giving support to the Christian Democrats, while the media that appears supported by the present government mentions the country's problems only in terms of "*Comunismo.*"

The regional war in Central America, of which Guatemala has been drawn in, seems to be more about poverty and repression than Communism. Hunger and misery are everywhere.

Just now as I turn the pages of the papers, I see a group of little people. Each pair of dark eyes stare straight at me, as they press their faces against the wide windows, and looks of longing are mirrored in the eyes of the children, looks that tell me that they are hungry.

I go to the take-out counter where the food is sold, just like in the fast food restaurants in the States, and order several cheeseburgers, a large bag of French fries and some cokes, all the junk food that every little kid loves. The waiter hands me my order, and while paying for it, I turn around in time to see one little devil grabbing my coffee. His eyes meet mine as I watch him dash for the door, the other urchins close on his heels. They all run down the street laughing, my coffee sloshing over the rim of the cup.

I begin running after them, high heels clicking on the sidewalk, calling as I run, "Hey, come back—really—it's okay. Really, please. This bag's for you."

They are of course wary, but the tempting smell of food to their hungry little stomachs prevails.

One by one they return to the "scene of the crime," but a rapid mutational process has taken place. The dirty beanie the leader wears is apparently only one of the hats he can wear with agility, as he is transformed from thief to gentleman. He immediately takes charge of things, distributing the cokes and cheeseburgers to his followers. From somewhere he digs out a handful of coins, offering them to me, probably more as a gesture of peace than anything else. I manage to choke out a few words to the effect that I don't want any money, but since I am lonely and my kids are in the United States, perhaps they could just give me a hug. They each extend their skinny little arms in generous affection, as I, too, reach for them and hold them close, feeling the prominence of their rib cages jabbing at extremity and heart—not possible to conceal the tears spilling down my face. It does not really matter. I surmise that in some vague way, the children know why I'm crying.

When the children leave, I return to my newspapers and a new cup of coffee. In the Prensa Libre, the November 9 issue, pictures of the presidential candidates appear. The large print reads: *AMPLIO DEBATE POLITICO—AMPLE POLITICAL DEBATE.* The candidates express their views and concerns as they relate to Guatemala, recognizing that a solution must be sought concerning the lack of economic growth, the need for better education, for housing and jobs. Vinicio Cerezo, while concurring with the need of political and economic reform, denounces the country's violence and simultaneously defends his position of having taken Guatemala's problems out of the country. He explains that Guatemala's interdependence with the United States is an actual phenomenon from which there is no escape. The Christian Democrats recognize this international interdependence and consider it a positive step toward democracy.

In the government-supported newspapers, which are practically all of them, even Vinicio is denounced as a "bad *Guatemalteco*" and everyone here knows what happens to bad Guatemaltecos.

Before I return to Gloria's home to collect my baggage and say adios, I have another stop to make, the home of Marina, my friend who both blesses and curses with equal enthusiasm. Before Marina and I part, I ask her, "Don't you think that you should think about leaving here with your family? The situation can only get worse." Typical of Marina, she answers me, "No, I'm a *Guatemalteca.* If everyone else is to die, then I must die with them."

With ticket in hand and bags parked in the doorway, it is time to say goodbye to Gloria and her family, and the sweet, elderly lady from among the Naturales working in her kitchen.

While at the airport, I see that the terminal, like the streets of Guatemala, is prolific with armed soldiers, presumably looking for people like the man from West Germany who got away.

I board the plane and take a long look about me, at the Guatemala I may never see again. I am at last on my way. The plane begins to soar away from the horror, away from the pain and misery that has befallen Guatemala.

Aboard, a league of Canadian athletes celebrates noisily. It seems that they are famous, accustomed to winning. They are on their way somewhere at which time they are confident of winning again. Standing near me is their coach and the players push him playfully in the seat next to mine. It must be that he is a confirmed bachelor—this being an ever-present concern of his team. One of the players tells me that I am their coach's new wife. The gentleman who has been forced on the seat beside me, I discover happily, is intelligent and good company, and while we are still flying over Guatemala, I feel compelled to tell him about Guatemala's horrible conditions. He seems shocked by the accounts I have just given him, and equally surprised when I begin to lower my voice to a whisper. (Two Guatemalan men occupy the seats ahead of us.) "Why be quiet about it?" the coach asks. "This is a free country." The territory over which we fly is Guatemala, and no, it is far from a free country.

I know that my task ahead is monumental. I have a lot of explaining to do...a lot of self-education to undergo, a complete revision of thought processes that I've held in the past, before I set foot on Guatemala's soil, so that what I have to divulge can be told in such a way that it will be acceptable to a North American's point of view.

The plane has landed in San Francisco, mere hours by plane, but centuries removed from our Latin American neighbors. I note happily the members of my family are at the gate waiting for me, proudly holding up a handsome grandson and a darling little girl as now family members. My sons and daughters have all married since I went to live in Guatemala.

On the way home from the airport everyone is talking at once.

Because the telephone calls in Guatemala had been monitored, I had told them on the phone, "The Cubans are here!" For this reason they are expecting some swashbuckling tale about my having come in contact with someone like Che Guevara—he and Fidel Castro were the heroes of the young people during the sixties, and still dangerously exciting subjects for conversation. "Was I kidnapped by any of these revolutionaries?"

My God! How to explain? "What I have to say," I tell them when it's possible to articulate my thoughts somewhat, "is not exciting. It is horrible beyond all imagination. I didn't see any Cubans and I didn't see any Russians. The people doing all the killing were the henchman of the Guatemalan Government."

I hear gasps from each family member, and I am so saddened to have to tell my daughter, Jeannette, that the people she found so fascinating are suffering horribly. Some of those she met are dead—others live in constant fear of being killed. When their family members leave home, they don't know if they will ever see them again, or indeed if they will all be killed in their homes.

Padre David's brother-in-law is dead, gunned down in Sololá while working in the government. (One of those killed by a jealous rival.)

My family, I see, is stunned, as were one of my sons and daughter when told of the truth of Latin American politics on the plane from El Salvador. This kind of information is hard at once to assimilate.

As for me, I realize that the plight of the Guatemalan people will never be very far from me—I will carry them in my heart until they have gained their freedom. It is but a single, anguished tear in a vast ocean of need, but it is all that I have.

THE NEWS

Since my return to the United States from Guatemala, November1980, what most surprises me is the absence of news coverage regarding Guatemala. Radio and television, however, are permeated with news of the political turmoil in El Salvador. Sometimes, being in another room, I think the reporters are broadcasting on the political situation in Guatemala, hearing only

205

portions of what is being said, only to discover later in the broadcast they are invariably talking about El Salvador…a very baffling situation. El Salvador we are hearing about; of Guatemala, little or nothing. There is a fierce anti-Communist campaign raging in both countries.

One day I discuss this puzzling state of political affairs with a friend. He works with the board of education and he hands me a newspaper to read, a Berkeley publication, in which one author of the articles declares that in the Latin American countries, there exists a structure so powerful, that occupancy of the presidential offices is determined years in advance—that there is a coalition that ties together this political network.

While still reading, segments of the puzzling picture fall into place. The remaining pieces seem to lie elsewhere, scattered and buried beneath mounds of lies and deceit.

At the end of 1980, the Guatemalan news media, the newspaper office and television and radio had undergone a total takeover. The members of the press resisting the brutal repression were ousted. The more outspoken, murdered and replaced with government supporters of the Lucas regime.

The only significant difference in the U.S. news media and the reports in Guatemala seem to lie in methodology, the truth snuffed out here through the subtler approach of propaganda rather than violence.

What little news of Guatemala that can be read about or heard markedly resembles the propaganda of Guatemala—the valiant struggle against Communism, but no mention of the horror and repression the people live with.

A few weeks into the year of 1981 some news is brought that is more consistent with my last experiences in Guatemala—news of the actual. situation. Factors other than Communism are mentioned. The grimness of poverty and repression are attributed to Guatemala's socio-political ills. Initially these are implications only—small pillars of smoke. The truth is often shrouded in mystery and euphemism. Many people confess they frequently don't know what is being said of whom. They don't know if the Guatemalan Government, the guerrillas or both sides are responsible for the violent conditions.

But the signals released by the press like all sensations begin to ignite. It is not long before it explodes into a raging flame. The vitriolic conditions of Guatemala's political climate have at last been brought to light. (Only four years since the devastating earthquake and Guatemala is again crushed.)

I watch and listen as the stories of the Guatemalan Government's cruelty and sadism are released by our broadcasting system. The military is seen in action on television screens across our nation as the soldiers open fire on the unarmed population of Guatemala. *Time Magazine, Newsweek* and other popular magazines—no longer just Berkeley publications—carry some very enlightening information.

Finally the truth is carried globally. (The news accessible in the U.S., I've been told, is the same information fed into an international system.)

The whole world is being made aware that the people of Guatemala are suffering horribly, but specifically through the hands of their own government. The public awareness will undoubtedly bring about some changes for the better.

But in spite of these revealing reports—the mass murders and other forms of repression by the military dictatorship—there are references to "Marxist-Lenin guerrillas," "Soviet-Cuban revolutions." "Leftist sympathizers among the clergy,"—phrases which seem designed to evoke fear and suspicion among us. But when these epithets are applied to groups or individuals in Guatemala, they target them for death.

The dread and anxiety I had experienced in Guatemala starts to return—the same dreadful feeling I had known when the army began its invasion of the pueblo where I lived. I feel an eerie sensation of déja vu, as if a weight is centered on my neck and shoulders, dragging me down into that huge hole in the ground, like the one just outside Santiago Atitlán—less than two kilometers from where I lived, the burial ground for the bodies of the "*Comunistas*," someone whose name was written on the death list.

More disturbing at this point than anything is the thought that if our government feels that Communism is the sole cause for the problems in Central America, will the practices of mutilation and terror be overlooked in the process?

Is it possible that the heads of government of El Salvador and Guatemala were both correct? They have both been quoted as saying that with the imminent change in the U.S. Government, Jimmy Carter no longer president, that they will be given full support. Can this be anything more than an arrogant assumption by these brutal dictators? Can they henceforth operate with complete impunity?

Articles to this effect had appeared in the right-wing newspapers in Guatemala, consistent with the time and chain of events that led to the civil war. These declarations, however, had become greatly exaggerated shortly after "full-scale guerrilla warfare" had been waged, and shortly before Ronald Reagan was to be elected president of the United States. Press releases by the U.S. Government do indeed seem to be swaying toward support of these tyrants—moving in this terrifying direction!

Just as the country of Guatemala is greatly divided, there seem to be two warring factions emerging within our government as well. A body of well-known statesmen, comprised primarily of Democrats, takes a very strong stand against continued support of the brutal Latin American dictatorships. The prominent members of the Republican Party begin to condemn, not the fascist countries in question, but their Democratic opponents in the United States.

But surely, I reason, when the focus of the newly-elected president has faded from the limelight, when the dramatic events of the returned American hostages from Iran will have ceased to be a prominent news item, an accurate assessment of U.S. foreign policy will be judged and acted upon fairly.

There seems to be some justification for this minuscule element of faith in the country's leaders. The stunning horrible news of the four murdered churchwomen in El Salvador is brought to the public and is being decried throughout the country.

Robert White, Ambassador to El Salvador at the time, in conjunction with Jimmy Carter at the White House, begins a full investigation of the murders, and the findings, when reported, are well substantiated. El Salvador's security forces committed the crime. These women had been tortured and raped before being killed. When reports of criminal investigation surfaces, it seems inevitable that the United States will immediately withdraw its support and demand (*something*) from the Salvadoran Government, even though Jimmy Carter is now vacating the House, having lost the election. (Since this latest well-known atrocity, it had begun to look as if President Carter might change his policies regarding El Salvador, although he had largely ignored all requests in the past by human rights workers and El Salvador's clergy, especially from Archbishop Romero, to withdraw support from the present Salvadoran military dictatorship.)

Another surprise awaits some Americans. Robert White, an expert on Central American affairs, rather than being sought for consultation by the new administration—Ronald Reagan's—is instead fired!

Since this crime occurred, many human pawns in El Salvador's military have been offered to the American public. The soldiers now in detention for these crimes reportedly are not the same ones initially jailed. Further incriminating evidence of El Salvador's guilt surrounds the death of Archbishop Romero. Ita Ford, one of the murdered nuns, in what was to become her ill-fated journey, arrived in San Salvador in time to see the archbishop murdered. Government soldiers—while the bishop was saying mass—gunned him down. Hundreds of parishioners watched in terrified silence. Sister Ita had come to El Salvador to assist the other three (churchwomen) who were Archbishop Romero's faithful supporters.

Torture and murder have become commonplace in both El Salvador and Guatemala, an undisputed fact...no one has been able to deny it. Yet the United States' relationship with these preposterous governments remains intact!

TENTACLES OF WAR

One year has passed and in 1981 the war stories of El Salvador begin to somewhat recede in the newspapers and articles of Guatemala cannot be found. Nicaragua begins to dominate the news. The United States Military, acting on the Pentagon directives, begins to move troops to the border of Nicaragua and Honduras. The country of Honduras, long noted for its repressive and corrupt regimes, is a bitter foe of the Sandinistas.

The internal enemies of the Sandinistas are called "Somocistas" with contempt, conveying that their leaders are part and parcel of the old regime of Anastasio Somoza. They do a lot of talking about their hatred of Communism, but if they are questioned further, it seems clear that their real objection with the Sandinistas involves money rather than politics, and their goal is to restore the "good old days" when the small, rich minority owned everything and the overwhelming majority owned nothing.

The Salvadoran majority (the people) by and large support the guerrilla movement. They say that victory could have been realized by now were it not for the continuing interference of outside forces. But with a fresh shipment of arms, exported from the United States on a punctual basis to their government, the insurgents believe that dialogue would have been possible. Reportedly they do not want a military victory. They seem to know that this would entail going to war with the United States as the Nicaraguans have been forced to do through the

United States contra-backed war.

We are reminded almost daily by the Reagan Administration that El Salvador and Guatemala enjoy democracies, while the people of Nicaragua, since the revolution, suffer from gross repression.

*Agosto Sandino, the revolutionary of whom the modern day Sandinistas have modeled themselves and who gave them their name, once told a reporter in the thick of battle, "The American Government desires to protect American lives and property. But I can say that I have never touched a pin belonging to an American. And no American who has come to Nicaragua without arms in his hands has been injured by us.

Nothing in Nicaragua's "new society" seems very much changed; those North American volunteers, many who make helping others a way of life, return from Nicaragua only with glowing reports. They say that they are overwhelmed by the welcome they receive there. They work in agriculture and in the schools. They pick cotton and coffee with the peasants and though the people are still poor, there is general agreement that fear, hopelessness and the condition of the citizens being without homes, has largely disappeared since the Sandinistas came to power. The officials of the government walk about freely, without bodyguards or arms, an unheard-of occurrence during the old Somoza regime.

Meanwhile El Salvador continues to kill off its school teachers, its progressive priests, doctors and trade unionists. In its raging, stormy courses the violence sweeps along many North Americans and Europeans.

Oliver Rebbot, photographer from France, lies wounded on a deserted street in San Francisco Gotera, a provincial capital of El Salvador. *Time Magazine* photographer, Harry Mattison, comes to the aid of his wounded comrade. Government troops of El Salvador, recapturing the town that had been a guerrilla stronghold, burned to death most of the opposition forces in the area.

*The Nation: 01-28-84.

In a separate "incident" two Americans who worked for the Free Labor Development organization, a branch of the AFL-CIO, are shot to death at the Sheraton Hotel in San Salvador, El Salvador's capital. Their role in El Salvador was to have included assisting in land distribution, a program in its infancy of Agrarian Reform. Mark Pearlman of Maryland and colleague Michael Hammer of Oregon, both attorneys, are gunned down in the hotel's cafeteria, along with Rodolfo Viera, the Salvadoran President of the Agrarian Reform Institute.

The U.S.-backed ruling junta, that includes Napoleon Duarte, a Christian Democrat, promises to get to the bottom of the murders. The ruling junta had been overthrown and replaced by the government rightist, General Carlos Humberto Romero.

Its critics scoff at Romero. "There have been no arrests in the December 3, 1980 murder of the four American churchwomen," obviously implying that there is little cause to believe that the assassins of these journalists will ever be brought to trial.

Colonel Adolfo Majano, considered the most liberal member of the party and military apparatus, and now in hiding for his dissenting views, states emphatically, "The very government is responsible for these killings and the high military commanders and those in charge of the government know how this incident occurred."

Paralleling atrocities continue unabated in Guatemala. As violent as were the conditions when I left (at the end of November 1980), conditions have steadily worsened.

Father Stanley Rother (Padre Francisco)—machine-gunned to death in Santiago Atitlán in August 1981. *The San Francisco Chronicle* publishes two successive articles about his tragic, untimely death. Sandwiched in between the accounts under "World," reprinted from the *L.A. Times*, a motive of robbery is attributed to his murder. Two Tzutuhil men are blamed for the crime. Long before the story is corrected and the military named as the assassins, I recognize the story as being completely false. The people of the pueblo loved Padre Francisco and we who were there knew he was targeted for death when he engaged in his first "seditious crime"—allowing the Tzutuhiles to sleep in the church.

A year prior to his murder Padre Francisco had gone back to Oklahoma, the state of his birth and formative years. He had been warned repeatedly that his name was on the death list circulating about the pueblo. But according to his friends in Oklahoma, he found separation from "his people" unbearable and returned to the Tzutuhiles. There the soldiers kept their promise of a year ago!

Entering the rectory in the middle of the night, they shot him twice, once in the left temple and once in the left cheekbones.

Two nuns who had recently come to Guatemala to work with Father Rother heard the blast of the gun fire in the church and, going to his room, found him lying in a pool of blood.

People who knew Father Rother say he was not a person greatly interested in politics, preferring to live his life apart from the conflicts that divide humanity—like the Naturales—and get on with the task at hand, which in his case was to make life better for the Tzutuhiles he had come to serve. This particular impression of those familiar with his work in Santiago Atitlán, like myself, can be corroborated.*

*Time Magazine—Requiem for a Missionary: 08-10.

THE WAR GOES ON (1982)

There are whole periods of time when my thoughts are elsewhere—in a land where the people's skin color is brown, not white, where tortillas are the daily bread, and where Spanish and Mayan dialects are spoken. All victories, whether trivial or significant, I count as my own. One evening in Mill Valley, along with my daughter and son-in-law, as we are about to enter the local theater, I hear my name being called. As I turn to see the caller, the voice belongs to a friend who is a social worker and the wife of a prominent attorney. She tells me somewhat breathlessly, from having had to run to catch up with me before I am lost in the sea of faces in the theater, that a friend of hers, a doctor, has just left for El Salvador to work behind the lines with the poor. My first response is one of complete surprise and so I say rather stupidly, "But doesn't he know that that's dangerous?"

The lady answers me teasingly, affectionately, "Yes, Bonnie, he knows it's dangerous."

And there in front of the theater, with people going by and while still on the sidewalk, I begin to cry. This is not a small victory, but a major triumph. The doctor is a former Air Force captain who flew fifty C-130 support missions in Vietnam. When he began to question U.S. policy there, he was given a medical discharge. We are told further that after returning from Vietnam he acquired a degree in medicine, and worked at a clinic in Salinas, California. While practicing medicine there where there were many migrant workers, he came in contact with the Latin American community from El Salvador, primarily the refugees who had fled the repression. He is said to have treated burns on small children that could have only been white phosphorous. Apparently the good doctor is already known in widely diversified circles, from the U.S. Air Force, to the residents of San Joaquin Valley, to the peace organizations, and by now, to the Salvadoran Government's opposition, and the Salvadoran Government, itself, whose peasants it burns with napalm and white phosphorous. I do not even know the man, have never met him. But I say with all my heart, "God bless you, Dr. Charles Clements!"

Though Dr. Clements went to El Salvador, not Guatemala, I think of the act as being for the same spiritual cause; it is the same war that afflicts both nations.

In Guatemala, April 1982, a former general and "born again Christian" comes to power in a bloodless coup. General Romeo Lucas is ousted and the new president, Rios Montt, thanks God that he is a chosen vessel. This gives rise to a ray of hope in the people. Perhaps there will be a change for the better, though any real expectations are looked upon with reservations, both by the citizens of Guatemala and those who embrace their cause in the United States. Consensus implies that he is, after all, an army general. For a while the death squad activity lessens in the capital. When further facts, however, are gathered, the governmental violence in the rural areas continues about the same as under the old Lucas regime.

Soon after Rios Montt takes office, a major event occurs in Guatemala, the Pope visits the country. His scheduled visit overlaps another schedule—a decree of Rios Montt. Fourteen men, all with Indian names, are about to be executed. The Pope begins to make intercession on behalf of these men high on his spiritual agenda, at the urging of the Catholic Clergy, to prevent these deaths from taking place. But the Pope makes no more of an impression on the Guatemalan leader than the Catholic faith he abandoned for fundamentalism. The men are put to death during the Pope's visit.

Late in 1982, I receive word that I am soon to have visitors from Guatemala—José and Francisca are coming to visit me! Ordinarily this news would bring to me sheer joy, but now it is mixed with ambivalence.

Did I know that Father Francis Rother (Padre Francisco) had been assassinated? These were among the first words the couple spoke. Apparently they believe that Guatemala is isolated from the rest of the world; indeed, this has sometimes been true, but I assure them that Father Rother's violent death was publicized here as well. I show them the articles I had saved concerning the village priest's death.

I have a new *Time Magazine* with coverage of the violence as it relates to the Christian Democratic Party. There is a rather blurred picture of Vinicio Cerezo, secretary general of this party and the party's candidate for president, Alejandro Maldonado. Only a week prior, a rocket had been fired into the passing cars of both men, and a grenade tossed into the home of Mr. Cerezo. As I read and translate simultaneously, feeling the couple's sadness, I cannot help but wonder, *Good Lord, Vinicio, how do you stay alive?*

Vinicio Cerezo was one of the first politicians to be labeled "a dead man" by his colleagues. Indeed, at the time, at the end of 1980 and the beginning of 1981, the Christian Democratic leaders were nearly all dead, two hundred of them.

In the second paragraph of the article, this remarkable man says that he doesn't know why he's still alive, but that it is a "little fluke." He tells the newsmen that he has stopped counting the attempts made on his life. At one point in the story, the eyes of the couple meet. Francisca looks at José with a knowing little smile.

The article is entitled "Caught in the Crossfire." The couple knows as well as I that the "leftists" bear Vinicio no grudge. They were not responsible for the deaths of his party's leaders. It is well known that the Lucas Government had them assassinated.

José and Francisca relate yet another account of the army's atrocities...A patrol had cornered about thirty Tzutuhiles in Santiago

Atitlán while working in their *milpa* (cornfields). The Tzutuhiles raised their hands in surrender, seeing that armed men surrounded them. It was then that ropes were put around their necks and they were strangled to death as the ropes were tightened. The women were saved until the last; they were first raped. One of the men among the Tzutuhiles managed to escape and re-entered his home unharmed…another witness to the government's atrocities. How long he can remain alive is anybody's guess.

At the time of the outrage, two schoolteachers from San Pedro La Laguna, Santiago Atitlán's neighboring village, came riding into the village on a motorcycle, unaware of any danger. They were living in that peculiar state of euphoria where they believed nothing could reach them…happy boy and girl in love. But something did—a shot in the back for each of them. When the commanding officer had given orders for them to turn around and go back in the direction they had come, they readily obeyed, but aware of the situation too late.

When the massacres took place, there were no guerrillas in the fields when the Tzutuhiles met with death—no leftists leaning persons who shot the cyclists, nothing about the deaths that could classify this situation as being in the middle of two political factions neither figuratively nor literally. They were killed by the Guatemalan military, like thousands of others.

After Francisca and José have gone, I realize that I've not asked when the massacre they spoke of occurred—under Romeo Lucas' Government or Rios Montt's. But it seems that Rios Montt's presiding power has made no appreciable difference in Guatemala. Though a "born again Christian" apparently he believes in all the commandments save one: Thou shalt not kill. During his Victory 1982 Program, the army or the paramilitary death squads between March 23 and September 30, left as many as 352 people dead in each village, an armed assault on one hundred and fifteen villages. Those who managed to get away fled across the border into Mexico.

By the end of the year, the reports from the Guatemalan section of the Urgent Action Committee, Amnesty International, could be taken from the pages of the history books describing the bloody battlefields of Genghis Khan. America's Watch, another international human rights organization, gives this report; "Those who do not aid the government by forming civil defense patrols or providing information on the whereabouts of the guerrillas may not be allowed to live."

...The government of Rios Montt is waging a type of counterinsurgency warfare, that is, in political and military terms, far more sophisticated than anything ever seen in Central America. His policy of "beans and bullets" involves not only military measures and a genocidal level of repression, but it is a total concept of counter-insurgency based on the U.S. model in Vietnam. What all this means in summary is that Guatemalan citizens must agree with the government or perish. While the Guatemalan Government has been labeled "authoritarian of a lesser evil," it is totalitarianism in the truest sense.*

A young woman with whom I'm acquainted, and who managed to escape from her country and cross the borders to Mexico and then the U.S., tells this story: "My brothers and father (along with other men of the pueblo) were forced at gun point to accompany Rios Montt's soldiers to the thick of the forest (in Guatemala's northern highlands) and there made to witness torture and murder of the other villagers (many of whom were our close relatives) and were then warned, 'This, too, will be your fate should you fail to cooperate.'"

In spite of these fiendish acts, which have affected the girl and her family, she tells me in defiant tones, "I'm on the side of the government," a chilling example of George Orwell's "Thought Police."

Since Jacobo Arbenz was deposed in 1954, 100,000 people (not including the disappeared) have been assassinated for so-called political reasons. Dire poverty and disease continue to be a lifelong reality for the majority of Guatemala's citizens. The government has only changed faces, not politics.

Although the Soviet Union is blamed for most of the global turmoil by the present administration in the United States, clearly Soviet Communism is not responsible for Guatemala's misery.

* Report: Peace and Justice Committee.

It seems, at times, a silent petition drops from Heaven over the inhabitants of the earth, asking, "Whose side are you on?"—a question that cannot any longer be ignored. But even in the churches where the believers are admonished by their God to obey His laws, rather than those of men, a person may be hard-pressed to find someone willing to hear the truth, and on that rare occasion when this does happen, unspeakable joy is the invariable outcome.

On a bright Sunday morning while at church and at coffee hour I reach for the sugar and find myself staring into the twinkling blue eyes of a visiting priest. He introduces himself to me as Bishop Mallory, Irish from head to toe, and young for a bishop. He asks if I am the lady who lived in Guatemala, and as we begin to talk about Latin America, it is obvious that he has a keen interest in the region. Before much time has elapsed I begin to weep as I recount the horrors, the dread, the hunger...all of it. I make no attempt to be refined or polite as I tell the grisly tale. The acts of the Guatemalan military are atrocious—obscene. Like Hitler's army they resort to killing infants. The babies are pried from their mothers' arms and thrown against the walls of the pueblos. If the mothers scream when they see the tender flesh torn apart from the impact, and make any attempt to interfere while watching their infants' skulls crack open, so much the better. The soldiers look on in sadistic satisfaction. Sobbing aloud now, I tell the bishop that the soldiers rape the women when they go to the fields...in the same fields the crops are burned...This is called the "scorched earth policy." No harvests in many areas are any longer possible, since the people of the pueblos are afraid to go near their fields to plant...the beginning of a famine without any drought.

It appears that the bishop does not disagree; he does not try to negate a single word I've told him; instead he places an arm around me. I lean back—slightly—and feel the strong arm of the church, the combined symbol of sanity and goodness, the healing of the individual and nations.

"Honey," the bishop responds with tender concern, "you're in the company of angels."

I am at the moment reminded of Mark Twain's statement: "I can live for a month on a good compliment." I understand you, Mr. Twain! I feel I can live an entire year on the kind of assurance the bishop has given me…I'm not only on the side of good men and women, I'm in the company of angels!

This sentiment, however, is not shared by everyone in the church where I attend and where I am also a member. Some of its congregation have even stopped speaking to me!

Our priest, after my having nagged him for a year about what I think the church's role should be concerning the socio-political situation in Central America, at last agreed to let me speak with the congregation about Guatemala. This was not because he necessarily agreed with my convictions, but rather he just wanted to be "unbiased." I think this was a fair assumption. A forum had been arranged with five speakers representing the Central American countries. My daughter, Jeannette, was designated as the Mistress of Ceremonies. We were given the room where people socialize over coffee, not as one parishioner who was allowed to speak, in the church where mass is held, about the "evil empire," the Soviet Union, where he had never been!

When the exciting day arrives for the meeting (exciting for me because I at least will be able to tell the Guatemalan story without argument or interruption—after all, the five of us have the microphone!) the five of us seat ourselves in place at the head of the table. I note with some surprise that a number of people, including members of the congregation, have come to hear us. A friend, Father George Dyer, a Catholic priest, sits nearby. His presence gives me more courage to say openly what I've come to tell.

The meeting is about to begin, when I decide it's time to take a last peek in the mirror of the restroom at the headband matching my blouse and skirt from Santiago Atitlán—to insure that it is not askew. Among the crowd, seated, I notice a group of people who appear to be Latin Americans. But judging by the expensive-looking clothes they wear and the air of confidence they emanate, they are not refugees!

I take the time to welcome them, asking their names. And while waiting for what I expect will be a polite exchange of interest, one man among them states, "We're the Contras! We're here to tell our side of the story."

Though I'm taken aback by this loud proclamation, I nevertheless go on my way to attend to my attire and tell him, "You can be assured you will get that chance here."

When I return to the room for our meeting a few minutes later, the room has been turned into an absolute bedlam. Everyone present seems to be upset and either arguing or talking loudly. My daughter's head is down as if she is crying, and indeed, I learn, that this is exactly what she is doing. Pete, her husband, stands behind her at the back of her chair, hovering over her, offering comfort while he caresses her neck and shoulders. It takes some minutes before I can ascertain the reason for this disrupting turn of events.

Jeannette apparently had made an attempt toward being hospitable to our Latin guests when she was greeted with the same information: "We are the Contras."

"Well, do you mean like raping women and killing babies?"

As evidenced by her present state, my daughter was soon to pay for her outspokenness.

"Mother, they shouted at me. They said that I had better not sleep with my back to a window or a door."

As I'm about to speak, our Contra guests hiss in the ear of Father Dyer, loudly enough for me to hear, "We know who and where you are and we're coming to get you."

I never fail to be amazed at the composure of Father Dyer. He says not a word in response to this threat against his life, but looks straight ahead, as if nothing at all happened.

We are all a bit shaken; we did not expect "their presence," much less that they would try to disrupt the whole meeting, practically shoving aside me and the other speakers when we arose to speak. But my daughter does regain her bearing, holds the meeting together and, in spite of the disruption, we continue as planned. I was able to tell our congregation about the sufferings and abuses inflicted upon the poor and defenseless in Guatemala, mainly directed at the Mayan population—and since our church believes in calling "a spade a spade," a gross wrongdoing a sin, I also state emphatically that our government's involvement is equal to committing a grave sin against humanity, against our helpless and unarmed brothers and sisters south of the border.

The other forum speakers are not so specific as I in their oratory, and who could blame them! They undoubtedly want to remain alive when they returned to these countries as missionaries and volunteers.

When we surrender the floor and microphone to the Contras (this was hardly necessary), they push their way to the front of the room, shoving the rest of us aside in the process. They give it their best shot, trying to convince our congregation that they were poor Nicaraguans persecuted by the Sandinistas. Nobody believed them! Their suits are of an expensive cut; they wear what looks to be Gucci shoes; their fingers are adorned with diamond rings, and one Contra seems to have a gun in the shoulder pad of his jacket. At the side of these men, their stylish women sit looking on as if they have merely come to "see the show."

The most convincing argument of all, however, is yet to come.

Our priest's sister notices the Contras while she appeals to him, "David, those are bad men who came in here; those are really bad men, David," all the while yanking on his vestments to further call his attention to these people. Though an adult, middle-aged woman, she is known to have the mentality of a child!

OF WAR AND PEACE

The year is now 1983. Angela visits me! She now works for the United Nations, but she tells me that she had abandoned her work in the Human Rights Division and transferred to another department. "It was making me too nervous."

When I tell her of some of the government's atrocities that I knew to be true of Guatemala, Angela has her own story to tell of El Salvador's government abuses. She knew of a friend and classmate at San Salvador University who was missing. The father's search for his daughter led him to the morgue, where he was questioned about his daughter's appearance.

"What did she look like? Yes, I think there is a female here meeting with that description. Was she pregnant?"

The father's fear and confusion only deepened. "She is missing from home. No, she was not pregnant when I saw her only a few days ago. But I would like to see the body anyway."

When led to the particular slab of bodies where the dead young woman lay, the father looked at the victim, and immediately recognized the face to be that of his daughter. Her abdomen was hugely and monstrously bloated, however. Unable to understand the reason for the obvious pregnancy, he began to explore the source of this hideous phenomenon. Bringing himself to look at the rest of his daughter's mutilated body, it was seen that her abdomen had been sliced open and in the abdominal cavity, the head of her lover was discovered.

At the end of this horrifying tale, Angela and I both agree that probably we should talk of something else, because to continue in this vein would be to relive the pain and stress we were trying to overcome from our personal knowledge of the two Central American countries, therefore rendering us useless to help in any possible way.

When Angela leaves the house where I now live with my daughter, son-in-law and grandchildren, I nevertheless return to my rumination of the sad situation, of which there seems to be no end in sight.

Three years have passed since the country of Guatemala was caught in the violence and destruction of Central America's regional war. Despite all the optimistic reports here in the States, no significant change has taken place in the intervening years. We the citizens are led to believe our country is taking care of everything in the Central American nations and the small countries of the Caribbean. The truth of the matter is that no one living in these areas is doing very well.

Only the sophistries of the cold war have been advanced—the "propaganda machine"—meant to offer an exclusive course in desensitization to the American people, so that our nation's intensified war—like activities against the suffering people of El Salvador and Guatemala—have become acceptable to a large faction of people. The war against the Sandinista Government in Nicaragua is bought and sold as defense of our nation.

The "Contras" launch their largest and most vicious attack to date!—destroying food distribution centers, grain silos, coffee warehouses, a bank and office buildings. Many citizens of Nicaragua, including the children, are murdered in these attacks.

Meanwhile the women and men of peace mobilize their forces. They seem to be in very dignified company. John Quinn, Archbishop of the San Francisco Diocese, writes a letter to every Catholic in the Bay area and to the people of all faith; he implores, "...Resist the activities of the United States Government in Central America." He asks that the churches open their doors as sanctuary to the refugees, that we write to our senators and congress people condemning the actions of the present administration in Central America. It can be noted that among the members of the religious community, the churches have already begun to offer sanctuary to the Central American refugees. Many new peace groups in support of the persecuted Central Americans spring up across the country and join in solidarity.

The ghosts from other wars hover near. They return to the military scene and join ranks with the new names and faces. They understand the mechanics necessary for the disruption of nations and toppling of governments. They are the architects of the Bay of Pigs, the engineers of the overthrow of Salvador Allende.

They are the forces behind the overthrow of Guatemala's short-lived democracy, the deposing of Jacobo Arbenz, freely-elected President in 1954.

Stakes are higher now. Bananas have lost much of their exotic appeal. Oil was discovered in Mexico in 1980 and flowed into Guatemala's northern boundaries. The smelly, thick commodity gushed forth under the giant spade of Texaco—no coincidence that Guatemala's heaviest fighting broke out in this region.

On August 9, 1983, another coup takes place in Guatemala. Rios Montt is replaced with another general, his former minister of defense, Oscar Humberto Mejia Victores. The new dictator is determined to succeed where his predecessors failed. His "Firmness 1983 Program" declares that it is designed to bring peace, security and development in Guatemala, but it is simply a continuation of the genocidal counterinsurgency policies, developed and implemented while serving in the government under Rios Montt.

At least fifty-four people were reported kidnapped or disappeared by the local newspapers and fifty cadavers were found scattered throughout the country during the first six weeks of Mejia's government. * In late September 1983 the Mejia regime is condemned by the United Nations, of which the United States is a leading member nation. The majority of the other nations request from the United States that it withdraw its support to Guatemala. (Jimmy Carter had cut off aid to Guatemala under General Romeo Lucas' government entirely because of its blatant human rights abuses.) Early during Rios Montt's presidency, aid had been re-instituted and, although it was labeled economic aid, it was little more than funded repression. When Mejia came to power, full military aid was restarted.

The United States now issues a warning to Guatemala that aid will again be withdrawn, if they do not show some signs of improvement in their human rights abuses.

Dictator Mejia is either deaf or arrogantly sure of his own power. "SWAT teams" make house-to-house searches, looking for traces of anti-government activities. 3,500 people are detained in the man's prison and death squad activity only increases.

Dire poverty and disease continue to be a reality for the majority of the Guatemalan citizens.

*Excerpts from The American Friends Service Committee, 1983.

THE CAMPS
AT CAMPECHE

The year is 1984—election year in the U.S.—a year that possibly can change things for the better for the Central Americans. With little effort we can now obtain an ample amount of information about Central America. There are the numerous peace groups and the religious communities, all involved with the refugees, directly or indirectly.

I fret and worry when I read the reports of the men and women killed while just engaging in activities necessary for survival...women who are raped and killed while going to the lake to do their family wash...husbands and sons murdered while tending to their *milpa*: how much longer can they produce enough food to avoid famine under these conditions? Who among these growing numbers of victims do I know? The faces of each person known to me rise before me daily.

The pain of separation becomes unbearable to me. Perhaps it is possible to visit the camps at Campeche where they are said to be relocated. I had heard that Dr. Juan and Susan work in this area, never having abandoned the Naturales they love so much though they were forced to flee Guatemala. Perhaps it is possible to help the Naturales interned at Campeche.

Money does not seem to be a problem with the residents of Mill Valley where I presently live, one of the few places where social consciences and purse-strings are tied together.

Once more I begin to make plans to quit my job and this is not so easy this time. I had promised my employers never again would I desert my typewriter where I turn out dozens of words per hour…fancy things physicians say about their sick and well patients.

Off again—this time to find the refugees. I have no clear picture of how to find these interned Guatemalans once I arrive in Mexico nor what to expect, but I have a ticket to Mexico that I bought for half-price through a friend, and that's a start. In just a few hours after purchase of my bargain plane ticket, I am on my way to Mexico.

When landing at the airport at Guadalajara, the airport personnel inform me that there is a first-class train running from here to the city, and once aboard, it does prove to have all the comforts of home. In my half of the rented pullman, there is a comfortable, cushioned lounge, and seated across from me an attractive man opens a bottle of champagne, though it is still early in the day. He keeps the cork contained in a white cloth and he doesn't allow the spumy liquid to spew all over the place when he uncorks it—one of the few people I've seen performing this ritual without a mess. He pours two glasses and hands one to me. The foamy, vinegary liquid looks cold and good, especially enticing when it has been offered in a pleasant a manner, for its host extends the glass smilingly, saying to me, "*Salud.*"

I refuse the offer—there is something about his presence that disturbs me. I sense that I've seen him before and his appearance seems associated with the Contras of Nicaragua.

All travelers seem to have a need to know about the people they meet in travel. My fellow traveler and I engage in the harmless exchange of data concerning our existence: where we are from, what we do for a living, etc. During the process the gentleman takes from his wallet a card and jots on it a phone number, apparently not on the card, and hands it to me. It reads that he is an executive with a local union engaged in agriculture. My guess at this point is that rather than being a Mexican he is a Nicaraguan.

As night comes the attendant on the train makes the beds. I sink my head down on the pillow and muse on life's ironies…the valise under my bed is stuffed with articles about men whose business is firearms, and about two feet away from me lies a man whose valise may be stuffed with those firearms—a tall and handsome man trying to pick me up!

The next morning while having breakfast, the "Contra" comes through the door of the dining room. I reprimand myself a bit for the foregone conclusion, as I really have no way of knowing that my assumption is in any way correct. I have slept well and am willing to give up my suspicions about his occupation, willing to be friendly. I say in what I hope is a friendly voice, *"Buenos dias."* He does not even look in my direction and behind him I immediately see the reason. Behind him are four North American men, tall and blond, and not unlike in appearance the other man I had met in the hotel in Guatemala and where I was given an accommodation in the furnace room. But these men are austere appearing, as though they are engaged in important and significant business.

The five of them huddle with their heads close together, talking, and at times appearing agitated. I watch with my peripheral vision, hearing tuned in their direction. I cannot help but wonder once more what it is about these people that causes them to be enemies of the poor—those who have suffered so much already, and the Central American—why does he betray the revolution?

When all five have dispersed, the man occupying my thoughts comes to my table and asks my permission to sit with me, once again friendly and a little flirtatious. Simultaneously I reach for the Mexican newspapers that another traveler has left behind after finishing breakfast. They are chock full of articles, as ours are in the States, of the war going on in Central America.

"What do you think of the situation in Central America?" asks the man of my suspicions.

"Well…the people of the left say one thing, while the people on the right say something entirely different," a good and safe ground for anyone.

"Si, pero que cree ud?" (Yes, but what do you think?)

"Yo…yo no se nada." (I don't know anything about the situation.) I'm just a woman.

This seems exactly the right answer, a little woman who knows nothing, save feminine and frivolous things, a woman who may respond to his masculine charm. He suggests a hotel where I might like to stay since we will soon be in Mexico City, one nearby and not too expensive, where they make good margaritas. Hallelujah—good margaritas!

The train stops—Mexico City—and comes to the end of the line. I must find another method of travel to go to Campeche. I gather my bags and start walking toward the terminal, more slowly than I want to, but the weather is scorching hot and I need to devise a plan of how I might reach my destination the most easily.

While still mentally planning, the man who had occupied my thoughts back there in the train, and whom I had now forgotten, falls in step with me. The bag he carries, though small, is set down several times, so that its owner can rest his hand and arm, as if very, very heavy.

I mention in that context that his "*hierros*" appear to be heavy. And at that he throws back his head and begins to laugh. *Hierros* can mean iron, something made of iron, more than one meaning…tools or weapons of war. I suppose that it seems ludicrous that I could think that the contents of that bag contain implements of agriculture. I say adios to him and keep walking.

I go through the side door of the train station where there are many waiting taxis. The driver explains that he must take another passenger to his destination in order to earn his full fare. He opens the door and the other passenger he feels compelled to take with us is none other than the man with whom I thought I had parted company. We are soon dropped off in front of a pleasant-looking hotel when I realize that I've not had a word to say about where I'm going, and furthermore, the taxi driver mumbles something about another stop he must make and says I must get out here.

The hotel lobby looks like the PX of an army base. Men in uniform, fatigues and full dress fill the stairway, coming and going.

While I inquire about a room, the only person I know here, the "Contra" offers me his. He states that he has a lot of business to do and that I need not even pay for its use.

I tell him that this is very kind of him, but that I really prefer to have a room of my own. While we are still speaking, my voice becoming firmer about my decision to be alone, there is considerable commotion following some item from the television at the front desk of the hotel. I had entirely forgotten—today is Election Day.

The young man's announcement to the only North American in the hotel by no means brings the desired results. Not for the first time do I begin weeping in a public place...Mr. Reagan's words—"I need four more years to accomplish what I set out to do." I've buried my head on the suitcases that I've set down on the counter and it must be that someone has asked what is the matter with me, as I hear the desk clerk reply, "Who knows? She's *loca.*"

I look up and retort, "Oh no, I'm not. I'm probably the sanest person here. At least I don't advocate destruction of the poor."

For his answer the tall young man raises a fist and shouts, "*Ataca!*" A pretty girl stands near him at this point and he draws her to him by putting his arm about her small waist, and shouts again, "*Ataca!*"

While I glare at him, he glares back, and like most hotel employees in a position that deals with the public, he probably has something more destructive at his disposal than a glare.

I know that it's time to get the hell out!—to get going while the going is still good. I feel like I'm back in Guatemala.

Outside the hotel, a taxi pulls up with hotel guests and I push and kick my luggage out of the hotel lobby and through the revolving door to the waiting taxi, once more having placed myself in a position of urgency, not going to, but away from—I was a threat to someone in Guatemala because I was a witness to its brutality and it seems that there is little difference here among this faction of people. I am in trouble for crying!

I tell the driver that I would like to be taken to the offices of the government, the branch where I may obtain permission for visiting the refugee camps of Guatemala. He at first looks at me as if he has picked up a crazy passenger, an assumption that doesn't particularly set well with a person. I feel the need to explain to him that I come here by own volition, and would like to help if I can, adding, "Perhaps they don't even have enough to eat."

His expression changes somewhat after this explanation and contains more respect. He tells me that I must go the office of the Minister of Interior. He will tell me what I can do—legally—to find them. But he admonishes me to be extremely tactful in my approach.

When I reach the designated office I think that I will get involved in a series of long and lengthy red tape just to get to see someone at the minister's offices, and that seeing him personally won't be possible, but after giving my name and stating my business to his secretary, to my complete amazement she escorts me directly to the office of the Minister of Interior where he receives me most graciously, getting to his feet and taking my hand. He is young and handsome and not for the first time am I delighted with someone's appearance. His face contains none of the arrogance sometimes associated with extreme good looks.

When I utter my first sentence, that I am here about the Guatemalan refugees, I begin to sob. "I'm very sorry," I tell him through gulps, and murmur something of the reason.

"I know, my secretary told me," he says, through eyes that have become tearful and he, too, begins to weep.

We sit and cry together for a very long time—that is, a long time as far as this kind of interaction goes, and share a box of tissues between the two of us.

When I leave the office I am not really sure what, if anything, has been accomplished for the Guatemalans. The Minister tells me that he is profoundly sorry, but he can't help me with the problem—that he would if he could (and I believe him), but that only the bishop in Campeche can address my request.

Though the refugees have not been helped as yet through my efforts, I have been wonderfully helped. The bitterness I've had to deal with since I left Guatemala has been bathed with the tears that have just been shed, flooded out with this kind man's compassion for his neighbors. The encouragement I needed in my quest has been generously given.

Since no permission to visit the refugees can be given here from Mexico City, it becomes clear that I must go to Campeche, to the area where they are housed. The secretary calls me a taxi and I instruct the driver to take me to the bus station where I might buy a ticket for Campeche.

The luxurious ride on the first class train from Guadalajara to Mexico City seems to be where comfort ends and gross exploitation of Mexico's poor takes a ride. On just surface evaluation, the bus looks modern and comfortable. After many hours, however, without stopping for a break, I ask the driver if he plans to stop so that we, the passengers, may use the bathroom, or if I may use the one on the back of the bus. (I had seen the man collecting tickets go to that bathroom.) He says that the rest room on the bus is not for public use. It would be just too dirty to allow that, and that only the employees have that privilege. Without turning his head the bus rolls on.

I return to my seat, my bladder feeling as if it will burst. I see that I'm not the only uncomfortable passenger here. There is a young mother-to-be who looks to be in absolute agony.

Finally, after hours of frequent complaints on my part—the *gringa*, the bus driver agrees to stop for a short break, but lets it be known that he is greatly inconvenienced by this unreasonable request.

This particular bus company takes me only halfway to my destination. I find I must take another train to reach the Yucatan. The condition of the train would make the heartiest person ill. The stench alone causes me to want to vomit, and use of the bathroom is completely out of the question. They are one huge outhouse, no place to sit or stand. In all my travels it is the filthiest, most degrading sight I have ever seen passed off as a washroom.

I am impressed with the thought of how horrible it is for people to have to live without money, but especially vile to the person who lives in a third-world country.

When I reach the town of Campeche, I realize that I've made a grave error. There is the town of Campeche and the District of Campeche, where there are hundreds of miles of federal lands. The Guatemalan refugees are not housed here in town, as I had imagined, but are somewhere out in the wide-open spaces.

While at the bus terminal, I ask the taxi driver to take me to an inexpensive but nice hotel. It is now the middle of the night and the hotel he takes me to proves to be inexpensive, but anything but nice.

In times past, we used to politely call a place like this "a house of ill-repute." South of the border they are just called *casas de las Putas*—whore houses. A look around me tells me that these scantily clad ladies do not do as well as some of their counterparts in the United States. In the States there is at least about them a facade of pleasurable living, stylish in their furs and diamonds. As they traipse down the stairs to buy their soft drinks from a tired, overworked coke machine, one look at the faces of these girl-women tells you that if they were ever really young, all youthful joy had disappeared during their childhood.

Theirs are not the expressions of violence or resentment, or hatred, not even sullenness, but nothing, complete apathy, the dreariest of all emotions.

The room I'm given smells of urine and Lysol, and the bed sags in the middle, springs jabbing me in the back. It is impossible to leave right now, in spite of this place making me just plain sick. There's no place to go; the taxis have stopped running for the night I'm told by the maid in the hotel. The next morning I wake, finding another hotel room the first item on my agenda. I learn from another taxi driver outside this miserable building that just a few blocks away there is a lovely colonial hotel that rents for just a few pesos more.

The managers prove to be a nice man and woman who are brother and sister, and it isn't long before I tell them of my "mission." They tell me the cathedral where the bishop resides is but a few blocks away; Presumably he is not there presently, but away on official business, but that I might make an appointment now or talk with a representative.

The church, like those in Guatemala, is constructed from adobe, rustic and unadorned and the main rooms surround a large courtyard. In one of the offices a man greets me with a humble grace and when I tell him I've come, he tells me that he is from Guatemala, but seems reluctant to talk about the situation and offers no encouragement as to my seeing the bishop concerning the refugees. He says rather guardedly that there is a young priest here, an assistant to the bishop, and that he may talk with me. When I inquire at the door of his office, he is either not in, or just too busy to see me.

I hang around the town for about ten days; mostly I am bored and want to get at the task at hand, if indeed there is a task. I seem to have acquired the reputation as a person looking for the refugees and someone from the hotel informs me that the bishop has returned. After this piece of news, I go to the cathedral as early in the morning as decorum permits. I am soon escorted into a wing of the church that bears no resemblance to the rest of the humble adobe structure. The offices are modern, recently painted, and the desks are fashioned of fine wood, shining with varnish. I'm shown to the office of a young priest. As I stand over his desk, he looks up with extreme annoyance. I'm unable to interpret a reason for his behavior, but he is bent ever a huge pile of money, and perhaps doesn't welcome the distraction. A look of sheer greed shines from his dark eyes as he fondles the dirty, green pile of paper. He only looks up again as a young, attractive woman enters the room and it appears that they are well acquainted by the way they greet one another. And by now the priest's attention is divided.

"Oh well," I tell myself, "I've not come to see him, but the bishop."

In a few moments, the assistant priest grudgingly escorts me to the Bishop's office. The Bishop stands and his countenance is as formidable as those pictures of God that used to scare the devil out of us when we were all little kids. He raises an arm and by this simple gesture I can see if I let him, he will reduce me to the dust from which I came. In an absolute rage, he demands to know who sent me here—just why I come here asking about those refugees.

I gather all the courage that I can muster, and answer, "Sir, no one sent me here. I used to live in Guatemala and because the Guatemalans are here in your country, I am determined to find them if I can. I have a couple of questions to ask you...First I would really like to know why you've not greeted me as Christian? I have come a long way and waited a long time to see you. Secondly, I would like you to explain to me why you are so hostile to me when I am only inquiring about my Guatemalan brothers and sisters?"

His manner does seem to be a bit more restrained, if not any less hostile.

He tells me that he has nothing to do with those refugees—he only gives them communion!

These helpless and displaced refugees seem to be a source of many problems for those who keep them contained. It is by now obvious that no one is going to give me permission to visit the camp, and that my options are narrowed to just two choices. I can go home and try to forget about those refugees who I cannot seem to help anyway, or I can just go and take my chances of seeing them. There is a third-class train, I learn, going somewhere near the camps, and in a matter of hours I am on one, going through a dense forest. This is where I'm let out. Aside from a little general store, which is closed, and a couple of houses that look empty, the place is completely deserted. I begin to walk in the direction where I think the camps should be, although I don't really know why I've chosen this route; few people have a worse sense of direction than I. I begin to walk along, singing like I did as a little girl. I feel like one now, alone in a vast forest and not knowing exactly where I'm going. After about an hour or so I hear the unmistakable sound of an engine and turn to look at its origin, and I see that to the side of the path and up a little knoll is a road, and it really is a vehicle I hear, a huge truck.

I run as fast as I can, clawing my way up the embankment, my heart beating out of fear of the unknown, not knowing which will turn out worse—accepting a ride from a total stranger in the middle of nowhere or taking my chances here in the forest. The truck is as large as any moving van; it rolls to a stop as I stick out my thumb in its direction. I get in the front with the two men and right away I notice that across the whole expansive top of the truck there is a life-size painting of the Virgin Mary and the Christ Child—a good sign already, I feel. The van seems to be used for transporting the refugees. I tell the men why I've come so far and they tell me that they understand—another good sign. "What must if do?" I inquire. "I don't seem to find the right person."

There is a mischievous little grin on the driver's face as he looks at me and replies, "Don't do anything. Nothing!"

In just a few minutes, I learn the reason; he instructs me to get down underneath the dash and we just roll into the refugee camp. There they are now, hundreds of them in their *traje tipico*. Beautiful, fantastic

Naturales! I see the little wooden huts with wee gardens of green things, clothes hanging out to dry and the long, black, illustrious hair adorning the heads of women, the little girls and boys also working, always working. Wherever the Mayas go they seem to populate, form a community—find a way to create out of so little.

I just stand there staring in awe. For four years I have thought of them constantly, and now as in a dream, here they are. My reverie lasts but a few moments, however. The men who brought me here leave and a man in a white coat hurries toward me, angry, demanding to know what I'm doing here. He tells me that I could go to jail for what I have done.

The reasonable approach that I had applied with the bishop (and to some degree had worked) I try again.

"Sir," I respond, "I lived in Guatemala among murderers. I am not really afraid of what a nice man like you will do to me, a good doctor like yourself who comes here to help these poor Guatemalans, your neighbors," my heart pounding all the while. (In truth I'm not looking forward to spending the rest of my life in Mexico's filthy jails.) That he is a doctor is probably a safe assumption; a stethoscope dangles from the pocket of his white jacket, but other than just this superficial observation about his appearance, I feel that my assessment of the man in other aspects of his personality and character is probably correct. There is a vulnerability about him, and in the face that is rapidly losing its anger, there is kindness. Indeed, he begins to apologize to me in a short while, explaining that he has been beset by many problems while working here in the camps. There is an overwhelming job to do, a million Guatemalan refugees, half of them here in Mexico and they are still crossing the border. He says that when "outsiders" come here, it is mainly out of curiosity, not really trying to understand their predicament of how difficult it is to take care of this many people. Reason tells me that he speaks the truth. If greed and exploitation have entered the camps along with the refugees then they do not seem to motivate this man. He lives here.

Very soon the doctor and I are surrounded by the Naturales. They are from Quiché and Sololá, from Huehuetenango, each wanting to talk about the repression, about their becoming *"desplazados"* (displaced persons) having lost their homes, separated from their places of birth and families, a devastated peoples. They, if no one else, seem to welcome my presence here. I even receive a few hugs and, coming from a generally stoic people, that's pretty good. Their assessment of me has been correct. I am on their side. I took sides when Nicolas first came to me saying, "Bonnie, did you know they killed another family last night?"

I am not in the camp very long and I see that it is time to go. The men who brought me here have arrived in their truck and the doctor tells me that I can't stay longer anyway. He says that he has no authorization for me to be here, and if he allows me to stay longer he'll be in trouble, and he adds that he believes that I am sincere in really wanting to help the Guatemalans.

I never do see the doctor again and after I arrive back at the city of Campeche, it is plain that the management of the hotel does not thoroughly approve of any activities involving the refugees. While there is an admonishing tone in the lady's voice when she tells me this, she informs me that she can put me in touch with the authorities responsible for the refugee camps, but I must promise never to mention her name in any of this.

Before leaving Campeche I do come in contact with others who are involved with the Guatemalan refugees. They, however, will not speak freely, some of the personnel literally running away from me. A young woman doctor whose office I'm directed to on the fourth floor speaks to me as we hurry toward an elevator, and talks hurriedly on the way down to the lobby. There does seem to be a lot of secrecy and intrigue involving the refugees, almost matching the description of the Guatemalan camps, where I understand they are held as virtual prisoners, as are the residents of Rios Montt's "model villages."

Before I take my leave of Campeche entirely, a group of people involved with the refugees comes to visit me at the hotel. They seem a bit more willing than the others to share some information with me and I learn the name of their organization is COMAR and they are largely supported by the United Nations.

Though I am but a "committee of one," and have never felt a need to join an organization, I had nevertheless anticipated someone asking me to identify myself. I decide to call "my organization," P.E.A.C.E. I am still in the process of trying to think of what this abbreviation might represent when I discover it is not necessary. It is enough that I represent something, some body of people.

It's time to go home. I feel that I have in some way accomplished what I came for, however tediously the information that I sought was acquired.

After returning to the States, my daughter, my son-in-law and I go into a family huddle, thinking of ways that we might help the refugees. Along with our brain-storming ideas, we put in a call to Dr. Charlie Clements, now a close friend and "ally." He puts us in touch with some people who work for Guatemala and apparently in direct contact with them. Their organization is Washington-based and its leader, a 28-year-old Philadelphian having hitch-hiked from his home state to Guatemala during the 1976 earthquake, raised money along the way to help the poor. Still active in Guatemala we learn his name is Eddie Fischer (no relation to the singer and actor) and that he was, or still is, studying for the priesthood.

The name of their organization, when given, is P.E.A.C.E. for Guatemala. How did this happen!

Soon after we make contact, my daughter and son-in-law are hosts to an interesting group of people devoted to helping Guatemalans. Three are from Guatemala, a nun and two men who all work with the refugees in Mexico City. There is a charming North American young woman devoted to Guatemala's poor and with them Eddie Fischer himself, supposedly. It takes a few minutes before anyone can really convince me that this is truly Eddie Fischer! Priests are mystics. They somehow look as if they never get enough to eat, pale and with that "other world" expression in their eyes, as if any moment they will pass from this life to the next from so much praying. But this man! He could teach a course in physical fitness. He is the image of a North American hero, tall and glowing with health.

One of my first questions to him, "Are you still a priest, Eddie?" is met with an answer, "No, Bonnie, they won't let me be a priest anymore. I'm married and have a baby."

As always when we are in the presence of people we like, the evening passes quickly. Before it ends, my son-in-law, Pete Sears, commits himself and the popular band he plays with, the Jefferson Starship, to the project. Quite naturally our guests are gratified. It has been a pleasurable and successful evening for all concerned.

When the Starship Band tunes up its electric guitars and the sound equipment men test their acoustics, even the shrillness of the noise is tolerable to me, but when they belt out their rock 'n' roll notes, they are angel music to my ears. This concert is for Guatemala! Like Otto René Castillo, *they make me the happiest of all sad people who still live on this planet.*

THE LEFT AND CENTER

The year of 1985 is ushered in and draws to a close. Due to the country's gross repression, it would seem the fire fueling Guatemala's revolutionary process would have been put out long ago and the "status quo" accepted. The latest grim statistics indicate that the death toll is moving toward 150,000 people—445 villages wiped out completely, the country left with one million refugees, both internally and in other countries, primarily in Mexico. But when all facts are gathered, all reports tabulated, the people of Guatemala are more determined than ever in throwing off their yoke of bondage. They are cognizant as never before that freedom can be theirs. They know that a democracy, despite all outward events to the contrary, is still a reality. It was theirs once (from 1944-1954) during that brief and heady period when tyranny ceased—when two successive presidents released a positive power on the nation for the common good.

The ruling class is not unaware of the revolutionary change occurring, either, the change that will free Guatemala's poor from their chains of slavery—hence the stepped-up repression. They know that in order for the poor to be less poor, they will have to be less rich.

The proposed constitution of the "New Guatemala" seems clear in its intent to have a just and fair government, and in the excerpts, the Guatemalan people's deep yearning can be felt; the similarity of their proposals and the words of our own Constitution is easily recognizable. The concepts of the revolutionary constitution by the Guatemala

241

National Revolutionary Unity (URNG) essentially states that the revolution will eliminate once and for all the repression against the people and will guarantee to all the citizens the supreme right to life and peace; the Revolution will guarantee equality between Indians and Ladinos and will end cultural oppression and discrimination.

The revolution will guarantee the creation of a New Society in which all patriotic, democratic sectors will be represented. In the New Society women will have the same rights as men and even greater rights in their roles as mothers. The revolution recognizes the Christian population as one of the pillars of the New Society since they have placed their belief and faith at the service of the struggle for the freedom of all Guatemalans. In today's complex and interdependent world it is necessary to maintain a position of non-alignment with the great powers and strive for international cooperation. Poor countries need foreign investment and this must be agreed upon on the basis of respect for each country's sovereignty.*

Political stability is, in this respect, indispensable, as without it there can be no internal cooperation.

The revolutionary concepts ask for restoration of the spiritual equilibrium, which, for centuries, it seems, a great part has been lost to the world.

By inviting the church to assist in governing in the "New Guatemala" once more it is accepted as a symbol of hope and sacrificial love, rather than in the past when the church embraced only wealth and power. As shown by its actions, its position has been exactly reversed.

Through the desolation, horror and gripping fear, a leader of the Christian Democratic Party survives, Marco Vinicio Cerezo Arévalo, the attorney who stuck out a cloth shoe for a little boy to shine, and his neck out for his country by condemning the institutionalized violence. In early December, Vinicio Cerezo becomes Guatemala's first civilian president in thirty-two years. Again the American journalists recognize a hot item for their magazine articles. Vinicio is seen in all the popular magazines, smiling, exultant, while his attractive wife kisses his cheek; he had won the presidency by a landslide of votes.

*Guatemalan News and Information Center—Los Angeles, CA.

Just how long this one bright star in Guatemala's politically blackened skies can continue to shine depends upon whether Mr. Cerezo will be allowed to govern (if he will even be able to exercise the 30% of power he claims as president)—or will have any control over the army.

The proposed constitution of the "leftists" and the aspirations of Vinicio Cerezo as president seem minuscule in their differences. Conversely, a close scrutiny is unnecessary to realize that no dialogue with the right is presently possible.

Clearly Mr. Cerezo is not a man who would command the death squads against an enemy, much less a friend or helpless victim. Yet only two days after the election in December, the bruised and battered body of Beatriz Eugenia Barrios is found. Her hands have been cut off at the wrist and a note pinned to her body: *MORE TO COME*, undoubtedly a clear warning to the new president.

Guatemala, a land where death awaits the person who tries to effect even the slightest change, still screams under the weight of its burdens, still calls for response.

The United States could greatly contribute to a democracy in Guatemala if they were to begin to court the oppressed, rather than the oppressors, but barring this possibility, it would be far better were they to be left alone to "work out their own salvation."

The indigenous people and the *campesinos* need those who will help them till their fertile soil, who will bring them tools of agriculture, not the implements of war.

Many willing hands and many pure hearts are necessary to Guatemala's peace, that time when the only disappearances will be greed and a lust for power…a time when there will be an end to the blood in Guatemala's cornfield.

AFTERWORD (1992–1993)

I did not exist to write poems,
to preach or to paint,
neither I nor anyone else;
all of this was incidental.
Each man has only one vocation—
to find the road that leads to
himself.

—Herman Hesse

If one were to look only at the grim statistics afflicting Guatemala which report 200,000 dead since 1960 (more than half since 1980), one million homeless within the country, another million in exile, the neglect and abuses of the street children, the continued torture and disappearances, the majority of whom are among the indigenous people, a conclusion would be drawn that no such road the famous author spoke of exists for the Mayas. But a look beyond this seemingly hopeless situation would reveal the same sense of communal spirit as always in this race of people, the perennial belief in self. They would see the Mayas quietly working behind the lines toward the day when they can take control of their own lives, live in dignity as a race of people.

Two civilians have been the latest presidents to take office in Guatemala (the only two "not connected" with the army since the overthrow of Jacobo Arbenz's government in 1954) the latest of whom was Jorge Serrano, elected on January 6, 1991 (and was still president in 1993) when Vinicio Cerezo's term expired as Head of State. For a brief period it began to look as if there might be a change for the better in Guatemala, as if there might be some chance of reviving the democratic Arévalo-Arbenz era following the election of Mr.Cerezo.

Almost immediately after assuming office, Mr. Cerezo opened talks with the other Central American presidents, which originally included the presidents of Mexico and two South American countries, Venezuela and Columbia. The photographers of the leading newspapers in the United States show Vinicio Cerezo taking the hands of the other Central American presidents, rather than accepting the presidential sash at the inauguration ceremonies; the draping of the president with the presidential sash is a long-time initiating rite in Guatemala.

During this time, Mr. Oscar Arias devised a plan to carry the Peace Process forward, and came to be recognized by the world community, first as a presidential candidate and later as president of Costa Rica, as a leader who would pursue regional peace and whose political dynamics have undoubtedly contributed greatly to its cause in Central America, and for which Mr. Arias was awarded the Nobel Peace Prize.

The first of a series of meetings, organized by Vinicio Cerezo, was held at Contadora, a beautiful Pacific island, where the presidents of Central America assembled in search of a solution to the regional political turmoil and the troubled economies. These summit meetings opened the way for more talks.

Esquipulas I, held on August 7, 1987, promised to be the zenith for these meetings. It was at that meeting that the National Reconciliation Committee was established and there the government (and the military) met with the representatives of the *Unidad Revolucionaria Nacional Guatemalteca* (URNG)—The Guatemalan Revolutionary Unity—and where agreement was reached for the guerrillas and the government to meet directly at a date in the near future. Although the talks following each successive meeting broke down, the guerrillas brought two main proposals to the bargaining table and considered tantamount to peace—those of reducing the army and dismantling the civil patrols entirely, which had been unequivocally rejected by the military—the struggle on the part of the people went on.

Throughout the periods of negotiation over the years, the violence never lessened to any great degree, and in spite of what may have been Mr. Cerezo's good intentions, the disappearances and the extra-judicial executions continued under his presidency, and in a matter of a year or so, the political violence was again released full force on the population. Because of the continued atrocities, President Cerezo's reputation as a reformer began to lose its significance. It is presumed by those kindest to Mr. Cerezo—since the United States failed to support him during his term in office as promised—so that eventually his government and the military had meshed into a single unit in many people's minds and burdened by an army out of control, that he had simply given up.

The ubiquitous presence of the army continued to be a threat to the citizens of Guatemala, particularly in the rural areas, and its troops that had established camp ten years earlier in Santiago Atitlán remained. The troops made regular raids on the pueblo at the whim of the commanding officer.

But on December 3, 1990, the Tzutuhiles of Santiago Atitlán experienced a stunning and major victory, one that would become an example for all pueblos in Guatemala living under the dominance of the military's harsh rule, and an act on Mr. Cerezo's part that undoubtedly has helped to re-polish his tarnished image. The people of Santiago Atitlán, with the assistance of President Vinicio Crerezo, (just before Mr. Cerezo's term as president expired) kicked out the army!

On Saturday, December 2, 1990 at about 11:00 P.M. two army officers in civilian clothes, and very drunk, had gone to the home of a prosperous merchant with the intent of breaking and entry. They first began banging on the door, awakening the family from sleep. The businessman, of course, had no intentions of opening the door, and when the two drunken men realized the door would remain shut, they demanded entry by shouting out an ultimatum that either the door would be opened or they would break it down.

The merchant had a very attractive daughter, so it was open to speculation whether the drunken officers' motive was one of rape or robbery. During the assault on his home, the merchant began to shout for help and, unlike the past when the villagers hid in their homes during the attacks on their neighbors, listening fearfully to the screams and shouts, or sneaking glances through the cornstalk walls of their homes, they came running and shouting from all directions, throwing stones as they advanced. The officers then began firing shots, at first aimlessly in the air, then directly at the merchant's home, injuring a teenage boy in the process. The whole scenario was visible under a full moon. A group of well-armed, uniformed soldiers arrived from the base to escort the drunk officers back to the base, apparently having been alerted to the disturbances.

Blending with the screaming and the gunshots, the shouts of neighbors spread like a flame on a hill of dry leaves. The town representatives demanded that the mayor-elect immediately lead a protest march to the army base. But the newly-elected official declined, stating it would be better to wait until morning and awaken the outgoing mayor. This delayed action in no way satisfied the pueblo. They then marched to the home of the mayor-elect, taking along the man who was still mayor. After awakening the mayor-elect they pushed both of them in front of a crowd, that had now swelled to thousands, and begun to gather on the grounds of the church. The bells had been ringing non-stop and without the priest's permission.

The mayors, aware that they had no alternative but to act immediately, with white flags in hand, began to lead a crowd of four thousand men, women and children on a march to the army base a kilometer away. The villagers carrying hoes, machetes and shovels reached the army base where the elected spokesman intended to demand an explanation for the officers' outrageous behavior in their town and to warn them that these abuses must end, and now! But as the procession reached the gate of the base (it was then after midnight) and tried to present their grievances, the soldiers opened fire with automatic weapons on the crowd, killing thirteen people and gravely injuring eighteen more, some of whom died from their wounds at a later date.

On this horrible occasion, the Tzutuhiles, as in the past, did not quietly bury their dead, but invited the press to come and see for themselves the injuries the pueblo sustained and to come and look at the bodies that were still lying on the ground in front of the army post.

An army spokesman who issued a statement that the guerrillas had started the shooting was replaced the following day, but this was hardly a recompense for the abuses visited on the pueblo for the past ten years. A petition of thirty thousand signatures and thumb prints demanding the removal of the army and the national police from Santiago Atitlán was ready by the following morning. The petition contained the signatures of children from other pueblos, union representatives, university students, and a member of Guatemala's Human Rights Committee arrived along with the press. There photographs were taken of the bodies still lying where they were shot. The Tzutuhiles won! *Mr. Cerezo* announced on the day following receipt of the petition that the army would be removed from Santiago Atitlán within fifteen days.

The shrines of the murdered victims lie just outside the pueblo, containing the epitaphs, if adults: "Do not be afraid of those who can kill the body but cannot kill the soul…" And if children: "Let the little children come unto me for of such is the kingdom of Heaven."

Opposite the narrow dirt road of this small, newly-formed memorial is a monument signed by President Vinicio Cerezo Arévalo, expressing his solidarity with the people of Santiago Atilán, and his profound sorrow for the tragedy, and containing a decree stating that the army can no longer occupy this village.*

During the two successive years of Jorge Serrano's occupancy of the presidential office, the incidence of human rights abuses waxed and waned, but considering the overall picture, never really abated.

*As told by an eye-witness, name withheld.

Among the more prominent incidents of violent death in Guatemala were the two popular politicians, Alberto Fuentes Mohr and Manuel Colom Argueta, the indigenous men from Quiché, burned to death in the Spanish Embassy but whose names were little known at the time. Others are Héctor Oqueli, Salvadoran political analyst and attorney; Myrna Mack, anthropologist, North American; here in the pueblo, Father Francis Stanley Rother, priest; Edgar Bauer, *finca* owner and conservationist; Antonio Ramirez, former mayor; and Juan Sisay, famous indigenous artist. But there have been scores of people murdered by the military or paramilitary death squads whose untimely deaths have never found their way to the news media, and the dead are known and mourned only by those who loved them.

But just as the modern-day archaeologists are uncovering the identity of murdered victims in war-torn countries by digging up their bones, so are the more revealing methods of testimony by the relatives of the known dead or "disappeared," and the Quiché leader who was burned to death in the Spanish Embassy was none other than the father of Rigoberta Menchú, winner of the 1992 Nobel Peace Prize. She lost not only her father to the violence but her mother and brother as well, and because, like the pueblo of Atitlán, unarmed and non-violent, having kicked out the army, she was a first in Guatemala's rural history. Rigoberta Menchú is the first Nobel Peace Laureate who springs from among the indigenous people of Guatemala, an event that not only maintained Guatemala's status on the world map, but caused her beauty and accomplishments to bask in the limelight of global attention!

The year of 1992 has been declared "500 YEARS OF RESISTANCE" by the indigenous people of the world community, commemorating the five-hundred year anniversary of Christopher Columbus' discovery of the Americas. It has represented only poverty and hunger, dominance and exploitation, occupied land—to the indigenous people—a condition they are still fighting against.

The year of 1993 has been named, out of respect and recognition of the plight of the American Indians, *El Año Internacional de las*

Poblaciones Indigenas—The International Year of the Indigenous Population, engendered and promoted by the United Nations.

A Mayan Quiché man, living in exile in Costa Rica, tall and dignified, both scholar and mystic, states that peace could come any day in Guatemala, and when it does the Naturales are ready. "Among us are a myriad of professionals—doctors, sociologists, educators." In his modesty he fails to mention that they also have in their midst attorneys and brilliant writers of Mayan culture and history, the man having educated himself, in two areas of study, the law and literature. When asked during conversation, "Is it true then that the indigenous people of Guatemala, as rumored, have plans for self-governing?" he replies, "Yes, that is very true."

"But isn't that a little difficult for you to believe?" he is asked, "in view of the fact that the atrocities have continued in your country till this present date, and the countries successfully instituting revolutionary processes have been overturned." It is understood that the countries being alluded to are Nicaragua and Grenada. His expression saddens. "Yes, I am aware of all that you say, but the doubt and pessimism stem from occidental thought, not from our people. The Maya's philosophy is circular, not linear, and its history cyclical." The man from Quiché goes on to point out that El Salvador has attained a great victory through negotiations, and that Guatemala has the right to expect the same results as the talks continue between the guerrillas and the Guatemalan Government. A light comes into his eyes as he repeats the hopeful and affirmative words, "When peace comes we are ready!" Guatemala deserves peace.

APPENDAGE

As in its virulent beginning, the decade of the 80s ends in a state of political chaos and traverses into the 90s with no relief in sight for the war-torn Central American countries. These continued atrocities, which at earlier times would have had a great impact on the world community, by and large, shock no one. One of the popular magazines features a story in which the author offers a series of palliatives to combat the panic and pain to the victims undergoing torture. * The most blatant atrocities to date are those of the massacre of the six Jesuit priests, a woman attendant and her teenage daughter, in El Salvador, and the brutal slaying of Myrna Mack, anthropologist, in Guatemala—crimes that occurred less than a year apart.

In the case of the murders of the six Jesuits and the two women, a witness who had managed to hide during the massacre, and later escape, tells this story: *In the early morning hours, just before dawn, on November 16, 1989, approximately forty armed men entered the rectory of the Central American University. The priests and the women had been asleep in there when they were dragged from their beds by the armed men to a large room outside the dormitories. There they were forced to lie on the floor, face downward, and were clubbed about the head and then shot close range in the back of the head and body.*

An autopsy later revealed that five hundred bullets had been pumped into their bodies and that among the dead was Father Ignacio Ellacuria, a Spaniard known to be a progressive priest who had aligned himself with the poor. He had been targeted for death by the military upon his arrival to El Salvador from Spain.

At the church where the funeral rites were held for the Jesuits and the cook and her daughter, a life-size portrait of Archbishop Romero hung overhead, lending to the sorrowful atmosphere a chilling sense of déja vu. Their enemies in the military called the priests at the trial for the crime "intellectual terrorists."[1]

Myrna Mack was murdered as she left her office on the evening of September 11,1990. She had been stabbed by an assailant 225 times and left to bleed to death on a sidewalk in Guatemala City. Myrna Mack was a cofounder of a research center where she dedicated her education and energies to the investigation and reporting on the human rights abuses of the Guatemalan national refugees.

Reporters covering the story and the family of Myrna Mack have all received death threats following her murder, and the police officer, José Merida, who filed the report of Myrna Mack's death, was himself murdered in the daylight hours less than a block from the headquarters of the National Police.

What sets these two cases apart from all the other grisly human rights abuses is that a conviction was secured in each instance. Nearly two years after the assassinations of the priests and the two women, on September 28, 1991—what Salvadorans refer to as the "trial of the century," a five-member jury found Army Colonel Guillermo Benavides guilty and was sentenced to prison for twenty or thirty years.

Myrna Mack's murderer was brought to trial in February of 1993. In a historic decision, Noel de Jesus Beteta, one-time member of the presidential military staff under Vinicio Cerezo, was given a 25-year sentence for the murder and five years for an additional crime.[2]

The Guatemalan Government and the leading opposition party, (URNG) *la Unidad Revolucionaria Nacional Guatemalteca*, again came together during four days in March 1994 (24-28) in Puebla, a Mexican town 340 Kilometers from Mexico's capital, to resolve their differences, if possible, and to seek a solution to Guatemala's continuing turmoil. Unlike the past, when over the years the negotiations ended in failure, the accords were actually signed by representatives of both parties.

Some very positive results were obtained in Puebla, including the creation of an international verification commission—to be ratified by the United Nations, which mediated at the meetings.

The agreement was reached in spite of a major contradiction on the part of the Guatemalan Government. A proposal by the guerrilla party (URNG) for a truth commission, which in essence called for an investigation of the numerous atrocities committed over the last thirty odd years in Guatemala, was flatly rejected by the negotiators of the government, while at the same time, the agreement committed the government to guarantee protection of the population and fight impunity of the security forces.

The presidential office during the signing of the accords was now occupied by Ramiro de León Carpio, a former human rights leader, appointed by Congress to replace Jorge Serrano Elías, who was ousted following an attempt to seize complete control of the country in an *auto-golpe*, a self-motivated coup d'etát. Serrano had suspended the constitution, with the dissolution of Congress and the Supreme Court! This action not only evoked the wrath of his countrymen, but was an act that discredited him in the eyes of the world community.

Soon after taking office, President De León began to sound like his predecessors that he had once criticized, and to negate the principles of the people he had once upheld. In his statements to the press, he blamed the guerrillas for the continued unrest in the country and implied that if further negotiations failed to achieve peace, the recalcitrance of the left would be responsible.

Since De León became president of Guatemala, the people of Santiago Atitlán have lived with the threat that the army would again occupy their village. President De Leon has, on more than one occasion, indicated that he had intentions of reinstating the presence of the military, the same that Vinicio Cerezo had ordered out.

Both major political events, the installation of Ramiro De León in the presidential office and the signing of the "peace accords," have been accompanied by future acts of violence.

A first cousin of the president, Jorge Carpio Nicolle, was killed in an ambush as his motorcade left the highlands in Quiche. Jorge Carpio was a judge, a former presidential candidate and an owner of the newspaper, *El Gráfico*. Two other leaders and his chauffeur were killed in the foray, and Carpio's nephew severely wounded.

Following the signing of the accords, another judge and President of the Constitutional Court, Epaminodas Gonzalez, died on April 2, 1994, after having been attacked by gunmen outside his home the night before. In less than a week, a congressman, Obdulio Chinchilla, was shot and wounded when an attempt was made on his life. Some observers have attributed the continued violence to the military, that they say, may have been trying to thwart the peace process.

But in spite of the violence, and despite the ambiguities that would have to be clarified, the process of peace remained valid. It was anticipated that Guatemala would see the end of hostilities between the government and the guerrillas in September 1994, and that the peace accords would be finalized in December of the same year.

[1] A well publicized story in the news media.
[2] *Tico Times*, San Jose, Costa Rica, 02/19/93.

OTHER AFFAIRS

The year 1995 has brought some changes to the political scene in Guatemala. The violence, though not having ceased, has loosened its grip on the population as a whole.

The recent decrease in tensions has been attributed to various causes, among them being that many factions have speculated that the United States has grown weary of supporting governments that are placed among those who kill and torture their own citizens on a regular basis. Even the Guatemalan soldiers are widely believed to have grown tired of the killing, and the army has been reported worn down by its own war. By the first part of April, the Guatemalan Government and the leading guerrilla faction were back at the bargaining table in Mexico.

But above and beyond the unreasonableness of maintaining an unpopular war, one that could never have been won; in all probability the underlying cause for the decrease in hostilities lies in the widespread publicity Guatemala has received. Undoubtedly, the efforts of the United Nations, various U.S.-based organizations that monitor human rights in Latin America and individuals who have brought to light the gross abuses in Guatemala have played an important role. In so doing they have exposed the Central Intelligence Agency for its involvement in the activities that have led to the deaths and disappearances of Guatemalan citizens and North Americans alike.

Overlapping a summit meeting in El Salvador in which President Ramiro De León, Guatemala's president, cut short his participation (no reason was given in the news media for his walkout), U.S.

Congressman Torricelli openly charged a Guatemalan army colonel, Julio Alpirez, of having been in the pay of the CIA when he ordered the murders of U.S. rancher, Michael De Vine and Efrain Bamaca Velasquez, a Guatemalan guerrilla commander and husband of U.S. lawyer, Jennifer Harbury.

Although the murders were actually thought to have been committed earlier in the decade (the murder of Michael De Vine in 1990 and Efraín Bamaca's murder in 1992), at the time they were abducted, Ms. Harbury held the hope that her husband was still alive until the early months of 1995. Her fasting and willingness to discuss with reporters the assassination of her husband have added momentum to the pending investigations of the CIA and its role in the two murders.

UPDATE
(2001)

I arrive in Santiago after having been absent from the pueblo for many years to the tune of music and speech-giving in the plaza. A gala affair, with banners waving, the whole town is celebrating a joyous occasion. My family and I join the happy throng. One of my sons-in-law, Pete, the musical one from birth, gives the marimbas a few strokes and soon plays with ease along with the band of indigenous musicians.

On December 29, 1996, the Peace Accords, which had been nullified by the military in 1994 and subsequently broken down, were again signed on December 29, 1996. The guerrilla's two main stipulations were once more brought to the bargaining table—that the army would reduce its size and the civil patrols be dismantled entirely before any concession on their part would be made. The Mayas having equal rights was high on the list of mandates.

Finally, after so many "peace talks " that had ended in failure and after many years of war, the army agreed to these proposals and the guerrillas conceded to a laying down of arms.

In Santiago Atitlán, there is an additional reason for celebration. The Atitecos had successfully expelled the army from their town, an act that has continued to be an example for all other pueblos in Guatemala, and a decree signed by the outgoing president, Vinicio Cerezo, stating that the army can never come back, has helped to sustain their cause.

Many villagers ask me upon my return visit, "Bonnie, did you know we kicked out the army!?"

I can only answer "*Si, yo se*," nothing more. The magnitude of their great accomplishment defies conversation!

Tragically, not all the efforts of those working so diligently toward peace have been met with success, but rather have ended in sorrow and tragedy.

Monseñor Juan Gerardi Conedera, long an advocate of human rights and called "an apostle of truth," was assassinated on April 26, 1998 in the garage of his parish home, San Sebastian, Guatemala City. The outrageous act occurred just fifty-four hours after releasing an exposé condemning the human rights abuses in Guatemala. In a document entitled, "Guatemala: *Nunca Mas*," he had listed the names of those he knew to be victims of assassination; many were members of the clergy and other religious persons of the community. Interestingly, the parochial house was situated three blocks from the Palacio Nacional, and one of the men mentioned in the document for having been a collaborator in these atrocities was one of the army men later convicted for the archbishop's murder.

The trial dragged on for more than three years and it had begun to look as if no conviction was imminent.

Meanwhile, over the years, this crime was being denounced globally, unlike the death of Archbishop Romero of El Salvador, gunned down in church while saying mass, and whose assassination was largely ignored by the world communities—that is, of course, with the exception of the church and other human rights workers who were saddened and deeply concerned that a murder of this magnitude would be committed.

Since the death of Archbishop Gerardi, all eyes have again been turned on Guatemala. President Clinton and Kofi Annan, Secretary General of the United Nations, are shown together by the press denouncing the crime that led to the death of this religious leader. There was a quote by Rigoberta Menchú, stating that this latest atrocity involving the clergy in high places is proof that impunity still exists.

Three years later the suspects in the case of Archbishop Gerardii were brought to trial, considered one of the firsts in Guatemala's history. On June 9, 2001, three army men, el Capitán Byron Lima

Oliva, Coronel Byron Disrael Lima Estrada and José Obdulia Villanueva Arévalo were sentenced by the courts to thirty years in prison. Padre Mario Orantes Nájera, named as an accomplice in the crime, received a sentence of twenty years. Many people believe that the priest was innocent of the murder of the archbishop, but conceded that he had probably known about it and had concealed the facts from the courts and the public, perhaps out of fear of reprisals toward him and his family, following any information that he would have divulged.

In the years of 2001 and 2002, the country seems to be moving toward a resurgence of the political violence of the 80s and 90s; Santiago Atitlán has become a center for street crime and housebreaking. Initially it appeared that the tourists were mainly the targets for robbery. But as the lawlessness progresses, Santiago's poor, both Maya and Ladino, have become victims. These crimes range from a simple holdup on the streets where no one is injured, particularly when there is no resistance, to the atrocious crime when a group of young thugs sliced off a Mayan woman's arm at the shoulder when she attempted to defend her employer's possessions by trying to prevent the young thugs from entering the household while the owners were away.

These street crimes are so brazenly rampant that they are committed during the daytime hours and sometimes witnessed by several onlookers. Young ladies are known to be robbed of their jewelry during the daylight hours, and robbed of their *huipiles* and *cortes* after dusk, making it necessary to return home naked.

Many people speculate as to the cause of the crimes. Drugs are frequently named as the underlying problem. Crack cocaine has been introduced to the youths of the pueblo. Attributed by others are the lack of jobs that leads to poverty; both reasons must be considered valid. But there arises in my mind a question that would tend to refute the theory of "poverty-crime syndrome." The pueblo is no less poor than it was in the past, when very little crime was known in it, particularly no violent crime. A scene surfaces in my memory from the 70s when I had waited for Francisca and José to return home from a party in the village. It was 4:00 A.M. when I waited alone on the doorstep of the pension

Chi-Nim-Ya and felt no fear at all. To the contrary, I watched the parade of Dads at daybreak going by with their cattle, steering whips in hand, dressed in their *traje tipico,* and their little boys walking beside them with their miniature whips.

A local artist, one of the now famous Chavez brothers, Miguel, describes what he believes to be the source of the rampant crime afflicting the pueblo: "The seeds of violence were sown during the 1980s and we are reaping the fruits thereof...." As I listen to these eloquent words, I think of Charles Dickens whose poetic expressions Miguel Chavez of Santiago Atitlán has just repeated almost verbatim, and muse. Most probably Miguel has never even heard of Charles Dickens!

Elsewhere in Guatemala the degree of political violence and impunity have lessened, but sadly, they have not ceased. Within a year's time, a leader of the opposition party and a radio journalist were assassinated. These murders followed closely on the heels of both men, having denounced the corruption of the federal and local governments.

The assassins convicted of the murder of Myrna Mack, anthropologist, were recently released. A number of the leaders (or perhaps all) of human rights organizations have been threatened, and on May 7, 2002, it is reported by the local newspapers that Fredy Peccerelli, President of the Forensic Anthropology Foundation of Guatemala, involved in exhumation of graves, will leave the country for the same reason. The director of the Rigoberta Menchu Foundation, Guillermo Ovalle, was murdered on April 29, 2002; although arrests were made for this despicable act, along with similar acts of violence that are consistent with political motivation, the real perpetrators of the crimes are seldom brought to trial. If the crime receives enough publicity internationally, so that a conviction can't be successfully avoided, then the "hitmen" usually are given over to the Guatemalan authorities and are named as the criminals.

What is now May 2002, greater cultural changes in Santiago Atitlán have occurred.

The quaint little huts with their thatched roofs and walls of stone and bamboo, like the covered wagons in the United States, have all but disappeared, replaced by cement and concrete, less charming to be sure, albeit more practical than in years past.

The pueblos at Atitlán in general have undergone radical changes. They are no longer occupied only by the indigenous population, but have become a home for many foreigners. There are now language schools, elegant hotels, and Internet cafés, fancy restaurants, Western clothing shops—in the process of becoming modern cities and still growing.

Many groups, mainly from the various churches, Catholic and Protestant alike, and those groups who claim no religious affiliation come to the pueblos from the United States, Europe and Asia to build homes for the widows, to assist in dental and medical care, education, nutrition; they bring with them engineers who install potable water supply systems. Agronomists come to teach organic agriculture. All these volunteers, who radiate friendliness and good will, seem to experience satisfaction and fulfillment in working with the indigenous people, happy to add their talents and abilities toward helping those in need. The Naturales from various sectors of the villages cooperate with the volunteers' efforts to affect changes for the better, and, of course, the visitors never fail to comment on the beauty of Atitlán and the fascination derived from its people.

The work of the anthropologists and archaeologists is now acceptable, and indeed, greatly appreciated by the people of the pueblos; they have, over the years, begun to realize how important this work is to Guatemala and to the world in general. Many *pueblerinos* are now pleased that these interesting groups of intelligent people would devote so much time and attention to their geography, their soil, their artifacts…and find their environment so fascinating that they would come from all over the globe to study their culture.

One day, ceremonies of a school, now occupied by students, was held at San Lucas, Santiago's neighbor, and a celebrity philanthropist and his volunteer co-workers had funded and supervised the construction. What a thrill it was to be standing just inches away from the most famous tenor in the world, Luciano Pavarotti, at San Lucas Toliman. He came by helicopter for the inauguration for the great occasion. It is rumored that Santiago Atitlán is next on their agenda. Meanwhile, there are directors and teachers, both Guatemalan and foreign, who are working diligently to build schools in order to educate the people of the pueblo. One young student enthusiastically stated, "If we can read and write, we can accomplish anything!"

UPDATE
(2003)

The presidency of Alfonso Portillo terminates at the end of the year. During his six-year tenure, no real changes for the better in the political spectrum are evident. Widely believed by most Guatemalans is that he is merely a puppet in the presidential office—that Rios Montt, President of Congress, elected to the congressional office when Alfonso Portillo became president—still wields the power. Nepotism is rife—the government offices are filled with Montt's relatives including his own daughter. Portillo seems more interested in the accumulation of wealth than having his position of president usurped.

Those who condemn the corruption and nepotism of the government openly put their lives in grave danger, but even a mild disagreement spells trouble for the politician or journalist.

While the president bilks the country, millions of quetzals are missing from the treasury; the Guatemalans are not only hungry, but are actually in the middle of a famine. Appearing in the *Prensa Libre* on April 29, 2003 are photographs of mothers holding their children while they lie starving to death. In the reports, they are without any means to improve their situation. Due to a drought a famine occurred that brought on the desperate situation, making it impossible for any sustenance of life.

Many sympathetic Guatemalans come to their aid—an abandoned and forgotten society until the press made the public aware of their critical situation—they come with thousands of pounds of food and truck loads of clothing. The photos show thin hands and bony arms outstretched to receive their packages from the trucks when they arrive. The doctors respond to the needs of these people with medicine and treatment.

The vice-president of the country, Francisco Reyes Lopez, also visits these camps during this horrible period. What he has to contribute, however, is harassment, not help. He asks of one doctor rendering aid, "And you, sir, are you here on a vacation?"

He calls a little boy "fat," with all the symptoms of starvation, swollen belly and the rest of his body showing nothing but skin and bones, his face and head shrunken on frail shoulders. Documentation of these acts by the second leader of the country brings many criticisms by various sectors of society. Outside the Posada de Santiago, while sitting on a padded bench underneath the trees, comfortable and enjoying the August sunshine, an open page of the *Prensa Libre*, photographs showing starving babies who look like wizened gnomes, lie open before me. A youthful couple take the path that passes my way and look in my direction as if they want to talk with me. The young woman notes my reading material and asks, "What is your impression of all this?"—a hand motioning toward the articles and photographs, demonstrating the critical situation in Alta Verapaz.

"Well, truthfully, this makes me ill—very painful to look at."

"That's exactly my intention," she responded. "I took the pictures and my fiancé here wrote the articles."

The three of us then engage in conversation to some length. The young couple ask me to show their work to anyone I might know of who have not yet seen these articles.

"You know," the journalist adds, "we have to make the world aware."

As voting time draws near and the year comes to a close, there is renewed hope along with a resurgence of widespread fear and violence. The streets are filled with violent crime, that may or may not be associated with the political crimes. Robberies committed by youth gangs are rampant. The streets are unsafe, and the highways have become a chance-taking risk when traveling by buses, private van or automobiles.

*On July 24 and 25 Guatemala City is aflame with rioting and violence. Supporters of Rios Montt and "paid dissidents"—state employees, in fear of losing their jobs if they did not comply, participating *campesinos* who were paid 50 *quetzales* (the equivalent of $6.50) turn the city into utter chaos. The ruling FRG party (The Guatemalan Republican Front) had bussed thousands of *campesinos* to the scene and, according to the press, many did not appear to know the purpose of the protest, or even that a protest was planned. The demonstrators smashed windows and burned cars. The judges and journalists were targeted by the rioters. These riots are led by none other than Rios Montt's daughter!

The Supreme Court of Justice had earlier handed down an unfavorable verdict to Rios Montt in regard to his bid for the presidency. (The constitution forbids a candidate who comes to office other than by popular vote to become president. Rios Montt had come to power through an overthrow of the ruling government of Romeo Lucas Garcia.) This legal ban proved to be temporary. On July 30, the Constitutional Court stuck down the Supreme Court injunction. Rios Montt was again on the ballot. This injunction undoubtedly gave impetus to the ensuing riots.

Journalists were also a particular target of the protests and two photographers from El Periodico and *El Siglo XXI* were reported to be targets of these attacks. One sixty-five-year-old reporter, Hector Martinez, died of a heart attack while attempting to flee from his pursuers. Presumably the riots were aimed at demonstrating the general's power and sowing fear into the population.

But in spite of the widespread violence, the scare tactics did not work. The voters both in the city and pueblos, by the hundreds of thousands, streamed to the polls on November 9 to reject former dictator, Efrain Rios Montt, accused of genocide for his role in the massacres of the 1980s. Two candidates, Oscar Berger, former city mayor of Guatemala City, and Alvaro Colom of the Unity of Hope

Party, defeated Montt by a wide margin. In a runoff election between the two candidates, on December 28, Oscar Berger ran in the election and is now the president of Guatemala!

While the results of the election are less than satisfactory to some Guatemalans, particularly the ex-guerrilla faction and their supporters, and a certain number of the human rights workers, nevertheless this turn of events represents a new start for the Guatemalans, and hope for a new era of democracy and peace that has never really been theirs apart from the short-lived decade of Juan Arevalo and Jacobo Arbenz. Oscar Berger was well favored while a mayor in Guatemala City.

*A portion of this information was taken from *NISGUA*, The Network in Solidarity with the People of Guatemala, November 23, 2003 issue.